ALLUSIVE SOUNDPLAY
IN THE HEBREW BIBLE

ANCIENT ISRAEL AND ITS LITERATURE

Thomas C. Römer, General Editor

Editorial Board:
Mark G. Brett
Marc Brettler
Corrine L. Carvalho
Cynthia Edenburg
Konrad Schmid
Gale A. Yee

Number 28

ALLUSIVE SOUNDPLAY IN THE HEBREW BIBLE

Jonathan G. Kline

SBL PRESS

Atlanta

Copyright © 2016 by Jonathan G. Kline

All rights reserved. No part of this work may be reproduced or transmitted in any form or by any means, electronic or mechanical, including photocopying and recording, or by means of any information storage or retrieval system, except as may be expressly permitted by the 1976 Copyright Act or in writing from the publisher. Requests for permission should be addressed in writing to the Rights and Permissions Office, SBL Press, 825 Houston Mill Road, Atlanta, GA 30329 USA.

Library of Congress Cataloging-in-Publication Data

Names: Kline, Jonathan G., author.
Title: Allusive soundplay in the Hebrew Bible / by Jonathan G. Kline.
Description: Atlanta : SBL Press, [2016] | Series: Ancient Israel and its literature ; number 28 | Includes bibliographical references and index.
Identifiers: LCCN 2016024603 (print) | LCCN 2016029247 (ebook) | ISBN 9781628371444 (pbk. : alk. paper) | ISBN 9780884141716 (hardback : alk. paper) | ISBN 9780884141709 (ebook)
Subjects: LCSH: Hebrew language—Paronyms. | Bible Old Testament—Language, style. | Bible as literature. | Allusions in the Bible.
Classification: LCC PJ4815 .K63 2016 (print) | LCC PJ4815 (ebook) | DDC 221.6/6—dc23
LC record available at https://lccn.loc.gov/2016024603

Printed on acid-free paper.

for Joanna, Eva, and Thea

with love

Contents

Acknowledgments ix
Abbreviations xi

1. The Role of Soundplay in Innerbiblical Allusions 1
   1.1. Introduction   1
   1.2. Innerbiblical Allusion   1
   1.3. Paronomasia in the Hebrew Bible   6
   1.4. The Role of Paronomasia in the Expression and
        Development of Israel's Theological Traditions   13
   1.5. Identifying Allusive Paronomasia in the Hebrew Bible:
        Methodological Considerations   17
   1.6. How This Study Is Organized   41

2. Theodicy 43
   2.1. What Are Human Beings?   43
   2.2. Looking Upon the Punishment—or Prosperity—of the
        Wicked   53
   2.3. Extinguishing the Lamp of the Wicked   64

3. Judgment 73
   3.1. Setting Babylon on Fire   73
   3.2. Denying Oneself on the Day of Atonement   80
   3.3. Defiling and Defrauding YHWH   88

4. Salvation 101
   4.1. Bringing the Destruction of Assyria on Babylon   101
   4.2. Creating, De-creating, and Re-creating   106
   4.3. The Day of Devastation from Shaddai   112

5. Conclusion 119

Bibliography 129
Ancient Sources Index 145
Modern Authors Index 153

Acknowledgments

I am indebted to Thomas Römer and the other members of the editorial board of the Ancient Israel and Its Literature series for their kindness in accepting this book into the series and to Bob Buller and Nicole Tilford of SBL Press for their graciousness throughout the production process.

I am grateful to Andrew Teeter for encouraging me to pursue this project when the idea for it was still inchoate and for his wise guidance throughout the period during which I conducted most of my research and writing. His enthusiasm for the material and his ability to relate it to broader discussions in the field of biblical studies provided me with a wide perspective and contributed to the enjoyment I experienced throughout the time I spent working on the project. I am also thankful to Jon Levenson and Gary Rendsburg, who provided me with helpful feedback that improved the work and who also encouraged me with their kindness and good cheer. I have sought to improve this study whenever possible on the basis of the criticism offered by these wise experts, but none of them should, of course, be held responsible for the deficiencies and limitations that remain in this work.

Various ideas found in this book were tested out in papers that I presented in the Harvard Hebrew Bible and Semitic Philology workshops and at regional and national meetings of the Society of Biblical Literature. I am grateful to the kind individuals who attended those talks for their encouragement and their helpful questions and criticisms.

A supportive group of friends and colleagues encouraged me while I worked on this study and discussed various aspects of the project with me. I am particularly grateful to Brian Doak, Maria Metzler, Gabe Hornung, Cian Power, and Michael Lesley for sharing their wisdom with me and for helping make the time I worked on this project enjoyable.

I am grateful to my family—especially my parents and my brother and his family—for their love and support throughout the years. Most of all, I am thankful to my amazing wife and fellow biblical scholar Joanna

Greenlee Kline, who has sustained me with her love and support while I have worked on this book and who has improved it with her incisive feedback. I dedicate this book with profound love and gratitude to her and to our two wonderful daughters, Eva and Thea.

JGK
March 2016

Abbreviations

AB	Anchor Bible
ABD	*Anchor Bible Dictionary*. Edited by David Noel Freedman. 6 vols. New York: Doubleday, 1992.
AnBib	Analecta Biblica
ANES	*Ancient Near Eastern Studies*
ANETS	Ancient Near Eastern Texts and Studies
AnOr	Analecta Orientalia
AOAT	Alter Orient und Altes Testament
AOS	American Oriental Series
AuOr	*Aula Orientalis*
BEATAJ	Beiträge zur Erforschung des Alten Testaments und des antiken Judentums
Bib	*Biblica*
BibInt	*Biblical Interpretation*
BIWL	Bibliographies and Indexes in World Literature
BZABR	Beihefte zur Zeitschrift für altorientalische und biblische Rechtsgeschichte
BZAW	Beihefte zur Zeitschrift für die alttestamentliche Wissenschaft
CBQ	*Catholic Biblical Quarterly*
CBR	*Currents in Biblical Research*
CIS	Copenhagen International Series
CurBS	*Currents in Research: Biblical Studies*
DCH	*Dictionary of Classical Hebrew*. Edited by David J. A. Clines. 9 vols. Sheffield: Sheffield Phoenix Press, 1993–2014.
DSD	*Dead Sea Discoveries*
EHLL	*Encyclopedia of Hebrew Language and Linguistics*. Edited by Geoffrey Khan. 4 vols. Leiden: Brill, 2013.
FAT	Forschungen zum Alten Testament

FRLANT	Forschungen zur Religion und Literatur des Alten und Neuen Testaments
FTS	Freiburger Theologische Studien
HALOT	*The Hebrew and Aramaic Lexicon of the Old Testament.* Ludwig Koehler, Walter Baumgartner, and Johann J. Stamm. Translated and edited under the supervision of Mervyn E. J. Richardson. 4 vols. Leiden: Brill, 1994–1999.
HAR	*Hebrew Annual Review*
HBS	Herders Biblische Studien
HCOT	Historical Commentary on the Old Testament
HThKAT	Herders Theologischer Kommentar zum Alten Testament
HUCA	*Hebrew Union College Annual*
ICC	International Critical Commentary
IDBSup	*Interpreter's Dictionary of the Bible: Supplementary Volume.* Edited by Keith Crim. Nashville: Abingdon, 1976.
JAAR	*Journal of the American Academy of Religion*
JBL	*Journal of Biblical Literature*
JCS	*Journal of Cuneiform Studies*
JHS	*Journal of Hebrew Scriptures*
JQR	*Jewish Quarterly Review*
JSJSup	Journal for the Study of Judaism in the Persian, Hellenistic, and Roman Periods Supplement Series
JSOT	*Journal for the Study of the Old Testament*
JSOTSup	Journal for the Study of the Old Testament Supplement Series
JSPSup	Journal for the Study of the Pseudepigrapha Supplement Series
JSS	*Journal of Semitic Studies*
KAI	*Kanaanäische und aramäische Inschriften.* Herbert Donner and Wolfgang Röllig. 2nd ed. Wiesbaden: Harrassowitz, 1966–1969.
KTU	*Die keilalphabetischen Texte aus Ugarit.* Edited by Manfried Dietrich, Oswald Loretz, and Joaquín Sanmartín. AOAT 24/1. Neukirchen-Vluyn: Neukirchener Verlag, 1976.
LHBOTS	Library of Hebrew Bible/Old Testament Studies
NEchtBAT	Neue Echter Bibel: Altes Testament

NIDB	*The New Interpreter's Dictionary of the Bible*. Edited by Katharine Doob Sakenfeld. 5 vols. Nashville: Abingdon, 2006–2009.
NJPS	*Tanakh: A New Translation of the Holy Scriptures according to the Traditional Hebrew Text*. Philadelphia: Jewish Publication Society, 1985.
NSKAT	Neuer Stuttgarter Kommentar, Altes Testament
OBO	Orbis Biblicus et Orientalis
Or	*Orientalia (NS)*
OTL	Old Testament Library
OTS	Old Testament Studies
PEPP	*The Princeton Encyclopedia of Poetry and Poetics*. 4th ed. Edited by Roland Greene. Princeton: Princeton University Press, 2012.
PTL	*PTL: A Journal for Descriptive Poetics and Theory of Literature*
RevQ	*Revue de Qumran*
RTT	Research in Text Theory
SBLDS	Society of Biblical Literature Dissertation Series
ScrHier	Scripta Hierosolymitana
SEÅ	*Svensk exegetisk årsbok*
Sem	*Semitics*
SJ	Studia Judaica
SJOT	*Scandinavian Journal of the Old Testament*
STDJ	Studies on the Texts of the Desert of Judah
SubBi	Subsidia Biblica
THB	Text of the Hebrew Bible
VT	*Vetus Testamentum*
VTSup	Supplements to Vetus Testamentum
WMANT	Wissenschaftliche Monographien zum Alten und Neuen Testament
ZKT	*Zeitschrift für katholische Theologie*

1
THE ROLE OF SOUNDPLAY IN INNERBIBLICAL ALLUSIONS

1.1. INTRODUCTION

This book investigates the way various biblical writers used paronomasia, commonly referred to as "soundplay," in order to allude to and interpret earlier literary traditions that are also found in the Bible.[1] The focus of my investigation will lie on the biblical writers' use of allusive paronomasia specifically for the purpose of constructing theological discourse, that is, in service of their efforts to describe the nature of God and his relationship to humanity. By showing that a variety of biblical texts contain examples of allusive paronomasia employed for this purpose, I will demonstrate that this literary device played an important role in the growth of the biblical text as a whole and in the development of ancient Israelite and early Jewish theological traditions.

1.2. INNERBIBLICAL ALLUSION

During the past several decades, biblical scholars have emphasized the fact that interpretation of the texts that constitute the Hebrew Bible did not begin after the process of canonization had come to an end; rather, interpretation was a productive compositional factor in the literary development of the biblical writings. As James Kugel has put it, in ancient Israel "what we might call biblical interpretation, or *exegesis*, was going on centuries before 'the Bible' existed."[2] Often this kind of innerbiblical exegesis or interpretation involved the transformation—by means of various kinds

---

1. Unless otherwise noted, the term "Bible" in this study refers exclusively to the Hebrew Bible or Old Testament, not the Christian Bible.
2. James A. Kugel, "Early Interpretation: The Common Background of Late Forms of Biblical Exegesis," in James A. Kugel and Rowan A. Greer, *Early Biblical*

of adaptations and even sometimes rejection—of earlier traditions.³ The process by which the scribes of ancient Israel adapted, redacted, renewed, and sublimated earlier texts could take a variety of forms, including rewriting, glossing, emending, and more.⁴ One of the more prominent modes of innerbiblical exegesis involves the interpretation of earlier texts by means of tacit reference, a process normally referred to as "innerbiblical allusion."⁵

Literary allusion has helpfully been defined as "a kind of referencing in which an author uses material from another source (or from another

---

Interpretation (Philadelphia: Westminster, 1986), 17; italics original. See also Kugel, *The Bible as It Was* (Cambridge: Harvard University Press, 1997), 1–2.

3. The bibliography on innerbiblical interpretation is vast. Helpful introductions and overviews that have appeared in the last decade alone include: G. Brooke Lester, "Inner-Biblical Interpretation," in *The Oxford Encyclopedia of Biblical Interpretation*, ed. Steven L. McKenzie, 2 vols. (Oxford: Oxford University Press, 2013), 1:444–53; Yair Zakovitch, "Inner-Biblical Interpretation," in *A Companion to Biblical Interpretation in Early Judaism*, ed. Matthias Henze (Grand Rapids: Eerdmans, 2012), 27–63; Konrad Schmid, "Innerbiblische Schriftauslegung: Aspekte der Forschungsgeschichte," in *Schriftgelehrte Traditionsliteratur: Fallstudien zur innerbiblischen Schriftauslegung im Alten Testament*, FAT 77 (Tübingen: Mohr Siebeck, 2011), 5–34; Schmid, "Schriftgelehrte Arbeit an der Schrift: Historische Überlegungen zum Vorgang innerbiblischer Exegese," in *Schriftgelehrte Traditionsliteratur*, 35–60; Schmid, "Ausgelegte Schrift als Schrift: Innerbiblische Schriftauslegung und die Frage nach der theologischen Qualität biblischer Texte," in *Die Kunst des Auslegens: Zur Hermeneutik des Christentums in der Kultur der Gegenwart*, ed. Reiner Anselm et al. (Frankfurt am Main: Lang, 1999), 115–29; Geoffrey D. Miller, "Intertextuality in Old Testament Research," *CBR* 9 (2011): 283–309; Karl W. Weyde, "Inner-Biblical Interpretation: Methodological Reflections on the Relationship between Texts in the Hebrew Bible," *SEÅ* 70 (2005): 287–300; Reinhard G. Kratz, "Innerbiblische Exegese und Redaktionsgeschichte im Lichte empirischer Evidenz," in *Das Judentum im Zeitalter des Zweiten Tempels*, ed. Reinhard G. Kratz, FAT 42 (Tübingen: Mohr Siebeck, 2004), 126–56; Esther M. Menn, "Inner-Biblical Exegesis in the Tanak," in *The Ancient Period*, vol. 1 of *A History of Biblical Interpretation*, ed. Alan J. Hauser and Duane F. Watson (Grand Rapids: Eerdmans, 2003), 55–79.

4. For classification and extended discussion of these processes, see Michael Fishbane, *Biblical Interpretation in Ancient Israel* (Oxford: Clarendon, 1985).

5. Unless otherwise noted, in this book I use the term *allusion* as shorthand for *literary allusion*. Literature can, of course, contain allusions to nonliterary "sources" (e.g., art, music, architecture, etc.) as well, though most would not describe such references as *literary* allusion. (Contrast Pasco: "I plan to concentrate on … literary allusion, by which I mean simply allusion that occurs in literature" [Allan H. Pasco, *Allusion: A Literary Graft* (Toronto: University of Toronto Press, 1994), 6]).

text-segment in the same literary work), but without mention of the act of referencing."[6] The two primary features that characterize allusion are, therefore, that it is *implicit* (not marked by a citation formula, in contrast to quotation) and *intentional* (deliberate on the part of the author).[7]

As far as the first of these characteristics is concerned, scholars have identified, in addition to allusion, several other commonly used techniques of implicit literary referencing. Such techniques—which are denoted by terms such as *echo*, *influence*, and *reverberation*—describe the varying degrees of implicitness (i.e., the spectrum from the more obvious to the subtler) that can be found in the ways authors use sources in order to create their own texts. Because this book is about how the biblical writers used *paronomasia* in their allusions to other parts of the Bible and is not primarily concerned with identifying innerbiblical allusions per se, I will give little attention to the degree to which allusion, echo, influence, reverberation, and other, similar categories are to be distinguished from one another (even though the distinctions between these categories are interesting and worth making).[8] In addition, the second defining

---

6. Michael Lyons, "'I Also Could Talk as You Do' (Job 16:4): The Function of Intratextual Quotation and Allusion in Job," in *Reading Job Intertextually*, ed. Katharine Dell and Will Kynes, LHBOTS 574 (New York: Bloomsbury, 2013), 171. Lyons's next sentence is: "It is this feature that distinguishes allusion from quotation; allusion lacks the marking present in quotation, and presumes the reader's knowledge of the source referred to." See similarly Rachel Wetzsteon, "Allusion," *PEPP*, 42, and William A. Tooman, *Gog of Magog: Reuse of Scripture and Compositional Technique in Ezekiel 38–39*, FAT 2/52 (Tübingen: Mohr Siebeck, 2011), 5–6. One advantage to differentiating allusion and quotation by their respective implicit and explicit natures—in addition to being the way literary theorists outside biblical studies tend to define the terms (Tooman, *Gog of Magog*, 5)—is that this circumvents the difficulties involved in attempts to differentiate the two based on such criteria as the number of words the target text reproduces from the source text, the morphological fidelity with which these words are reproduced in the target text, or the order in which they appear: "In biblical studies, the line between quotation and allusion is blurry. There is no standard for how many borrowed words are required to qualify an allusion as a quotation. Nor do biblical scholars agree on whether identical morphology and order of elements are required in a quotation" (4–5).

7. Wetzsteon, "Allusion," 42. Wetzsteon also defines allusions as being "brief." Because allusions can sometimes be extended over large portions of text, however, and because what "brief" means is open to question, I do not consider brevity to be a definitive trait of allusion.

8. On echo and influence, see Tooman, *Gog of Magog*, 4–10; Benjamin D. Sommer,

characteristic of allusion, its intentional nature, has led me to avoid using the term "intertextuality" in this study, since that term is often used to describe relationships between texts that are not characterized by literary dependence but rather that exist primarily in the minds of readers.⁹

A Prophet Reads Scripture: Allusion in Isaiah 40–66 (Stanford, CA: Stanford University Press, 1998), 10–17. On reverberation, see Stephen Hinds, *Allusion and Intertext: Dynamics of Appropriation in Roman Poetry* (New York: Cambridge University Press, 1998), 32. See also Gian Biagio Conte, *The Rhetoric of Imitation: Genre and Poetic Memory in Virgil and Other Latin Poets*, trans. Charles Segal (Ithaca, NY: Cornell University Press, 1986), 24–25. The situation is complicated because scholars often use terms such as *allusion* and *echo* in different ways (David Shaw, "Converted Imaginations? The Reception of Richard Hays's Intertextual Method," *CBR* 11 [2013]: 241–42). Although in this book I have tried to discuss only examples of textual referencing that I believe can properly be described as allusions, the use of this specific label (as opposed to *echo, influence, reverberation*, etc.) is ultimately less important than the relationships that actually obtain between the texts under discussion and their functions. The broad definition of allusion given by Abasciano is helpful in this regard: "In its broad sense, allusion will refer to any intentional reference to a text, person, event etc. On this definition, allusion encompasses quotation and can refer to it. To quote is to allude but to allude is not necessarily to quote. In its narrower sense, 'allusion' will refer to informal, intentional reference to a text, person, event, etc. other than quotation" (Brian J. Abasciano, *Paul's Use of the Old Testament in Romans 9:1–9: An Intertextual and Theological Exegesis* [London: T&T Clark, 2005], 16; cited by Shaw, "Converted Imaginations," 242).

9. Wetzsteon, "Allusion," 42. On the theoretical problems surrounding the use of the term *intertextuality* in biblical studies, Brooke Lester writes: "In hindsight, it is clear that 'intertextuality,' as coined by Kristeva (1969), is different enough from the diachronic study of inner-biblical interpretation that the use of 'intertextuality' as an umbrella term for literary dependence has only bred confusion" (Lester, "Inner-Biblical Interpretation," 445). See further John Barton, "*Déjà Lu*: Intertextuality, Method or Theory?" in *Reading Job Intertextually*, ed. Katharine J. Dell and Will Kynes, LHBOTS 574 (New York: Bloomsbury, 2013), 2–16; Will Kynes, "Job and Isaiah 40–55: Intertextualities in Dialogue," in Dell and Kynes, *Reading Job Intertextually*, 94; Miller, "Intertextuality in Old Testament Research"; Christopher B. Hays, "Echoes of the Ancient Near East? Intertextuality and the Comparative Study of the Old Testament," in *The Word Leaps the Gap: Essays on Scripture and Theology in Honor of Richard B. Hays*, ed. J. Ross Wagner, C. Kavin Rowe, and A. Katherine Grieb (Grand Rapids: Eerdmans, 2009), 20–43; Patricia K. Tull, "Intertextuality and the Hebrew Scriptures," *CurBS* 8 (2000): 59–90; E. J. van Wolde, "Trendy Intertextuality?" in *Intertextuality in Biblical Writings: Essays in Honour of Bas van Iersel*, ed. Sipka Draisma (Kampen: Kok, 1989), 43–49; Benjamin D. Sommer, "Exegesis, Allusion and Intertextuality in the Hebrew

For the purposes of this book, therefore, I define *allusion* (which I use as shorthand for *literary allusion*) quite broadly, following the basic definition of Michael Lyons above, as referring to *any implicit, intentional reference in a text to an earlier text, whether obvious (overt) or subtle (covert)*.

A literary allusion differs from the text it alludes to (the source text) in *context* and usually (though not necessarily, in cases when the source text is reproduced verbatim) in *content*. Because by definition an allusion points back to an earlier text, what is highlighted in an allusion is the way the later text *differs from* (for example, omits from, adds to, or reconfigures) the earlier text—in other words, how the alluding text *transforms* its source text.[10] This is true even in the most minimal cases in which the source text is reproduced verbatim in the alluding text, since the act of providing the earlier text with a new literary context itself constitutes a transformation.[11]

Allusion therefore involves continuity with a difference. As I have just observed, the similarities between the source text and the alluding text are precisely what brings the differences between them—that is, what is new in the alluding text—into relief. Some scholars emphasize the fact that these differences that allusions create vis-à-vis their source texts often involve discontinuity or rupture with tradition.[12] Although this provides an adequate

---

Bible: A Response to Lyle Eslinger," *VT* 46 (1996): 479–89; Sommer, *Prophet Reads Scripture*, 6–10.

10. Allusion relates two texts, the alluding text and the source text, and produces something that is greater than the sum of the two (Pasco, *Allusion*, 13–14; Conte, *Rhetoric of Imitation*, 24).

11. Pasco, *Allusion*, 39–40. Allusions' transformation of source texts by putting them into a new context is actually just one of several kinds of possible transformations of a source text through textual reuse; see Meir Sternberg, *The Poetics of Biblical Narrative: Ideological Literature and the Drama of Reading* (Bloomington: Indiana University Press, 1985), 390–93.

12. In biblical studies this tendency can be seen particularly in the work of Bernard Levinson, according to whom the biblical tradents were compelled to honor and to continue handing down the traditions they received even as they sought to supersede and, in some cases, to invalidate them. Thus, Levinson speaks of "the hermeneutics of innovation" in order to describe the way in which the biblical authors found it necessary to appeal to the authority or wisdom of their predecessors' words precisely in order to surpass or undermine those very same words. Levinson defines "the hermeneutics of innovation" specifically as "the extent to which exegesis may make itself independent of the source text, challenging and even attempting to reverse or abrogate its substantive content, all the while under the *hermenutical mantle of consistency* with or dependency upon its source. *Exegesis is thus often radically transformative*:

and helpful framework for understanding some examples of innerbiblical allusion (as well as other kinds of innerbiblical interpretation that do not involve allusion), other allusions in the Hebrew Bible appear, in contrast, rather strongly to affirm the traditions to which they allude even as they transform them. In such instances, the authors of the alluding texts appear to have sought not (primarily) to undermine the tradition they inherited but rather *to mine it for incipient meanings that they believed could only be understood in the light of new circumstances*.[13] Many of the examples of allusive paronomasia that I discuss in this book will illustrate this point.

1.3. Paronomasia in the Hebrew Bible

The literary device known as paronomasia is pervasive in the Hebrew Bible, and it functioned as a productive compositional factor on the level of phrases, sentences, paragraphs, and even entire books, especially in the poetic literature, but also, as recent studies have demonstrated, in prose.[14]

---

new religious, intellectual, or cultural insights are granted sanction and legitimacy by being presented *as if* they derived from authoritative texts that neither contain nor anticipate those insights" (Bernard M. Levinson, *Deuteronomy and the Hermeneutics of Legal Innovation* [New York: Oxford University Press, 1997], 15, emphasis added). See also Levinson's *Legal Revision and Religious Renewal in Ancient Israel* (Cambridge: Cambridge University Press, 2008). Interest in the innovative aspect of innerbiblical interpretation is also apparent in the work of Levinson's teacher, Michael Fishbane (see, e.g., *Biblical Interpretation*, 86–87). Similar notions of literary dependence exist outside of biblical studies as well; for example, "W. J. Bate described the 'burden' that literary trad. [i.e., tradition] places on poets while also allowing them the chance to achieve maturity and originality by wrestling with it" and "Harold Bloom's theory of the 'anxiety of influence' put forth an Oedipal account of poetic borrowing" (Wetzsteon, "Allusion," 43).

13. This appears to be the case not infrequently in the literature of the Qumran community and in the New Testament. Although modern scholars have often understood both of these literatures to be reading their own ideas into the Hebrew Bible, a more nuanced perspective understands them as attempting to read the texts of the Hebrew Bible in the light of new circumstances (most notably, in the light of the appearance of the Teacher of Righteousness and Jesus of Nazareth, respectively).

14. The most recent overview of paronomasia in the Hebrew Bible is Scott B. Noegel, "Paronomasia," *EHLL* 3:24–29. On paronomasia in biblical prose, see, e.g., Moshe Garsiel, *Biblical Names: A Literary Study of Midrashic Name Derivations and Puns* (Ramat Gan: Bar-Ilan University Press, 1991); Ronald L. Androphy, "Paronomasia in the Former Prophets: A Taxonomic Catalogue, Description, and Analysis" (DHL

A typical definition of paronomasia is provided by the *Oxford English Dictionary*: "Wordplay based on words which sound alike."[15] Although—based on definitions such as the one just provided—paronomasia is often referred to as *soundplay* or simply equated with the more general term *wordplay*, it is well known that, as elsewhere in the ancient Near East, in the Hebrew Bible paronomasia was used for a wide variety of purposes, some of which were humorous or playful (in the common sense of that term) but many of which were quite serious.[16] As Scott Noegel has observed,

> Most cases of paronomasia in the Hebrew Bible bespeak a worldview on par with that of the literati of ancient Egypt and Mesopotamian [*sic*], who deemed words inherently powerful and manipulated them for their cosmological charge. Indeed, paronomasia often served the needs of ritual and performance more than it did the arenas of rhetoric and ornamentation.[17]

---

diss., Jewish Theological Seminary, 2011); and the references in Noegel, "Paronomasia," 25.

15. Similar is the definition in the most recent (2012) edition of the standard reference work *The Princeton Encyclopedia of Poetry and Poetics*: "Wordplay based on like-sounding words, e.g., a pun" (Eleanor Cook, "Paronomasia," *PEPP*, 1003). Entries on "wordplay" in biblical studies encyclopedias, which typically equate the terms "wordplay" and "paronomasia," tend to contain similar definitions (see below). My approach reflects that taken by *EHLL*, which does not contain an article on "wordplay" but instead treats paronomasia and polysemy as distinct (though related) phenomena. See also Cook's statement that "in the analysis of puns, the most familiar division is between homophonic puns (like-sounding, as in 'done' and 'Donne') and homonymic or semantic puns (different meanings in one word, as in railed 'ties' and 'ties' of the heart in Bishop's 'Chemin de Fer')" (Cook, "Paronomasia," 1004).

16. Noegel lists the following functions of paronomasia in the Hebrew Bible: "aesthetic, onomatopoeic, emphatic, rhetorical, referential, allusive, humorous/satirical, hermeneutic, and performative" (Noegel, "Paronomasia," 28). Interestingly, "allusion," the other main focus of this study in addition to paronomasia, originally denoted literary play that was intended "to mock" or "to make a fanciful reference to" (the term "allusion" derives from Latin *ad-* "to" + *ludere* "to play"; see Wetzsteon, "Allusion," 42). While allusions can be playful or comical, many are not, and thus allusion should not be thought of as inherently playful if by "play" something comical or nonserious is meant: "Despite its etymology, allusion need not be playful" (Wetzsteon, "Allusion," 42). As the present study emphasizes, the same is true of paronomasia or sound*play*.

17. Noegel, "Paronomasia," 24–25.

For these and other reasons, the terms *soundplay* and *wordplay* are not ideal synonyms for paronomasia in the Hebrew Bible.[18] Because the use of these terms is so entrenched, however, I will acquiesce to popular usage and sometimes employ the term *soundplay* in this study or refer to one word *playing* on (the sound of) another. However, I use these terms with the qualification that they are intended only as *formal* descriptions of the relationship that obtains between words that sound similar but differ in meaning and not as *functional* descriptions of the effect(s) created by this relationship.

To broaden the basic definition provided above, paronomasia is normally understood to describe the relationship that obtains between two or more words that sound similar, differ in meaning, occur in close proximity, and have been deliberately juxtaposed in order to draw the reader's attention.[19] Each of these four characteristics requires comment. To anticipate the conclusions of the following discussion, only the first two of these characteristics (similar sound, dissimilar meaning) should be seen as essential to the definition of paronomasia.

---

18. Scott B. Noegel, "'Word Play' in Qoheleth," *JHS* 7 (2007): 3–4; Noegel, preface to *Puns and Pundits: Word Play in the Hebrew Bible and Ancient Near Eastern Literature*, ed. Scott B. Noegel (Bethesda, MD: CDL, 2000), xvi. Compare Benjamin R. Foster, *Before the Muses: An Anthology of Akkadian Literature*, 3rd ed. (Bethesda, MD: CDL, 2005), 16.

19. The best overviews of paronomasia in the Hebrew Bible are Noegel, "Paronomasia"; Edward Greenstein, "Wordplay, Hebrew," *ABD* 6:968–71; Jack M. Sasson, "Wordplay in the Old Testament," *IDBSup*, 968–70. See also L. J. de Regt, "Wordplay in the OT," *NIDB* 5:898–99; J. J. Glück, "Paronomasia in Biblical Literature," *Sem* 1 (1970): 50–78; A. Guillaume, "Paronomasia in the Old Testament," *JSS* 9 (1964): 282–96; Wilfred G. E. Watson, *Classical Hebrew Poetry: A Guide to Its Techniques*, 2nd ed. (Edinburgh: T&T Clark, 2004), 222–29; Luis Alonso Schökel, *A Manual of Hebrew Poetics*, SubBi 11 (Rome: Pontifical Biblical Institute, 1988), 20–33. The modern study of paronomasia in the Hebrew Bible is usually traced back to Immanuel M. Casanowicz ("Paronomasia in the Old Testament" [PhD diss., Johns Hopkins University, 1892/1894]; Casanowicz, "Paronomasia in the Old Testament," *JBL* 12 [1893]: 105–67). Most standard articles on paronomasia by biblical scholars use *wordplay* and *paronomasia* as synonyms: Greenstein ("Wordplay, Hebrew," 968), Sasson ("Wordplay," 968), de Regt ("Wordplay," 898); see also Androphy, "Paronomasia," 3, and Alonso Schökel, *Manual*, 29.

1.3.1. Similarity of Sound, Difference in Meaning

What constitutes similarity of sound? Paronomasia can be (1) homonymic (referring to words that sound identical and are spelled identically but differ in meaning; e.g., "bear" as noun or verb) or (2) homophonic (referring to words that sound identical but differ in spelling and meaning; e.g., "bear" and "bare"), or (3) can involve words that sound similar but not identical and that differ in spelling and meaning (e.g., "bear" and "pear"). These three categories are differentiated by increasing degrees of markedness: the first is unique in that examples can be identified only on the basis of semantics (but not visually or orally/aurally); examples of the second category can be identified on the basis of semantics as well as visually (though not orally/aurally); and examples of the third category can be identified on the basis of semantics, visually, and orally/aurally. Given these differences in markedness, a useful distinction can be made between homonymic paronomasia (the first category) and nonhomonymic paronomasia (the second and third categories). The relevance of this distinction for identifying examples of allusive paronomasia in the Hebrew Bible will be discussed below.

Paronomasia can operate on the level of consonants (consonance) or vowels (assonance).[20] For simplicity's sake and also because the text of the Hebrew Bible was originally written without vowels (the Masoretic pointing being a later, interpretive tradition), in this book I will focus almost exclusively on examples of consonantal paronomasia.[21] Therefore, in the pages that follow the word *paronomasia* should be considered shorthand for *similarity of sound on the level of consonants, not vowels, between words that differ in meaning*.

---

20. Some biblical scholars use the term *alliteration*, in keeping with the way it is defined with respect to its use in Western languages, to refer only to the repetition of the same or similar (consonantal) sound(s) in different words *in initial position* only, but others employ the term with respect to Hebrew to refer to the repetition of the same or similar sound(s) in different words *in any position* (e.g., Gary A. Rendsburg, "Alliteration," *EHLL* 1:86; Noegel, "Paronomasia," 24). According to the latter understanding, "alliteration," "consonance," and "consonantal paronomasia" are interchangeable terms. In order to avoid confusion, I have preferred in this book to use the term *paronomasia* rather than the term *alliteration*.

21. Occasional examples of assonance (between words in close proximity, not allusive examples) will be noted and will be labeled as such.

Although a few scholars insist that words can be said to sound similar (and thus be related by paronomasia) only if they contain identical phonemes in a different order, most scholars consider this too restrictive a definition and also define as paronyms words that contain phonemes that are similar, but not identical, *with respect to place or manner of articulation* (and such sounds may occur in the same or in a different order in the words in question).²² On the other hand, words that sound similar but share the same etymology should not be considered paronyms,²³ nor should by-forms of the same word (such as שמלה and שלמה, both of which mean "garment").²⁴

1.3.2. Proximity

Most biblical scholars assume or state explicitly that paronomasia in the Bible can only exist between words in close proximity. Edward Greenstein, for example, defines paronomasia as the "use *in proximity* of words that display similarity of sound with dissimilarity of meaning,"²⁵ and according to L. J. de Regt, paronomasia "involves two (or more) words with different meanings, but almost coinciding in sound, that occur *in the same context*."²⁶ What precisely *proximity* and *same context* in these definitions mean, however, is not stated.²⁷ On the other hand, Jack Sasson observes

---

22. Greenstein, "Wordplay, Hebrew," 969; Noegel, "Paronomasia," 25. This can also include the use of identical graphemes that were pronounced differently because they represent different Proto-Semitic consonants (Gary A. Rendsburg, "Word Play in Biblical Hebrew," in Noegel, *Puns and Pundits*, 149–50, 154–55; Sasson, "Word Play," 969).

23. E.g., an infinitive absolute and a finite form from the same verbal root (*figura etymologica*) as well as other occurrences of more than one verbal form derived from the same root or a verb and a noun object from the same root (cognate accusative); see Noegel, "Paronomasia," 24; Greenstein, "Wordplay, Hebrew," 968–69.

24. For similar apparent orthographic variants found in parallel texts and allusions in the Bible that may or may not be paronyms, see below.

25. Greenstein, "Wordplay, Hebrew," 968, emphasis added. This is the definition Greenstein provides for "wordplay," which he uses as a synonym of "paronomasia."

26. De Regt, "Wordplay," 898, emphasis added.

27. Consider, as a random example, the fact that the word נשפך in Lam 2:11 (חמרמרו מעי נשפך לארץ כבדי, "My insides are in anguish, my being [lit., 'liver'] is poured out on the ground") appears to be a deliberate paronym of נהפך in Lam 1:20 (מעי חמרמרו נהפך לבי בקרבי, "My insides are in anguish, my heart is overturned in my midst"), a verse from which it is separated by twelve intervening verses. Do Lam

that the Bible contains "extended wordplay"—that is, paronomasia that extends "beyond the confines of paragraphs or even chapters"[28]—and this longer-range use of paronomasia has been extensively documented in the Former Prophets in a recent study by Ronald Androphy.[29] Indeed, even Greenstein, whose basic definition of paronomasia appears the most restrictive of those I have just cited with respect to the scope in which the device may occur, recognizes that paronomasia can also operate at great textual distances; that is, it can function as a marker of allusion.[30] By creating a nexus between words that are not in close proximity, allusions create the possibility for paronomasia to operate at (sometimes large) textual distances.

Although most cases of paronomasia in the Hebrew Bible do occur in proximity, recent studies of innerbiblical allusion have made it clear that the Bible also contains many examples of allusive paronomasia as well.[31] The existence of allusive paronomasia outside the Bible is well known, and the recognition that it occurs in the Bible is not new, occa-

---

1:20 and 2:11 belong to the same context—i.e., are these two verses in proximity—or are we dealing here with a case of allusive paronomasia? This example suggests that the boundary between *the same context* and *allusion* is not always easy to define. In any case, Morier's view that paronomasia is a "figure par laquelle on rapproche, *dans la phrase*, des mots offrant des sonorités analogues avec des sens différents" is certainly too restrictive, at least for the Hebrew Bible (which, it should be noted, is not his concern; see Henri Morier, "Paronomase," in *Dictionnaire de poétique et de rhétorique*, 5th ed. [Paris: Presses Universitaires de France, 1998], 868, emphasis added).

28. Sasson, "Wordplay," 970.

29. Androphy, "Paronomasia."

30. "Wordplay may serve to allude to another passage, adding an association to the present one" (Greenstein, "Wordplay, Hebrew," 970). Greenstein cites one example of this, Tur-Sinai's proposal that the verb פרע in Exod 32:25 alludes to the בעל פעור episode in Num 25 (ibid.). The referential and allusive uses of paronomasia are also noted by Noegel, "Paronomasia," 28, though unfortunately he does not provide any examples.

31. Especially noteworthy in this regard is Sommer, *Prophet Reads Scripture*, who demonstrates that paronomasia, which he consistently refers to as "sound play" (along with polysemy [Sommer's "word play"] and what he calls "the split-up pattern," whereby a phrase is broken up and intervening words added), is a common allusive technique in Isa 40–66. Sommer's study constitutes the most systematic treatment of allusive paronomasia in the Hebrew Bible that has appeared to date, though by design it is limited to only a relatively small corpus in the Bible, and, as noted, allusive paronomasia is but one of several literary devices on which he focuses.

sional examples of it having been noted not only by modern scholars but also by much earlier biblical interpreters.[32] However, biblical scholars are just beginning to recognize the extent to which paronomasia was used allusively in the Bible and the importance this phenomenon has for our understanding of the way the biblical writers interacted with the traditions they inherited.[33]

De Regt observes that paronomasia "creates a special effect: it intensifies the message and draws attention to a certain point."[34] Because paronomasia, like allusion, is characterized by relating words that are similar (in sound) and different (in sense) in a way that brings the difference between their meanings into relief, the use in an allusion of one or more words that invoke one or more words in the source text *by means of paronomasia* is a particularly striking way of (to adapt de Regt's statement) intensifying the allusion's message and drawing attention to the allusion's point; that is, it highlights the difference in meaning between the alluding text and the source text.

---

32. Unfortunately for the scholar who wishes to study allusive paronomasia in the Hebrew Bible systematically, most suggested instances of the phenomenon have been made incidentally in works focusing on other subjects and are therefore scattered throughout a very wide literature.

33. Scott Noegel explains the general failure on the part of modern scholars to appreciate allusive polysemy in the Bible, and his remarks apply, mutatis mutandis, to allusive paronomasia. He writes: "The inability fully to appreciate internal references and punful allusions applies not only to the modern philological approach within historical linguistics"—which, according to Noegel, generally ignores polysemy in the Bible—"but to the discipline of socio-linguistics as well. Specifically, socio-linguistic studies on polysemy begin with the assumption that puns are effective only when in close proximity. While this certainly is true for those of us dependent on computer chips and calculators, it cannot be said of the ancients, whose well-practiced memories, without such aids, were far superior" (Scott B. Noegel, *Janus Parallelism in the Book of Job*, JSOTSup 223 [Sheffield: Sheffield Academic, 1996], 16). Allusive paronomasia occurs throughout human speech, often outside of literary contexts. Much of the entry on paronomasia in Morier's *Dictionnaire de poétique et de rhétorique* is devoted to examples of "paronomase allusive," and most of the examples he cites appear in nonliterary contexts and allude to axioms, not literary compositions (Morier, "Paronomase," 869–70).

34. De Regt, "Wordplay," 898.

1.3.3. Deliberate Juxtaposition

To say that paronomasia involves the *deliberate* juxtaposition of words that sound similar but differ in meaning *for the purpose of* drawing the reader's attention is to stir up a hornet's nest of questions regarding the ability of (modern) readers to discern (ancient) authorial intention (and, for some literary theorists, even more radical questions about the degree to which authorial intention is relevant for interpretation or exists at all). The relevance of authorial intention for instances of paronomasia that occur in close proximity is not my concern in this book, and it has, in any case, been discussed elsewhere.[35] In the rest of this chapter and in the following ones, I will address the issue of authorial intention only as it relates to *allusive* paronomasia. For reasons that will become clear shortly, however, further discussion of this topic must wait until several other issues have first been addressed.

1.4. THE ROLE OF PARONOMASIA IN THE EXPRESSION AND DEVELOPMENT OF ISRAEL'S THEOLOGICAL TRADITIONS

Research on allusive paronomasia in the Bible is still in its infancy, and no work devoted entirely to this literary device has yet appeared. The present study is intended as a modest effort to begin the process of redressing this lacuna in the scholarly literature; it is just a first step, however, and my hope is that other scholars will continue to expand our understanding of this interesting and, I would argue, important feature of biblical literature. A comprehensive treatment of this subject—if, indeed, one can ever be written—lies far in the future. My main goal in this book is much more modest: to present a relatively small (though, I hope, substantial enough) number of what I consider to be clear and interesting examples of allusive paronomasia in the Hebrew Bible for the purpose of demonstrating (1) that this device was employed by a variety of biblical writers and, more importantly, (2) that giving careful attention to the ways they put it to use can enrich our understanding of the growth of the biblical text as a whole and the development of ancient Israelite and early Jewish theological traditions.

---

35. Thomas P. McCreesh, *Biblical Sound and Sense: Poetic Sound Patterns in Proverbs 10–29*, JSOTSup 128 (Sheffield: Sheffield Academic, 1991), 17–22, esp. 17, 21–22.

In order to appreciate how the biblical writers used paronomasia allusively to develop their theological traditions, it will be helpful first to look briefly at how they used paronomasia for this purpose in isolated contexts, that is, between words that occur in close proximity.

Paronomasia has a variety of purposes in the Bible, from producing simple stylistic effects (such as euphony for the sake of literary pleasure) to achieving more significant literary goals (such as indicating irony, reversal, the appropriateness of a character's fate, and more). Because the Bible is a work of theological literature, it is not surprising that one of paronomasia's more pervasive and significant roles in the Bible is its use as a vehicle of divine revelation or as a tool the biblical writers employed to draw attention to—and, in certain cases, to help themselves and their readers conceptualize—God's relationship to humanity (whether individuals, Israel, or the nations).[36]

That paronomasia is employed in individual texts throughout the Bible to make a theological point or as a means of communicating divine revelation is well known. The deity's use of soundplay to reveal his plans for Israel, for example, is famously illustrated by several prophetic texts.[37] In the narrative of Jeremiah's call, immediately following YHWH's declaration that he has set the prophet "over nations and over kingdoms, to pluck up and to break down, to destroy and to overthrow, to build and to plant" (Jer 1:10), we find two visions of divine judgment against Judah that

---

36. As Scott Noegel has observed, the study of paronomasia and other wordplay in the Hebrew Bible (as well as other ancient Near Eastern texts) "raises important theological questions, since at the center of ... [these] puns and paronomasia lie sacred and/or magical texts. The illocutionary power of the word to transform reality is everywhere evident in ancient Near Eastern texts" (Noegel, preface, xvi). Sasson notes that paronomasia was used to express divine revelation in ancient Greece as well: "Paronomasia is the term employed by ancient Greek commentators when referring to rhetoric [sic] devices designed to engage the attention of an audience. The use of paronomasia promoted a certain aura of ambiguity, which was intended to excite curiosity and to invite a search for meanings that were not readily apparent. It is not surprising, therefore, that divine revelations were often couched in paronomastic forms" (Sasson, "Wordplay," 968).

37. The examples treated here are discussed together by Stefan Schorch, "Between Science and Magic: The Function and Roots of Paronomasia in the Prophetic Books of the Hebrew Bible," in Noegel, *Puns and Pundits*, 215–16. Jeremiah 1:11–12 and Amos 8:1–2 are also mentioned together by Greenstein, who observes that "the polysemy of language, as in these symbolic visions, conceals revelation" (Greenstein, "Wordplay, Hebrew," 971), and by de Regt, "Wordplay," 899.

are expressed in terms of paronomasia.[38] In the first, YHWH shows Jeremiah "the branch of an *almond tree* [שָׁקֵד]" in order to reveal that "I am *watchful* [שֹׁקֵד] to bring my word to pass" (Jer 1:11–12).[39] In the second, YHWH shows Jeremiah "a *steaming* [נָפוּחַ, *qal* of נפח] pot" as a means of disclosing that "from the north disaster *will break loose* [תִּפָּתַח, *niphal* of פתח] on all the inhabitants of the land" of Judah (Jer 1:13–14).[40] Later in the book of Jeremiah, YHWH once again declares judgment on Judah by punning on the name of a cooking vessel: after instructing the prophet to "*buy a jug* [וְקָנִיתָ בַקְבֻּק] made by a potter," YHWH declares, "*I will empty/ lay waste* [וּבַקֹּתִי, *qal* of בקק] the plans of Judah and Jerusalem" (Jer 19:1, 7).[41] Another well-known example in which YHWH uses paronomasia to express his will (specifically for judgment) is found in Amos 8:1–2, where YHWH shows the prophet "a basket of *summer fruit* [קָיִץ]" as a way of revealing that "*the end* [הַקֵּץ] has come for my people Israel."

These examples indicate that for at least some in ancient Israel, paronomasia was considered a worthy vehicle for YHWH's direct revelation. Moreover, inasmuch as the first two visions discussed above (Jer 1:11–12, 13–14) immediately follow Jeremiah's call to proclaim the divine word, they also provide direct divine warrant for the prophets' (or at least for Jeremiah's) use of paronomasia to convey revelation from God—a phenomenon that is reflected in the prophetic books' particularly rich use of soundplay.[42]

---

38. Most of the translations of the biblical text in this book follow the NJPS. When necessary, I have modified the NJPS rendering or provided my own translation in order to facilitate the argumentation. I have standardized all the translations, however, by not capitalizing pronouns referring to God.

39. YHWH's call of Jeremiah and his declaration that he will watch over (שקד) his people (Jer 1:10–12) is taken up again in Jer 31:28, where, significantly, the message of Jer 1:11–12 (which, given the subsequent context, focuses on the negative aspects of v. 10) is turned into a *redemptive* act focusing on the positive aspects of Jer 1:10. On the other hand, YHWH's determination to watch over (שקד) Judah *in order to punish* extends to the Judean exiles in Egypt, where they have fled from the Babylonian onslaught (Jer 44:27), and later appears to be taken up by Dan 9:14.

40. The effect of the soundplay is heightened by the presence of several more words that share the sounds /n/ and /p/ of נפוח: all the words of the clause ופניו מפני צפונה in v. 13 and the word צפון in v. 14.

41. The primary paronomasia is between בקבק and ובקתי, but וקנית enhances the effect.

42. On the prophets' penchant for paronomasia, see Sasson, "Wordplay," 970; Schorch, "Between Science and Magic," 205.

Also indicative of ancient Israel's belief that paronomasia was a particularly suitable vehicle of revelation about the nature or fate of a group or an individual is the widespread use in the Bible (whether by God, another character in the story, or the narrator) of paronomasia involving the name of a group, individual, or place in order to say something about its character or destiny.[43] This phenomenon, which scholars refer to as *nomen omen*, is so widespread that it needs no illustration for readers familiar with the biblical text.[44] In cases of *nomen omen*, the paronomasia unlocks or reveals meanings that the biblical authors thought were embedded or incipient in the names being played upon.[45] As I will demonstrate throughout the remainder of this study, allusive paronomasia in the Bible often has a similar function, serving to actualize or reveal meanings the biblical writers considered to be incipient or nascent in earlier

---

43. Although the idea that the meaning of the past, present, or future can be unlocked by means of paronomasia is particularly conspicuous in the Bible's use of paronomasia involving names (proper nouns), there is no real difference between this and the use of paronomasia involving common nouns. Greenstein distinguishes paronomasia involving proper and common nouns but admits that he does so simply "for convenience of organization" (Greenstein, "Wordplay, Hebrew," 970).

44. Ibid. Noteworthy studies on *nomen omen* are Andrzej Strus, *Nomen-omen: La stylistique sonore des noms propres dans le Pentateuque*, AnBib 80 (Rome: Biblical Institute Press, 1978); Russell T. Cherry III, "Paronomasia and Proper Names in the Old Testament: Rhetorical Function and Literary Effect" (PhD diss., Southern Baptist Theological Seminary, 1988); Garsiel, *Biblical Names*. See also the recent article by Christopher Rollston, "*Ad Nomen Argumenta*: Personal Names as Pejorative Puns in Ancient Texts," in *In the Shadow of Bezalel: Aramaic, Biblical, and Ancient Near Eastern Studies in Honor of Bezalel Porten*, ed. Alejandro F. Botta (Leiden: Brill, 2012), 367–86.

45. Greenstein writes: "When Jacob blesses his sons in Genesis 49, or a prophet condemns a nation, by interpreting their names through paronomasia, they may be more than merely playing with words. They may be releasing a hidden fate" (Greenstein, "Wordplay, Hebrew," 971). The biblical authors' use of paronomasia as a means of revelation—their exploitation of the potentialities of language to interpret the past, present, and future, and to generate theological discourse—reflects the ancient Israelite concept of the power of language, a belief with deep roots in Mesopotamia, one that possibly goes back to the very beginnings of writing: "As with riddle and charm, the pun is associated with very early writing. Possibly it gave birth to Western writing itself in the Sumerian alphabet [sic] of pre-3000 BCE Mesopotamia.... As Frye says, 'Paronomasia is one of the essential elements of verbal creation'" (Cook, "Paronomasia," 1004).

texts, meanings that in their view had become evident only in the light of new circumstances.

1.5. Identifying Allusive Paronomasia in the Hebrew Bible: Methodological Considerations

Despite the prevalence of paronomasia in the Bible, centuries of attention to the phenomenon among readers of the Bible, and the widespread recognition among biblical scholars of paronomasia's role in the development of Israel's theological traditions (in individual texts), the allusive use of paronomasia in the Bible has received only occasional attention, usually in the form of a passing notice of a possible example. Perhaps the major reason for this general neglect is the widespread assumption among biblical scholars, noted above, that paronomasia can only operate between words that occur in close proximity. Even when one realizes that this assumption is incorrect, however, certain methodological challenges can make it difficult to identify cases of allusive paronomasia or to construct a persuasive argument that what appears to be an example of allusive paronomasia actually is one and is not something else.

These challenges may involve either of the two basic steps necessary for identifying allusive paronomasia, the first of which is identifying an allusion and the second of which is identifying, within the allusion, the allusive paronomasia itself. In what follows, I will first briefly discuss some of the difficulties that can arise in the process of attempting to identify innerbiblical allusions and describe the methodology for doing so that I employ in the subsequent chapters of this book. However, the main purpose of the following discussion is to describe the challenges involved specifically in identifying allusive paronomasia in the Bible and to provide a methodology for doing so with a reasonable degree of confidence. I will devote more space to this latter pair of tasks since, as far as I am aware, this is the first study to deal with them explicitly and since they provide a theoretical framework that will allow the reader to evaluate the strength of the examples found in the following chapters. In addition, it is my hope that the framework and principles I provide for identifying allusive paronomasia in the Bible will encourage others to identify and describe further examples of the phenomenon beyond the relatively limited selection that I discuss in this book.

1.5.1. Identifying Innerbiblical Allusions

In recent years a number of excellent studies have appeared that discuss the principles by which innerbiblical allusions can be identified.[46] For this reason and because my primary concern in the remainder of this chapter is not how to identify innerbiblical allusions per se but rather how to identify allusive paronomasia in the Bible, the following remarks on how to identify innerbiblical allusions will be brief.

Any discussion on how to identify innerbiblical allusions must address at least two basic issues: what are the markers of literary allusion, and how does one determine the direction of dependence between texts considered to be related by means of allusion?

1.5.1.1. The Markers of Literary Allusion

Although scholars debate what markers, if any, are minimally necessary for an allusion to be identified,[47] the most basic and common markers of literary allusion are *thematic and lexical correspondences* (i.e., the presence of shared ideas and language, especially unique or distinctive ideas or language) between two texts.[48] In addition to such conceptual and verbal links, another strong marker of allusion can be *formal or structural connections*—for example, the presence in the alluding text and in the source text not only of the same or similar ideas or words but their presence *in the same or in a similar order*.[49] Furthermore, the argument for an allusion can sometimes be made more probable if it can be demonstrated that the proposed alluding text contains other allusions (i.e., if the text has *allusive density*), especially other allusions to the proposed source text (a phenomenon known as *recurrence*).[50]

Thus, allusions are often marked by semantic, syntactic, or structural connections between two (or more) texts—including the use of the same or similar words, locutions, imagery, concepts, rhetorical structures or devices, arguments, and the like—or a combination of such elements.[51]

---

46. See nn. 3 and 6 above.
47. For discussion, see, e.g., Shaw, "Converted Imaginations."
48. Tooman, *Gog of Magog*, 27–30.
49. Shaw, "Converted Imaginations," 236. See also Wetzsteon, "Allusion," 43.
50. Shaw, "Converted Imaginations," 235.
51. As the present study demonstrates, an allusion can also be marked by con-

Although, generally speaking, the most clearly identifiable allusions are those with the most connections as well as the most kinds of connections,[52] some allusions are subtle, being marked by only a small number of such elements (this can be especially true when the elements are unique to or distinctive of the two texts involved).[53] In fact, an allusion can exist even in the absence of shared language, which, as noted above, is often considered to be the most basic or essential marker of allusion.[54] Although some subtle allusions are easy to identify, at least for readers familiar with the source text,[55] many are not, and the very fact that subtle allusions exist implies that at least some of these will escape the notice of certain readers.[56]

Aside from subtlety, a further reason that allusions are sometimes difficult to identify—and a reason why different readers may disagree whether an allusion is present in a given case—is that connections between two texts that might appear to constitute an allusion are in certain cases attributable to other factors. These include but are not limited to: (1) coinci-

---

nections between the alluding text and its source text on the level of sound (the use of words that sound the same and are deliberately related by means of paronomasia), though such sound correspondences alone are not sufficient to demonstrate an allusion; semantic, syntactic, or structural connections between the two texts should almost always be established first. On the markers of allusion, see further Miller, "Intertextuality," 294–98; Jeffery M. Leonard, "Identifying Inner-Biblical Allusions: Psalm 78 as a Test Case," *JBL* 127 (2008): 241–65; Ziva Ben-Porat, "The Poetics of Literary Allusion," *PTL* 1 (1976): 105–28; Carmela Perri, "On Alluding," *Poetics* 7 (1978): 289–307; Udo J. Hebel, "Towards a Descriptive Poetics of Allusion," in *Intertextuality*, ed. Heinrich F. Plett, RTT 15 (Berlin: de Gruyter, 1991), 135–64; Udo J. Hebel, ed., *Intertextuality, Allusion, and Quotation: An International Bibliography of Critical Studies*, BIWL 18 (Westport, CT: Greenwood, 1989).

52. Pasco, *Allusion*, 18; Tooman, *Gog of Magog*, 27–29.

53. As Wetzsteon remarks, "allusion can vary widely in … degree of obscurity" ("Allusion," 42). See further Charles Halton, "Allusions to the Stream of Tradition in Neo-Assyrian Oracles," *ANES* 46 (2009): 51, 58. Pasco considers subtlety to be an intrinsic characteristic of allusion, though he readily admits that not all scholars who study allusion agree with this judgment (Pasco, *Allusion*, 9–10).

54. One must keep this issue in mind particularly when identifying allusions in texts written in one language to texts written in another (Hays, "Echoes of the Ancient Near East," 35).

55. Wetzsteon, "Allusion," 43.

56. Compare Pasco's remark that "in almost all cases, only the text can tell us whether an allusion exists. And that is good reason for entering a caveat. With nothing but internal evidence, how are we to know who created the allusion—the author … or the critic?" (Pasco, *Allusion*, 17).

dence, or the "accidental confluence" of elements in the two texts; (2) the use of a topos in one of the texts, that is, the simultaneous reference to many similar texts or traditions that include but are not limited to the other text in question;[57] (3) the deployment in the two texts of stock phrases or common themes or imagery; (4) the presence in the two texts of similar traditions that arose independently of each other; or (5) the independent reliance of the two texts on a third (now possibly unknown) text.[58] As Stephen Hinds observes, even the boundaries between genuine allusion and what he calls "accidental confluence"—which, of the phenomena listed above, appears to be most distant from allusion since it implies a total lack of genetic relationship between two texts—are not always clear.[59] Anyone who has studied allusion for any length of time is acutely aware that it is often difficult to differentiate between the various scenarios just described and cases of bona fide allusion, and it is not uncommon for readers to disagree with each other about how best to account for the connections that exist between or among texts.

The foregoing discussion makes clear that, despite the helpful principles that scholars have developed for identifying allusions, it should always be remembered that the process of identifying allusions depends on many factors, including the knowledge and competence of individual readers, and is more an art than a science.[60] Because every allusion is unique, some criteria will naturally be more helpful for identifying certain allusions than others. I am inclined to agree with Christopher Beetham that in many cases the most fundamental requirement for identifying an allusion is the

---

57. Wetzsteon, "Allusion," 42; Hinds, *Allusion and Intertext*, 34–37: "Rather than demanding interpretation in relation to a specific model or models, like the allusion, the *topos* invokes its intertextual tradition as a collectivity, to which the individual contexts and connotations of individual prior instances are firmly subordinate" (34).

58. Paul R. Noble, "Esau, Tamar, and Joseph: Criteria for Identifying Inner-Biblical Allusions," *VT* 52 (2002): 220.

59. "The fact that language renders us always already acculturated guarantees that there is no such thing as a wholly non-negotiable confluence, no such thing as zero-interpretability. This is the basic insight of the semiological intertextualist; and in principle, as well as for the more practical dividends which it can offer, it should be embraced within the philological allusionist's enterprise, not treated as irrelevant or (worse) as a threat to it" (Hinds, *Allusion and Intertext*, 34).

60. As noted by Sommer, *Prophet Reads Scripture*, 35 (cited in Bohdan Hrobon, *Ethical Dimension of Cult in the Book of Isaiah*, BZAW 418 [Berlin: de Gruyter, 2010], 153). See also Pasco, *Allusion*, 17; Tooman, *Gog of Magog*, 35.

ability to demonstrate that (unique or distinctive) lexical and thematic correspondences are present ("word agreement or rare concept similarity"), that the alluding text interprets or somehow transforms the source text ("essential interpretive link"), and that the source text is earlier than the alluding text ("availability").[61] These last two categories lead us to our next subject, the direction of dependence.

1.5.1.2. The Direction of Dependence

When two texts appear to be related by means of allusion, how does one determine which text alludes to the other? The simplest way to establish the direction of dependence between two texts is, in theory, to compare the texts' relative dates, if these are known. Although such dates are usually available in the case of modern works of literature, even approximate dates for biblical texts (whether books, pericopes, or specific verses) are often very difficult or nearly impossible to determine with certainty.[62] James Crenshaw offers the following rather pessimistic view of the situation:

> To some extent ... endeavors to establish a historical context for a biblical book constitute exercises in futility. Much of the argument moves in the realm of probability, often resting on one hypothesis after another about the development of the language and religion of the Bible. I do not think we can accurately date most books in the canon, nor do I believe it possible to determine the exact history of any Hebrew word. Even if one could fix a date for the composition of a book, Amos, for example, that would in no way establish a date for every verse, for the written text often evoked interpretive glosses and additions of various kinds.[63]

Although there is wisdom in this kind of caution, on some occasions critical scholarship has succeeded in producing strong arguments for the (approximate) dates of certain biblical texts, and in some cases a consensus has even been reached. In such cases, I do not hesitate to use these dates as part of my argument for the direction of dependence between texts in the

---

61. Christopher A. Beetham, *Echoes of Scripture in the Letter of Paul to the Colossians* (Leiden: Brill, 2010) (cited in Shaw, "Converted Imaginations," 238).
62. This is, of course, the case for most other ancient texts as well. For modern literature, on the contrary, relative dating is the normal way to establish the direction of dependence between an alluding text and a source text.
63. James Crenshaw, *Joel*, AB 24C (New York: Doubleday, 1995), 28.

examples I discuss in the following chapters, though I do so always with the realization that scholarly consensus is not the same as fact and that some dates are more certain than others.[64] Even when relative dates point, with more or less probability, to a certain direction of dependence between texts, and above all in cases where relative dates are very uncertain or unknown, one must always look to other criteria as well to determine the direction of dependence. Such criteria can include volume of use, modification, integration, conceptual dependence, and known scribal practices of reuse, which, as William Tooman has demonstrated, are particularly useful for identifying allusions in Ezek 38–39.[65] Unfortunately, however, one cannot predict in advance for any given allusion which or how many of these criteria—useful as they are as general principles—might prove helpful for determining the direction of dependence, especially for allusions that are brief (e.g., an allusion might be restricted to one verse or a part of one verse) or subtle (e.g., those involving minimal verbal connections to the source text).

Indeed, even after considering the principles just listed or similar ones, scholars may agree that two texts are related by means of allusion but disagree about the direction of dependence. A well-known case concerns the relative dates of Job and Second Isaiah, one of which clearly alludes to the other on a number of occasions.[66] Although I agree with the current scholarly consensus that Job alludes to Second Isaiah rather than vice versa, this question continues to be debated. In such cases, the most persuasive arguments concerning the direction of dependence usually involve the demonstration that the probability that one of the texts is interpreting the other makes more sense than the opposite scenario.[67] In other words, a particularly strong way to argue that one text alludes to another is to

---

64. For a cautiously optimistic view of our ability to date at least some biblical texts, see Sommer, *Prophet Reads Scripture*, 10.

65. Tooman, *Gog of Magog*, 31–35.

66. See esp. Kynes, "Job and Isaiah 40–55."

67. Thus, Kynes writes with respect to Job and Second Isaiah: "First, are the connections between Job and Isa 40–55 the result of literary dependence? Second, if so, which text is referring to the other? And, third, what is the purpose of those allusions? I believe the answers to these questions are interdependent, each contributing to solving the others" (ibid., 95). After discussing a number of connections between the two corpora, Kynes concludes that "Job's parody of the praise and promise in Isa 40–55 makes more sense than Isa 40–55 incorporating Job's complaint and accusation into his message" (104).

demonstrate that the connections that exist between the two texts serve a clearer *purpose* or possess a more demonstrable *function* if the proposed alluding text alludes to the source text rather than the other way around. This ultimately brings us back to the point that intentionality or deliberateness is one of the defining characteristics of allusion. Where intentionality can be demonstrated (and this is usually done by demonstrating function), a particularly strong case exists both for the presence of an allusion and for the direction of dependence between the texts involved.

1.5.2. Identifying Allusive Paronomasia

1.5.2.1. Principles

Any attempt to identify allusive paronomasia in the Hebrew Bible must address each of the four elements that defines paronomasia.

1.5.2.1.1. Similarity of Sound

How similar must two words sound in order for them to be paronyms? As Greenstein observes, "because Hebrew words comprise a consonantal root interspersed with changing vocalic schemes, we generally demand of wordplay [i.e., paronomasia] that at least half the consonants, usually two of the common root's three, are identical or phonologically similar."[68] Although this is a good rule of thumb, the Bible contains many instances of words that occur in proximity that meet this condition but do not appear to be genuine examples of paronomasia.[69]

The question of the degree to which the sounds of two words must be similar in order for paronomasia to be present ultimately raises the thorny question of authorial intention: that is, how do we differentiate genuine cases of paronomasia from words that sound similar because of "sheer coincidence (because it [their similarity in sound] is presumably unintentional)"?[70] Although the process of identifying paronomasia can involve an element of subjectivity, a few principles can help us decide between genuine examples of paronomasia and sound similarities that are due to coincidence. For example, if the text in which a possible example of paronomasia occurs contains a high density of other examples of

---

68. Greenstein, "Wordplay, Hebrew," 969.
69. See n. 71 below.
70. Greenstein, "Wordplay, Hebrew," 969.

paronomasia or if the possible paronomasia extends to multiple words in close proximity, it is generally more likely that the example in question is a genuine case of paronomasia than not.⁷¹ A less reliable principle is that biblical poetry tends to have higher concentrations of paronomasia than biblical prose—but there are also very many exceptions to this trend.

The foregoing principles are as true for allusive paronomasia as they are for paronomasia that obtains between words occurring in close proximity. A further principle that can strengthen the argument for a proposed instance of allusive paronomasia is as follows: if the corpus in which the proposed instance occurs contains (many) other established instances of allusive paronomasia, then the proposed instance is more likely to constitute a case of allusive paronomasia.⁷² For paronomasia in allusions, however, the strongest way to argue that similarity in sound between a word in the alluding text and a word in the source text is intentional—that it constitutes a genuine example of paronomasia and is not due to coincidence—is to show that the paronomasia performs a function. I will develop this point further below when I come to the final defining characteristic of paronomasia, deliberate juxtaposition.

1.5.2.1.2. Difference in Meaning

As noted above, paronomasia describes the relationship between words that not only are similar in sound but that differ in meaning. Determining whether two words differ in meaning is not always easy, however, particularly when these words occur in different texts (e.g., a source text and an alluding text) and especially when these texts were composed in different historical periods. This difficulty can be illustrated by comparing Lam 3:54, Ps 31:23, and Jonah 2:5:

---

71. Scott B. Noegel, "Drinking Feasts and Deceptive Talk: Jacob and Laban's Double Talk," in Noegel, *Puns and Pundits*, 167. Both of these points can be illustrated by two random examples. Given the very high density of paronomasia in the book of Lamentations, it seems difficult to deny that שמעו כי נאנחה אני אין מנחם לי in Lam 1:21 contains a genuine (i.e., intentional)—indeed, an exquisite—example of paronomasia. A similarly sonorous phrase, ולקחת את שמן המשחה ומשחת את המשכן, is found in Exod 40:9, but given the fact that this is prose and due to the paucity of paronomasia in the context, it is more difficult to decide if this constitutes a genuine (i.e., intentional) instance of paronomasia.

72. For example, an argument for a case of allusive paronomasia in Isa 40–66 can gain strength from the fact that this corpus has been shown to contain many examples of allusive paronomasia (as Sommer has demonstrated in *A Prophet Reads Scripture*).

Lam 3:54, 56

צפו מים על ראשי אמרתי נִגְזָרְתִּי: ... קולי שמעת אל תעלם אזנך לרוחתי לשועתי:

Ps 31:23

ואני אמרתי בחפזי נִגְרַזְתִּי מנגד עיניך אכן שמעת קול תחנוני בשועי אליך:

Jonah 2:3, 5-6

ויאמר קראתי מצרה לי אל יהוה ויענני מבטן שאול **שועתי שמעת קולי**: ... **ואני אמרתי נִגְרַשְׁתִּי מנגד עיניך** אך אוסיף להביט אל היכל קדשך: **אפפוני מים** עד נפש תהום יסבבני סוף חבוש **לראשי**:

Although some scholars have denied that these three texts are genetically related to each other,[73] the multiple verbal connections among them (indicated in boldface above) seem difficult to attribute to coincidence. Whatever the case may be in this regard, however, the important issue for the present discussion is simply whether the terms נגזרתי in Lam 3:54, נגרזתי in Ps 31:23, and נגרשתי in Jonah 2:5 have different meanings. The answer to this question—which is further complicated by the evidence of the manuscripts and the ancient versions for these verses[74]—is not immediately obvious. If, as seems likely, these three words share the same (basic) meaning, it would seem best to explain the orthographic differences among them as something other than paronomasia. Different possible explanations for such variation as we encounter here among נגזרתי, נגרזתי, and נגרשתי will be discussed later in this chapter.

As the foregoing example illustrates, when attempting to identify examples of nonhomonymic allusive paronomasia in the Hebrew Bible, it is sometimes difficult to determine if the proposed paronyms actually differ

---

73. Delekat considers the presence of אמרתי נגזרתי in Lam 3:54 in addition to the similar locutions in Jonah 2:5 and Ps 31:23 to be evidence that this is "a common phrase" ("eine geläufige Wendung") and on this basis concludes that Jonah 2:5 "is probably not dependent on Ps. 31[:23] or vice versa" ("Das Gebet, das ihm vom Dichter des Jona-Buches in den Mund gelegt wird, ist wahrscheinlich nicht von Ps. xxxi abhängig oder umgekehrt"; see L. Delekat, "Zum hebräischen Wörterbuch," *VT* 14 [1964]: 11).

74. Ibid.

in meaning.⁷⁵ This difficulty is always present and becomes even more acute in attempts to identify examples of *homonymic* allusive paronomasia, which involve words that appear in different texts and are spelled identically and sound identical but differ in meaning. In other words, because homonymic paronomasia is marked only on the basis of semantics (and not visually or orally/aurally), detecting and arguing persuasively for allusive cases of homonymic paronomasia must rely solely on the degree to which one can demonstrate that the homonyms bear different meanings in the texts in question. No doubt examples of homonymic allusive paronomasia exist in the Bible,⁷⁶ but since they are even more subtly marked than cases of nonhomonymic allusive paronomasia, I have chosen to discuss in this book only examples of the latter.

1.5.2.1.3. Proximity

As I mentioned above, the assumption that paronomasia can only be effective between words that occur in close proximity is incorrect since in the Bible (as in other literature, as well as in nonliterary speech acts) paronomasia can function allusively. Nevertheless, there is a way in which the principle of proximity is still relevant for paronomasia of the long-distance, allusive variety; in fact, by creating a nexus between two texts that are distant in space (i.e., across the pages of the Bible) and usually (though not always) also distant in time (if located, for example, in

---

75. On the distinction between homonymic and nonhomonymic paronomasia, see above.

76. See Sommer, *Prophet Reads Scripture*, 70 and passim for examples in Isa 40–66. Sommer refers to examples of homonymic allusive paronomasia and nonhomonymic allusive paronomasia as "word play" and "sound play," respectively. Although I find some of Sommer's examples of "word play" (i.e., homonymic allusive paronomasia) in Second Isaiah's reuse of earlier traditions convincing, some are so subtle that it is hard to be persuaded by them. For example, Sommer suggests that the word מצדיקי ("the One who vindicates me") in Isa 50:8 is an example of "word play" (i.e., homonymic allusive paronomasia) on the word צדיק ("righteous") in Jer 20:12, claiming that the verbal root צדק has a different meaning in each text (ibid., 64; the translations are Sommer's). Does this root actually bear a different meaning in these two texts? Rather, does it not have the same basic meaning in both ("righteous"), the distinction between מצדיקי ("the one who makes me righteous") and צדיק ("righteous") being attributable simply to the fact that מצדיקי is a causative verbal form meaning "to cause to be righteous" (i.e., "to vindicate")? Sommer may be correct that this is a case of "word play" (and that מצדיקי in Isa 50:8 interprets or transforms צדיק in Jer 20:12), but his argument strikes me as overly subtle.

different books or different redactional layers of the same book), an allusion adds another dimension to the criterion of proximity.[77] For example, Job 15:14 (מה אנוש כי יזכה) alludes to Ps 8:5 (מה אנוש כי תזכרנו), and, as I will argue in chapter 2, the verb יזכה in the former text was used intentionally as a paronym of the verb תזכרנו in the latter.[78] Because יזכה in the alluding text (Job 15:14) occupies the same syntactic slot in the text segment reproduced from the source text (Ps 8:5) as the word it plays on, תזכרנו—that is, it is the X-element in [מה אנוש כי + X]—the paronyms תזכרנו and יזכה do actually occur in close proximity, not within the same text but *with respect to the phrase that the alluding text reproduces from the source text*. To take a different example, Prov 15:18 and 29:22 are linked by shared vocabulary (איש אף יגרה מדון [29:22]; איש חמה יגרה מדון [15:18]), and the immediate contexts of both of the clauses just cited contain words that are similar in sound; this raises the possibility that the words in question in the later text (whichever that might prove to be) are examples of paronomasia (ארחת and ארח in 15:17, 19 and אחרית in 29:21; and ריב in 15:18 and רב in 29:22):[79]

Prov 15:17–19
טוֹב אֲרֻחַת יָרָק וְאַהֲבָה שָׁם מִשּׁוֹר אָבוּס וְשִׂנְאָה בוֹ: אִישׁ חֵמָה יְגָרֶה
מָדוֹן וְאֶרֶךְ אַפַּיִם יַשְׁקִיט רִיב: דֶּרֶךְ עָצֵל כִּמְשֻׂכַת חָדֶק וְאֹרַח יְשָׁרִים
סְלֻלָה:

---

77. On the difficulty of defining proximity, see n. 27 above. A text in a given book (e.g., Job) that alludes to an earlier text in the same book may not be separated from the latter in time, especially if the two texts were written by the same author (though in the case of Job, as with many other biblical books, this must be decided on a case-by-case basis since the book is very likely the product of multiple authors/redactors).

78. See §2.1.4 below.

79. I leave aside for the moment the question of which of the two texts may be alluding to the other if an allusion is present. On the special nature of repetition in Proverbs, see Daniel C. Snell, *Twice-Told Proverbs and the Composition of the Book of Proverbs* (Winona Lake, IN: Eisenbrauns, 1993); Knut M. Heim, *Poetic Imagination in Proverbs: Variant Repetitions and the Nature of Poetry* (Winona Lake, IN: Eisenbrauns, 2013). For discussion of when variants in repeated proverbs may be the result of oral or written transmission, see David M. Carr, *The Formation of the Hebrew Bible: A New Reconstruction* (Oxford: Oxford University Press, 2011), 25–34. On the relationship between Prov 15:18 and 29:22 in particular, see Heim, *Poetic Imagination*, 383–87.

Prov 29:21–22

מפנק מנער עבדו וְאַחֲרִיתוֹ יהיה מנון: אִישׁ אַף יִגְרֶה מָדוֹן וּבַעַל חֵמָה רַב פָּשַׁע:

In contrast to the Job 15:14/Ps 8:5 example noted above, in these two texts from Proverbs the words that are possibly related by means of paronomasia (i.e., ארחת, ארח, and אחרית; and ריב and רב) do not occur in the same syntactic positions vis-à-vis the text-segment that is common to Prov 15:18 and 29:22 (איש חמה/אף יגרה מדון). In comparison with the paronyms in the Job 15:14/Ps 8:5 example (יזכה and תזכרנו), because in this case the possible paronyms occur in relatively close, but not quite as close, proximity with respect to the clause that the two texts share, it is more difficult to decide if the words in question in Prov 15:17–19 (ארחת, ארח, and ריב) and 29:21–22 (אחרית and רב) constitute, in the case of whichever text is later, genuine instances of allusive paronomasia with reference to the similar-sounding words in the earlier text or if the similarities of sound are coincidental. In addition to the issue of proximity, the other factor that helps one build a persuasive case that the relationship between יזכה in Job 15:14 and תזכרנו in Ps 8:5 is one of genuine paronomasia rather than the product of coincidence has to do with the issue of intention. It is to this, the final defining characteristic of paronomasia, that I now turn.

1.5.2.1.4. Deliberate Juxtaposition

I have already noted de Regt's observation that paronomasia "creates a special effect: it intensifies the message and draws attention to a certain point."[80] This is true, though the degree to which this occurs in any given case varies; as Eleanor Cook has felicitously expressed it, "paronomasia runs from *piano* to *forte* effects."[81] The production by a proposed instance of paronomasia of a strong or (to follow Cook's musical analogy) *forte* effect often constitutes the most persuasive argument that the possible instance of paronomasia, in an individual text and especially in cases of allusive paronomasia, is a genuine instance of paronomasia and not the result of

---

80. De Regt, "Wordplay," 898.
81. Cook, "Paronomasia," 1004. This is as true for the Bible as for the modern literature Cook cites, and within the Bible it is true for paronomasia involving both words found in close proximity to each other and allusions. As I will show below, the most clearly identifiable examples of allusive paronomasia are those whose effects are, to employ Cook's terminology, *forte*.

THE ROLE OF SOUNDPLAY IN INNERBIBLICAL ALLUSIONS 29

coincidence. This can be illustrated by the example from Job 15:14 noted above. Although a full discussion of the effect of the paronomasia between יזכה in this verse and תזכרנו in Ps 8:5, its source text, must wait until the next chapter, here I will note simply that in Job 15:14 Eliphaz alludes to Ps 8:5 in order to tell Job that Job has, through his sin, abdicated the divine favor described in Ps 8:5. Both the allusion and the allusive paronomasia within it, the latter of which effectively reverses the sense of the source text, have a strong effect in the context of Eliphaz's overall argument; they "intensify his message and draw attention to his point," to paraphrase de Regt. To take the other example discussed above involving Prov 15:17–19 and 29:21–22, it is much more difficult in this case to demonstrate that the sound correspondences between ארחת and ארח in 15:17, 19 and אחרית in 29:21 and between ריב in 15:18 and רב in 29:22 have a particular effect or perform a specific function in either text. For this reason, it is more difficult to make the case that these sound correspondences constitute genuine paronomasia and are not simply coincidental.

To say that the most persuasive way to argue that a proposed example of allusive paronomasia in the Hebrew Bible was deliberately intended by the author of the text in which it occurs and is not simply the imaginative creation of the reader finally brings us back to the preceding three defining characteristics of paronomasia. This is so because the best way to demonstrate that a possible example of allusive paronomasia performs a clear function is to show that the word in the source text and its proposed paronym in the alluding text are in *close proximity* with respect to the words or text-segment(s) that the alluding text reproduces from the source text and, even more importantly, that the *similarity in sound* and *difference in meaning* between the word in the source text and its proposed paronym in the alluding text combine to produce a striking effect in the message of the alluding text.

1.5.2.2. Allusive Paronomasia and Formally Identical Phenomena

1.5.2.2.1. Typology

In many innerbiblical allusions, it is possible to find one or more words in the alluding text that sound like one or more words in the source text, which is hardly surprising given the limited number of sounds Hebrew (like any language) contains. As I illustrated in the preceding section, noticing such sound correspondences between or among words in the source text and the alluding text is by itself insufficient grounds for concluding that these words are related by means of paronomasia. Analysis of a given instance in which one thinks a case of allusive paronomasia may be present yields at least four possible scenarios (granting, for the sake of the argument, that one has been able to argue persuasively that an allusion is present).[82]

	1	2	3	4
Is an allusion (or other textual reuse) present?	yes	yes	yes	yes
Is paronomasia between the alluding (or later, parallel) text and the source text present?	no	possibly	likely	yes
Does the (possible) paronomasia have a function?	(N/A)	unclear	subtle	clear

This chart reflects the point made in the preceding section that the most persuasive argument for a proposed case of allusive paronomasia is one that can demonstrate that the proposed paronomasia has a clear function (category 4). At the other end of the spectrum from such examples are those (category 1) for which, while they are formally indistinguishable from examples in category 4, the similarity in sound between the words in the source text and the alluding (or, as is often the case, the later, parallel) text must be explained as something other than paronomasia.[83] Between these extremes are examples (categories 2 and 3) that, again, are formally indistinguishable from those in categories 1 and 4, but for which the presence of paronomasia is possible but uncertain, whether likely (category 3) or unlikely (category 2). My use of the terms "uncertain," "likely," and "unlikely" here makes it obvious that there is a degree of overlap among the categories, which are points along a spectrum, not air-tight distinctions, and that not all readers will agree about how to categorize any given example.[84] However, despite the fluid—and, it must be admitted, to some degree subjective—nature of the categories, I believe they provide a useful

---

82. Most of the examples that fall into what the following chart calls "category 1" appear in "parallel" texts. Since the later of a pair of parallel texts should not be described as "alluding" to the earlier one, I have added to the term "allusion" in the chart the vaguer qualifying phrase "or other textual reuse."

83. On these other possible explanations, see below.

84. Indeed, an individual interpreter may change his or her mind over time concerning the classification of a given example.

analytical tool that can enable us to differentiate bona fide cases of allusive paronomasia in the Hebrew Bible from similar phenomena with a reasonable degree of confidence.

In order to account for as many data as possible, in addition to the four categories just described I will also discuss a fifth category below, one that does not lie on the spectrum that comprises categories 1 through 4. Examples that fall into category 5 involve two texts that share similar or identical paronomasia; but, unlike the texts in categories 1 through 4, it is unclear whether texts in category 5 are related to each other by means of allusion.[85] I discuss examples that fall into this category because they show that in identifying paronomasia in allusion, one must always demonstrate not only that two texts have similar paronomasia but also that the texts are related by means of allusion.

1.5.2.2.2. Examples

In this section I will discuss selected examples that in my view fall into categories 1, 2, 3, and 5 of the typology above. (Because all the examples in chapters 2, 3, and 4 of this book are intended to illustrate category 4, I have omitted this category from the following discussion.) Although each of the examples presented below possesses its own intrinsic interest, my main purpose in discussing them is to provide a framework for identifying examples in category 4. In other words, the purpose of the following discussion is to hone our ability to recognize clear examples of allusive paronomasia in the Hebrew Bible and to differentiate such examples from subtler ones and from similar phenomena that do not actually constitute allusive paronomasia.

Category 1. The examples in this category, most of which involve not allusions but parallel texts,[86] illustrate the fact that many texts in the Hebrew Bible that clearly reuse earlier textual material that is also found in the Bible contain a word that sounds like a word in their source text

---

85. I have not included in my discussion examples of similar paronomasia in texts that appear clearly to be unrelated to each other, though of course many such texts do exist in the Bible. See Schorch, "Between Science and Magic," 210.

86. On parallel texts in the Bible, see, e.g., Abba Bendavid, מקבילות במקרא (Jerusalem: Carta, 1972); and Isaac Kalimi, *Zur Geschichtsschreibung des Chronisten: Literarisch-historiographische Abweichungen der Chronik von ihren Paralleltexten in den Samuel- und Königsbüchern* (Berlin: de Gruyter, 1995).

although the word in question in the later text is not an example of allusive paronomasia. Occasionally this is so because the later text has replaced a word in the earlier text with one that sounds similar *but that has the same or a nearly identical meaning*. In most cases, however, the later text has replaced a word in the earlier text with one that sounds similar *and does have a different meaning*. Because there is no doubt that the word in the later text is used in place of the word in the earlier text, such examples at first blush might appear to be cases of allusive paronomasia. What ultimately indicates that many of them are not, however, is the issue of function: most such variations can be explained as either *not deliberate* on the part of the author of the later text (and therefore lacking in function) or *deliberate but lacking in function* (in the case, for example, of the replacement of a word with a similar-sounding synonym).

What follows is a selected list of variations in Chronicles vis-à-vis that book's source texts that obtain on the level of sound (phonetics) and occasionally on the level of writing (orthography), along with several examples from outside Chronicles as well. Although some of the instances of sound variation that I cite below fall into category 1 and others do not, surveying all of these examples together will provide the basis for a discussion of how one can distinguish category 1 examples from those that belong to categories 2 through 4.

(1) Transformations may occur on *the orthographic or graphemic level*. For example: (a) A consonant may be substituted for a similar-looking one (whether in the Old Hebrew script or in the square Aramaic script), as when the proper noun ריפת ("Riphat") in Gen 10:3 is paralleled by דיפת ("Diphat") in 1 Chr 1:6, and when the proper noun ארם ("Aram") in 2 Sam 8:12–13 is paralleled by אדום ("Edom") in 1 Chr 18:11–12. (b) All the consonants of a word may be retained but their order rearranged (metathesis), as when תמנת סרח ("Timnath-serah") in Josh 24:30 is paralleled by תמנת חרס ("Timnath-heres") in Judg 2:9.[87]

For a similar example of a graphemic transformation outside Chronicles, consider the parallel between זרים ("strangers") in Ps 54:5 and זדים ("the arrogant") in Ps 86:14.

---

87. An interesting though in my view somewhat speculative explanation for this change is found in Avigdor Shinan and Yair Zakovitch, *From Gods to God: How the Bible Debunked, Suppressed, or Changed Ancient Myths and Legends* (Lincoln: University of Nebraska Press, 2012), 61–62.

(2) A variety of *substitutions of one sound for another* may occur. (a) A consonant may be replaced by one that is similar in place or manner of articulation: for example, the verb להשיב ("to restore") in 2 Sam 8:3 is paralleled by להציב ("to set up") in 1 Chr 18:3; שבטי ("tribes") in 2 Sam 7:7 is paralleled by שפטי ("judges") in 1 Chr 17:6. (b) Many more cases exist in which a consonant has been replaced by one that is *dissimilar* in place or manner of articulation (a few of these cases also involve the deletion of one or more consonants): for example, וישם ("he set") in 2 Sam 12:31 is paralleled by וישר ("he hacked") in 1 Chr 20:3; בית ("the temple") in 1 Sam 31:9 is paralleled by the *nota accusativi* את in 1 Chr 10:9; בית הלחמי את ("Bethlehemite" followed by the *nota accusativi*) in 2 Sam 21:19 is paralleled by את לחמי אחי ("Lahmi brother of" preceded by the *nota accusativi*) in 1 Chr 20:5; נסך ("you will flee"; lit., "your fleeing") in 2 Sam 24:13 is paralleled by נספה ("you will be swept away") in 1 Chr 21:11–12; במקדשו ("in his temple") in Ps 96:6 is paralleled by במקמו ("in his place") in 1 Chr 16:27; גְוִיַּת ("the body") and גְוִיֹּת ("the bodies") in 1 Sam 31:12 are paralleled by, respectively, גוּפַת ("the body") and גוּפֹת ("the bodies") in 1 Chr 10:12; ותכונן ("you have established") in 2 Sam 7:24 is paralleled by the contextually synonymous ותתן in 1 Chr 17:22.

Outside of Chronicles, sound substitution appears in the example described above involving נגזרתי in Lam 3:54, נגרזתי in Ps 31:23, and נגרשתי in Jonah 2:5;[88] in the parallel between וישמע ("he heard") in 2 Kgs 20:13 and וישמח ("he rejoiced") in Isa 39:2 (in these two examples the interchanged sounds are similar in place and, in the latter, manner of articulation); in the parallel between עליזה ("exultant") in Zeph 2:15 and עדינה ("pampered") in Isa 47:8; and in the parallel between עבות ("clouds") in Ps 77:18 and עבר ("passed over") in Hab 3:10 (in these two examples the interchanged sounds are dissimilar in place and manner of articulation).

(3) *Consonants may be deleted or added.* (a) Examples of deletion include the following: the proper noun מתג ("Metheg") in 2 Sam 8:1 is paralleled by the proper noun גת ("Gath") in 1 Chr 18:1;[89] מגזרת ("axes") in 2 Sam 12:31 is paralleled by the synonym מגרות in 1 Chr 20:3; נוטל ("hold over") in 2 Sam 24:12 is paralleled by נטה ("offer") in 1 Chr 21:10; השער ("the gate") in 2 Sam 10:8 is paralleled by העיר ("the city") in 1 Chr 19:9; מדין (*qere*: מדון; "stature") in 2 Sam 21:20 is paralleled by the syn-

---

88. On this example, see §1.5.2.1.2 above.
89. Note also the transposition of *tav* and *gimel* in this example.

onym מדה in 1 Chr 20:6. (b) Examples of addition include the following: the proper noun מש ("Mash") in Gen 10:23 is paralleled by the proper noun משך ("Meshek") in 1 Chr 1:17; ויבאו ("they came") in 1 Sam 31:12 is paralleled by ויביאום ("they brought them") in 1 Chr 10:12.

(4) A variety of *combined transformations* involving any of the aforementioned changes may also occur: for example, the verb ידעו ("they knew") in Josh 24:31 is paralleled by the verb ראו ("they saw") in Judg 2:7; the proper noun חלאמה ("to Helam") in 2 Sam 10:17 is paralleled by אלהם ("to them") in 1 Chr 19:17;[90] the verb מכרכר ("whirling") in 2 Sam 6:16 is paralleled by מרקד ("leaping") in 1 Chr 15:29; בכל עצי ברושים ("with all kinds of cypress woods") in 2 Sam 6:5 is paralleled by בכל עז ובשירים ("with all their strength and with songs") in 1 Chr 13:8;[91] והניחתי לך מכל איביך ("I will give you rest from all your enemies") in 2 Sam 7:11 is paralleled by והכנעתי את כל אויביך ("I will subdue all your enemies") in 1 Chr 17:10; וינטשו ("they spread out") in 2 Sam 5:18, 22 is paralleled by ויפשטו ("they raided") in 1 Chr 14:9, 13; קציר ("harvest") in 2 Sam 23:13 is paralleled by הצר ("the rock") in 1 Chr 11:15; the proper noun בטח ("Betah") in 2 Sam 8:8 is paralleled by טבחת ("Tibhat") in 1 Chr 8:8; השל ("the indiscretion") in 2 Sam 6:7 is paralleled by שלח ("he stretched forth") in 1 Chr 13:10; לא יכלו ... להחרימם ("they were not able ... to destroy them") in 1 Kgs 9:21 is paralleled by לא כלום ("they did not destroy them") in 2 Chr 8:8; ויעש ... תשועה ("he brought about [lit., 'made'] ... a victory") in 2 Sam 23:10 is paralleled by ויושע ... תשועה ("he brought about [lit., 'was victorious with'] ... a victory") in 1 Chr 11:14.

(5) There also exist cases in which (a) the sounds or graphemes of one word in the source text appear to have been *refracted across more than one word* in the later, parallel text: for example, the phrase אשר מראה (ketiv: "who was of appearance"; the qere is איש מראה: "a man of appearance"), said of the large Egyptian killed by Benayah ben Jehoyada in 2 Sam 23:21, is paralleled by איש מדה חמש באמה ("a man five cubits [tall] in size") in

---

90. On these two parallel verses, see Kalimi, *Geschichtsschreibung des Chronisten*, 346. On חלאם and its variants in Samuel, see Moshe Garsiel, "Word Play and Puns as a Rhetorical Device in the Book of Samuel," in Noegel, *Puns and Pundits*, 196–97; Garsiel considers the change from חלאמה in 2 Sam 10:17 to חילם in 2 Sam 10:16 an instance of what he calls "midrashic name derivation."

91. Note also the change of the word צלצלים ("cymbals") in 2 Sam 6:5 to the synonym מצלתים in 1 Chr 13:8. On these verses see Kalimi, *Geschichtsschreibung des Chronisten*, 58. Also relevant here are 1 Chr 15:28 and 2 Sam 6:5 (see ibid., 58–59).

1 Chr 11:23;[92] העויתי ("I have done wrong") in 2 Sam 24:17 is paralleled by הֲרֵעַ הֲרֵעוֹתִי ("I have indeed caused harm") in 1 Chr 21:17; תורת ("law") in 2 Sam 7:19 is paralleled by וראיתני כתור ("and you saw me as a line [of humanity]") in 1 Chr 17:17.[93] Correlatively, in at least three cases (b) the sounds of two words in a source text appear to have *coalesced* into one word in the later, parallel text: for example, מכרכר בכל עז ("he whirled with all [his] might") in 2 Sam 6:14 is paralleled by מכרבל במעיל ("he was wrapped in a robe") in 1 Chr 15:27; נתן אתן ("I will surely deliver") in 2 Sam 5:19 is paralleled by ונתתים ("I will deliver them") in 1 Chr 14:10;[94] ויעש דוד שם בשבו ("and David made a name [for himself] when he returned") in 2 Sam 8:13 is paralleled by ואבשי בן צרויה ("and Abishai son of Zeruyah") in 1 Chr 18:12. Similar to category (a) is an example in which (c) two paronyms from the source text are retained in the later, parallel text, which also plays on their shared sounds by adding yet another word: הוד והדר ("glory and majesty") in Ps 96:6 is paralleled by הוד והדר in 1 Chr 16:27, which plays on the shared sounds of these two words with the added word וחדוה ("and joy").

It may be tempting, at least at first glance, to explain most of the foregoing examples (and many similar ones found throughout Chronicles) as scribal errors or instances of lexical updating—that is, as noninterpretive in nature and belonging purely to the realm of text criticism. For example, the change of ריפת ("Riphat") in Gen 10:3 to דיפת ("Diphat") in 1 Chr 1:6 appears to involve scribal error, and the change of מגזרת ("axes") in 2 Sam 12:31 to the synonym מגרות in 1 Chr 20:3 seems to be an instance of lexical updating or of the substitution of one by-form for another.

Other examples that I have provided above seem to move more in the realm of interpretation than text criticism, however; that is, these changes seem to be deliberate on the part of the author of the later parallel text and intended to perform a function. A possible case is the change of בכל עצי ברושים ("with all kinds of cypress woods") in 2 Sam 6:5 to בכל עז ובשירים ("with all their strength and with songs") in 1 Chr 13:8. If this change is interpretive, though, what interpretive content it might convey is not immediately obvious. In other words, if this change has a function, the

---

92. On these parallel verses, see ibid., 57.

93. On this difficult phrase in 1 Chr 17:17 see, e.g., *DCH*, s.v. תּוֹר I (whence the translation "and you saw me as a line of humanity").

94. Note also that התתנם ("will you deliver them?") earlier in 2 Sam 5:19 is paralleled by the synonymous but slightly different construction ונתתם in 1 Chr 14:10.

function seems to be subtle. An alteration that probably has more exegetical import is the change of וישמע in 2 Kgs 20:13 to וישמח in Isa 39:2. By changing the neutral "he heard" to the more nuanced "he rejoiced," Isa 39 appears to provide a more explicit explanation than does 2 Kgs 20 of why Hezekiah is judged for displaying the treasures of his house and his realm to the Babylonian envoys.

Such variations between Chronicles and its source texts as have just been illustrated (as well as other, more extensive textual variations) can be explained in a variety of ways. Thomas Willi has described a spectrum of possibilities that includes the following (moving from noninterpretive to elaborately interpretive changes): errors in transmission (of either the text in Chronicles or its source text), orthographic and grammatical changes, minor omissions, clarifying additions and changes, adaptation, theological modification, harmonization with other biblical texts, and typology.[95] That so many explanations for sound variation in parallel texts are possible indicates that, although some of the changes described above are *not deliberate or deliberate but noninterpretive* and therefore are clearly not cases of allusive paronomasia (i.e., belonging to category 1), each example must be considered on its own to determine the reason(s) that gave rise to the sound variation.

Category 2. This category includes examples that in my judgment involve an allusion that may contain allusive paronomasia but for which this cannot be determined with certainty, primarily because a discernible function for the possible paronomasia cannot be clearly demonstrated. If for any of the examples in this category allusive paronomasia were ultimately judged to be absent, the example would belong in category 1; if, on the other hand, paronomasia were judged to be present, the example would belong in either category 3 or 4 (depending on one's evaluation of the strength of the paronomasia's function).

The example involving Prov 15:17–19 and 29:21–22 that I discussed above falls into the present category. Another example that in my view

---

95. Thomas Willi, *Die Chronik als Auslegung: Untersuchungen zur literarischen Gestaltung der historischen Überlieferung Israels*, FRLANT 106 (Göttingen: Vandenhoeck & Ruprecht, 1972), 67–68. Furthermore, even changes that were originally noninterpretive in nature, such as the change from ריפת to דיפת (a case of scribal error), were sometimes made by interpreters into productive principles of exegesis or interpretation.

THE ROLE OF SOUNDPLAY IN INNERBIBLICAL ALLUSIONS 37

belongs in this category involves Jer 4:13 and Hab 1:8. The phrase וקלו
מנמרים סוסיו ("its steeds are swifter than leopards") in Hab 1:8 appears
to allude to קלו מנשרים סוסיו ("its steeds are swifter than eagles") in Jer
4:13, and furthermore a few lines later in Hab 1:8 the word נשר appears
(Babylon's horsemen are likened to eagles rushing to eat: כנשר חש לאכול)
as well as several words related to it by means of paronomasia (ופשו פרשיו
ופרשיו ["their steeds gallop, their steeds!"]). One possible explanation for
the shape of Hab 1:8 and its connection with Jer 4:13 is that the former
relocated the word נשר from the phrase קלו מנשרים סוסיו in the latter,
played on it with the words ופשו פרשיו ופרשיו, and then played on the
word נשר again in a different way by substituting the paronym נמר in the
phrase taken from Jer 4:13, thereby creating the new phrase וקלו מנמרים
סוסיו. However, it is difficult to *prove* that this hypothetical explanation
for the composition of Hab 1:8, which posits allusive paronomasia in Hab
1:8 with reference to Jer 4:13, is correct. This is so primarily because, if
allusive paronomasia is indeed present in Hab 1:8, its main function would
seem to be simply that of expanding the animal imagery for the Babylonian army presented in Jer 4:13—a function that, while interesting, is quite
subtle and does not appear to contribute in a major way to the message
of the later text. Given the lack of a clearly demonstrable function for the
possible allusive paronomasia in Hab 1:8, it seems best to conclude that
the phenomenon may be present here but that this is uncertain.

Category 3. The examples in this category involve texts containing what
in my judgment are genuine cases of allusive paronomasia, though the
paronomasia's effect is subtle. Depending on one's judgment about the
proposed paronomasia's function or effect for any given example in this
category, one might wish to reclassify the example. For instance, if one
judged the effect to be particularly weak or unclear, one might conclude
that the example belonged to category 2 (allusive paronomasia is possible
but uncertain); on the other hand, if one judged the proposed paronomasia's function to be strong, one could classify the example under category
4 (clear allusive paronomasia with a strong function).

An example that I would place in category 3 involves Pss 115:4–6, 8
and 135:15–18, which discuss the futility of idols. Psalms 115:4–6a, 8 and
135:15–17a, 18 are nearly identical, with only a few minor differences. The
main difference between these texts (aside from the fact that Ps 115:7 has
no parallel in Ps 135) is found by comparing Pss 115:6b (אף להם ולא יריחון
["they have noses but cannot smell"]) and 135:17b (אף אין יש רוח בפיהם

["indeed, there is no breath in their mouths"]). Given that two clever plays appear to be present here—אף in 115:6b means "nose," but in 135:17b the same word means "indeed," and in the place of יריחון ("they smell," from the root ריח/רוח) in 115:6b we find רוח ("breath") in 135:17b—and that they are found in close proximity with respect to the text segments that both psalms share, it seems very likely that here we are dealing with a deliberate example of allusive paronomasia. The paronomasia does not produce a significantly new meaning, however. The source text and the alluding text (which one is which is irrelevant for the present purpose) say slightly different things, to be sure (namely, that idols cannot smell and cannot speak), but the basic message is the same in both texts: idols are worthless. For these reasons, I consider this pair of texts to present a genuine case of allusive paronomasia, but one without a very striking effect.

A similar example is found in the allusion in Ps 15:5 to Ezek 18:13, 17. Ezekiel 18:13 declares that the one who has lent at interest or taken accrued interest (בנשך נתן ותרבית לקח) will not live, emphatically stating that האלה עשה מות יומת ("the one who does these things shall surely be put to death"). Ezekiel 18:17, reflecting on the nature of transgenerational punishment, declares that if a wicked man of the kind described in verse 13 has a son who refrains from taking interest or accrued interest (נשך ותרבית לא לקח), the son will surely live; such a one לא ימות ("will not die") for the sins of his father. A similar perspective on the evils of lending or taking interest is found in Ps 15:5. The first two lines of this verse describe as follows the person who possesses the moral purity requisite for dwelling in God's presence: כספו לא נתן בנשך ושחד על נקי לא לקח ("he who has not lent money at interest or taken a bribe against the innocent"). Although the similarity of the language here with that found in Ezek 18:13, 17 is not sufficient to prove the presence of an allusion, the final line of Ps 15:5, combined with the first two, suggests that one is present: עשה אלה לא ימוט לעולם ("The one who does these things will never be shaken"). Indeed, it seems to me that לא ימוט in Ps 15:5 alludes, by means of paronomasia, to both מות יומת and לא ימות in Ezek 18:13, 17. This is suggested by the fact that עשה אלה לא ימוט in Ps 15:5 expresses the corollary of האלה עשה מות יומת in Ezek 18:13, that is, the same idea that is expressed by לא ימות in Ezek 18:17.[96] If my argument is correct that we are dealing

---

96. The change from האלה עשה in Ezek 18:13 to עשה אלה in Ps 15:5 is an example of Seidel's Law or "inverted quotation," which is a not uncommon marker of allusions in the Hebrew Bible (as well as in the New Testament and other literature).

with allusive paronomasia here, what is its function? As in the example involving Pss 115 and 135, whatever effect the allusive paronomasia in Ps 15:5 has appears to be subtle since this text reflects on the same basic realities treated in Ezek 18:13, 17 and offers a nearly identical point of view. As in the Pss 115/135 example, the paronomasia in the present example has a subtle or (to employ again Cook's musical analogy) a *piano* effect. If one considered this effect to be so subtle that the proposed paronomasia is possible but cannot be proven, this example would best be classified in category 2. If, on the other hand, one could demonstrate that the paronomasia contributed in an important way to the production of new meaning or the setting forth of a new idea in the alluding text vis-à-vis the source text, this example would best be classified in category 4.

Category 5. Here I skip over category 4 (which I will discuss briefly at the end of this chapter and which will be illustrated by the examples in chapters 2, 3, and 4) and proceed to category 5. This category involves texts that may or may not be related by means of allusion and that contain similar instances of paronomasia. As mentioned above, this category is therefore somewhat of an outlier: because texts in category 5 may involve allusions but cannot be demonstrated conclusively to involve them, this category does not fall on the spectrum that includes categories 1 through 4, all of which deal with texts that involve demonstrable allusions.

One example that in my opinion belongs to category 5 involves Job 26:13 and Isa 27:1. Although these two texts share the motif of YHWH's defeat of the primeval chaos monster and are the only two verses in the Bible that describe this primordial foe as נחש ברִ(י)ח ("the elusive serpent"),[97] it is unclear to me how one might demonstrate that one of

---

See Moshe Seidel, "Parallels between the Book of Isaiah and the Book of Psalms," *Sinai* 38 (1955–1956): 150 (Hebrew); Pancratius C. Beentjes, "Inverted Quotations in the Bible: A Neglected Stylistic Pattern," *Bib* 63 (1982): 506–23; Michael A. Lyons, "Marking Innerbiblical Allusion in the Book of Ezekiel," *Bib* 88 (2007): 245–50 (and bibliography at 246 n. 4).

97. Cyrus H. Gordon argued that בָּרִח in Isa 27:1 should be translated "evil," based on an Arabic cognate ("Near East Seals in Princeton and Philadelphia," *Or* 22 [1953]: 243; see also Gordon, *Ugaritic Textbook*, AnOr 38 [Rome: Pontifical Biblical Institute, 1965], 376; Mitchell J. Dahood, "Ebla, Ugarit, and the Bible," afterword to *The Archives of Ebla: An Empire Inscribed in Clay*, by Giovanni Pettinato [Garden City, NY: Doubleday, 1981], 288).

these texts alludes to the other.[98] Interestingly, however, both texts play on the word בריח: Isa 27:1 declares that YHWH will punish the נחש ברח with his cruel, great, and mighty sword (בחרבו). In Job 26:13, parallel to the declaration that YHWH's hand pierced the נחש בריח is the statement that YHWH calmed the heavens by his wind (ברוחו).[99] If one could demonstrate that one of these texts alludes to the other, this would open up the possibility (though would not prove) that the play on בריח in the later text constitutes an instance of allusive paronomasia (one that in fact builds on the paronomasia on בריח already present in the source text).

A second example belonging to category 5 concerns the noun ברית ("lye"), which appears twice in the Bible, in Jer 2:22 and Mal 3:2. These texts share a somewhat similar theme: Jer 2 uses the image of washing with lye in order to expunge the guilt of Judah, and Mal 3 speaks of washing with lye in order to expunge the guilt of the exilic community. Apart from this vague thematic connection and the use in both texts of the noun ברית as well as the verb כבס ("to wash"), Jer 2:22 and Mal 3:2 have no other prominent lexical connections; thus it is not clear to me how one might argue that one of the texts alludes to the other. Interestingly, however, both of these verses—again, the only ones in the Bible that contain the word ברית—play on this word: in Jer 2:22 YHWH declares that though the nation wash with natron and increase lye for itself (ותרבי לך ברית), its guilt will remain. In Mal 3, it is the appearance of the messenger of the covenant (מלאך הַבְּרִית [Mal 3:1]), who manifests himself like a refiner's fire and like fuller's lye (ברית מכבסים [Mal 3:2]), that will lead to the purification of the sons of Levi (Mal 3:3).

---

98. It is possible, for example, that Isa 27:1 and Job 26:13 hark back to a common tradition and therefore neither is dependent on the other (note the similar tradition in *KTU* 1.5 I 1–2, where Yam is referred to as *ltn btn brḥ ... btn ʿqltn*, which sounds remarkably like Isa 27:1: לויתן נחש ברח ... לויתן נחש עקלתון). Even if one could demonstrate that Isa 27:1 and Job 26:13 are related by means of allusion, the relative dating of these two texts would be difficult to determine. (On the date of Job, see n. 6 to chapter 2; and on dating Isa 24–27, see Jacob Stromberg, *An Introduction to the Study of Isaiah* [London: T&T Clark, 2011], 12–14.)

99. The use of רוח here seems to be a reflection on Gen 1:2. Interestingly, Job 26:13 appears to combine the image of the divine wind/spirit from the P account of creation (Gen 1:1–2:4) with the *Chaoskampf* motif that describes creation in other biblical texts but that is notably absent from Gen 1:1–2:4.

1.6. How This Study Is Organized

As I mentioned earlier, one of my main goals in writing this book has been to demonstrate that allusive paronomasia occurs in various books of the Bible; the phenomenon is not limited to one specific book or biblical subcorpus. In order to show that this is the case, in chapters 2, 3, and 4 I discuss nine examples (three per chapter) of what I consider to be demonstrable cases of allusive paronomasia (that is, examples that fall into category 4) from a number of biblical books. No doubt the reader, based on his or her own judgment about the strength or validity of any given example, might rather classify it in another category on the spectrum discussed in the preceding section. It should be obvious that the relatively small number of examples of allusive paronomasia in the Hebrew Bible that I discuss in this study in no way constitutes a comprehensive collection of this apparently widespread phenomenon, nor are my examples in any way intended to imply that allusive paronomasia occurs only in the books in which they are found. I chose to discuss the examples that are presented in chapters 2, 3, and 4 simply because—though some examples may be more convincing than others—I believe that, taken as a whole, they illustrate well the phenomenon of allusive paronomasia in the Bible and show that this literary device was used by multiple biblical writers. In theory, a completely different set of examples could have been used to make the same points.

At the same time, there is a specific principle that led me to include each of the examples found in this book and to exclude other examples that I might have treated instead. Each of the texts I discuss has a similar function in that it showcases a biblical writer using allusive paronomasia *as a means of generating theological discourse*—that is, playing on the sounds of tradition in order to reflect on and say something about the nature of God and his relationship to Israel, the nations, or individual human beings. Although paronomasia, whether allusive or not, has a variety of functions in the Bible (as noted above), one of the more important for our understanding of the development of Israelite religion and the compositional history of the biblical text is the role paronomasia plays in the construction of ancient Israel's theological discourse. The texts that I discuss in this book provide what in my view are interesting examples of this.

In order to highlight my point that the biblical writers employed allusive paronomasia in constructing their discourse about God and his relationship to humanity, I have grouped the examples in chapters 2, 3, and

4 according to three broad theological themes that are prominent in the Bible and that can provide an effective, if basic, shorthand for describing the relationship between God and humanity: theodicy (chapter 2), judgment (chapter 3), and salvation (chapter 4). I have organized my examples according to these themes not because they in any way *dictated* the biblical authors' use of allusive paronomasia, but rather because the use of allusive paronomasia in constructing theological discourse is well *illustrated* by these themes.[100]

Because in this book I focus not on identifying innerbiblical allusions per se but instead on identifying and describing cases of allusive paronomasia in the Hebrew Bible, I have generally limited myself to discussing examples of this literary device that are found in what I perceive, on the basis of my own judgment and in reliance on the opinions of other scholars, to be clearly marked allusions.[101] Some particularly interesting examples of allusive paronomasia occur in subtle allusions, however, and for this reason I also present a few examples found in allusions about whose identification scholars disagree. Regardless of the degree to which a scholarly consensus exists about the presence of an allusion in each of my examples, I always attempt to make a probable case that, first, the source text was available to the writer of the alluding text and, second, at the very least two markers of allusion are present: the source text and the alluding text share distinctive or unique lexical and/or thematic connections, and the alluding text can be shown to be interpreting the source text.[102]

---

100. Because theodicy is a major subject in the book of Job and because that book contains several striking examples of allusive paronomasia, two of the examples in chapter 2 come from Job. Likewise, because salvation is a major theme in Second Isaiah, two of the examples in chapter 4 come from Second Isaiah. Nevertheless, theological theme, not corpus, is the primary organizational principle in this study. This is simply one possible method of grouping the examples, however; one could organize them in a number of other ways—for example, according to corpus or by the specific literary function of the allusive paronomasia.

101. Such examples can be divided into (1) examples for which a consensus exists both regarding the presence of the allusion and the direction of dependence of the texts, and (2) examples for which a consensus exists that an allusion is present but not concerning the direction of dependence.

102. This follows what Beetham considers to be the most important criteria for identifying an allusion: "availability," "word agreement or rare concept similarity," and "essential interpetive link" (Beetham, *Echoes of Scripture* [cited in Shaw, "Converted Imaginations," 238]). See further §1.5.1.1 above.

2
Theodicy

2.1. What Are Human Beings?

2.1.1. Ps 8:5: "What Are Human Beings That You Are Mindful of Them?"

מה אנוש כי תזכרנו
ובן אדם כי תפקדנו:
ותחסרהו מעט מאלהים
וכבוד והדר תעטרהו:

What are human beings that you are mindful of them?
And mortals that you care for them?
You have made them a little lower than the heavenly beings
And have crowned them with glory and majesty. (Ps 8:5–6)[1]

This famous declaration is the central climax of a ten-verse poem that, particularly in its latter half, reflects on a creation tradition similar to—if not the same as—the one presented in the opening chapter of the Bible.[2]

---

1. Although the translations of biblical passages in this book generally follow the NJPS, I have introduced gender-neutral language when the text refers to humanity in general. Hebrew masculine singular nouns (e.g., אנוש, בן אדם) have been translated as, e.g., "human beings," "people," or "mortals" when they refer to humanity in general; the corresponding masculine singular pronouns (e.g., "his," "him") have been rendered as plurals (e.g., "their," "them").

2. For a discussion of the problems involved in the relative dating of Ps 8 and Gen 1, see Christian Frevel, "'Eine kleine Theologie der Menschenwürde': Ps 8 und seine Rezeption im Buch Ijob," in *Das Manna fällt auch heute noch: Beiträge zur Geschichte und Theologie des Alten, Ersten Testaments; Festschrift für Erich Zenger*, ed. Frank-Lothar Hossfeld and Ludger Schwienhorst-Schönberger, HBS 44 (Freiburg: Herder, 2004), 253–54.

Psalm 8:5-9 reflects on Gen 1:26-31 in particular, which describes God's creation of humankind and his granting them dominion over the rest of his handiwork.³ Psalm 8:5 has been said to epitomize the anthropology of the Psalter and the temple community, as well as of the wisdom tradition and indeed the Bible as a whole.⁴ As I will discuss presently, Ps 8:5 is drawn upon on several occasions in the book of Job and plays a central role in the debate between Job and his friends over the moral and existential place of humankind, and of Job in particular, in God's cosmos.⁵

2.1.2. Job 7:17–18: "What Are Human Beings That You Make Much of Them?"

The book of Job contains a network of texts that hark back to Ps 8:5.⁶ The Psalter, as Christian Frevel has observed, serves as the touchstone from

---

3. See Michael Fishbane, "The Book of Job and Inner-Biblical Discourse," in *The Voice from the Whirlwind: Interpreting the Book of Job*, ed. Leo Perdue and W. Clark Gilpin (Nashville: Abingdon, 1992), 88. In Jon Levenson's opinion, Ps 8:4–9 "is not necessarily dependent upon Genesis 1:26–28, but illumines it nonetheless" (Jon D. Levenson, *Creation and the Persistence of Evil: The Jewish Drama of Divine Omnipotence* [Princeton: Princeton University Press, 1994], 113).

4. Frevel, "Eine kleine Theologie," 249 (and n. 18 there); Melanie Köhlmoos, *Das Auge Gottes: Textstrategie im Hiobbuch*, FAT 25 (Tübingen: Mohr Siebeck, 1999), 172 n. 1. Frevel writes: "Die intensive Intertextualität, mit der Ps 8 aus dem Psalter herausgehoben wird, bestätigt die zentrale Stellung von Ps 8 im ersten Davidpsalter und in der Psalmengruppe 3–14. Der Psalm ist kontextuelles Widerlager gegen die Not des bedrängten Menschen in den individuellen Klageliedern. Ps 8 ist ein kanonisches 'Gravitationszentrum' im Psalter" (Frevel, "Eine kleine Theologie," 269–70). Frevel also speaks of the "herausragende Stellung von Ps 8 als anthropologischen Grundlagentext" (268). Regarding the central, unique place of Ps 8 in the group Pss 3–14, see also Konrad Schmid, *The Old Testament: A Literary History*, trans. Linda M. Maloney (Minneapolis: Fortress, 2012), 114.

5. On the reception history of Ps 8, Frevel writes: "Da die Anthropologie von Ps 8 durch die schöpfungstheologische Rückbindung eine basale Aussage auf sehr engem Raum macht, nimmt es nicht Wunder, dass gerade Ps 8 besonders stark rezipiert worden ist" (Frevel, "Eine kleine Theologie," 256).

6. Driver and Gray observe that, "as to the age of Job, opinions have differed perhaps more widely than with regard to any other book of the OT" (Samuel R. Driver and George B. Gray, *The Book of Job*, ICC [Edinburgh: T&T Clark, 1921], lxv); Pope has remarked, "the fact that the dates [for the book of Job] proposed by authorities, ancient and modern, span more than a millennium is eloquent testimony that the evidence is equivocal and inconclusive" (Marvin H. Pope, *Job*, AB 15 [Garden City, NY:

which the book of Job conducts its debate.⁷ More specifically, a number of scholars have argued that Ps 8 in particular is the most important Israelite tradition with which the book of Job interacts and that this psalm constitutes a key for understanding the entire book.⁸ This is not surprising, for the central concern of Ps 8 is basically the same as that of the book of Job: what is the existential and moral place of humanity in the world that God has created and over which he rules?

The most explicit reference to Ps 8:5 in the book of Job is found in Job 7:17–18, an allusion that is nearly universally recognized and frequently discussed.⁹ Here—in the midst of what began as a rejoinder to Eliphaz's

---

Doubleday, 1973], xl). Most modern scholars consider Job to be a postexilic composition, although a variety of dates within this period have been offered (Driver and Gray, *Book of Job*, lxv); I agree with Schmid that the book, at least in its final form, most likely dates to the Persian or Hellenistic period (Konrad Schmid, "The Authors of Job and Their Historical and Social Setting," in *Scribes, Sages, and Seers: The Sage in the Eastern Mediterranean World*, ed. Leo G. Perdue, FRLANT 219 [Göttingen: Vandenhoeck & Ruprecht, 2008], 153). Although Pope admits that the final form of the book is likely postexilic ("While the completed book may be as late as the third century B.C., it may also be several centuries earlier" [Pope, *Job*, xl]), in his view the main part of the book is likely preexilic ("The seventh century B.C. seems the best guess for the date of the Dialogue" [ibid.]). For the history of the dating of Job, see ibid., xxxii–xl. Although it is impossible to date Ps 8 with any precision, according to Briggs "the linguistic evidence [of Ps 8] favours [a date in] the Persian period" (Charles A. Briggs, *The Book of Psalms*, 2 vols., ICC [Edinburgh: T&T Clark, 1906], 1:61). Because the date of the book of Job is by no means an agreed-upon matter, arguments for the identification of a proposed allusion in the book to another biblical book must generally be made on grounds other than relative dating.

7. "Die Psalmen sind das Paradigma, an dem sich das Ijobbuch 'abarbeitet'" (Frevel, "Eine kleine Theologie," 257). On the connections between Job and the Psalter, see above and esp. Will Kynes, *My Psalm Has Turned into Weeping: The Dialogical Intertextuality of Allusions to the Psalms in Job*, BZAW 437 (Berlin: de Gruyter, 2012).

8. According to Köhlmoos (*Auge Gottes*, 362), "der wichtigste Intertext für die Hiob-Dichtung ist der mehrfach rezipierte Ps 8," a judgment with which Frevel concurs (Frevel, "Eine kleine Theologie," 268). On the important role played by Ps 8 in the book of Job, see Fishbane, "Book of Job," 86–98.

9. See, e.g., Fishbane, "Book of Job," 87–90; Fishbane, *Biblical Interpretation*, 285–87; Kynes, *My Psalm*, 63–67; C. L. Brinks, "Job and Deutero Isaiah: The Use and Abuse of Traditions," *BibInt* 20 (2012): 410–11; Karl-Johan Illman, "Theodicy in Job," in *Theodicy in the World of the Bible*, ed. Antti Laato and Johannes C. de Moor (Leiden: Brill, 2003), 316; Konrad Schmid, *Hiob als biblisches und antikes Buch: Historische und intellektuelle Kontexte seiner Theologie* (Stuttgart: Katholisches Bibelwerk, 2010), 52–53 (reproduced with minor revision as "Innerbiblische Schriftdiskussion

first speech but has become a complaint directed at God—Job, the beleaguered sufferer who finds himself not to be creation's master but rather to be at the mercy of hostile supernatural forces and destructive elements in God's creation and to be the object of the burning gaze of the deity himself, declares, "What are human beings that you make much of them, that you fix your attention on them? You inspect them every morning, and every moment you examine them" (Job 7:17–18):

Ps 8:5

מה אנוש כי תזכרנו ובן אדם כי תפקדנו:

Job 7:17–18

מה אנוש כי תגדלנו וכי תשית אליו לבך: ותפקדנו לבקרים לרגעים תבחננו:

Job's appeal to Ps 8 gives force to his complaint: if God has really exalted human beings above all creation and made them just a little less than the divine beings, then why does Job suffer so at the hand of God?[10]

Although Job 7:17–18 could be understood positively, at least on one level,[11] almost all scholars recognize that in these verses "the positive sense of the statement [in Ps 8:5] is overturned word for word and the reference to Ps 8 is transformed into a parody."[12] This is particularly clear in the

---

im Hiobbuch," in Schmid, *Schriftgelehrte Traditionsliteratur: Fallstudien zur innerbiblischen Schriftauslegung im Alten Testament*, FAT 77 [Tübingen: Mohr Siebeck, 2011], 259–60); Köhlmoos, *Auge Gottes*, 170–72; Leo Perdue, *Wisdom in Revolt: Metaphorical Theology in the Book of Job*, JSOTSup 112 (Sheffield: Almond Press, 1991), 130–31, 234; Moshe Greenberg, "Job," in *The Literary Guide to the Bible*, ed. Robert Alter and Frank Kermode (Cambridge: Belknap, 1987), 288–89. The book of Job's interaction with creation is seen not only in the response throughout the book to Ps 8 but also in the undoing of the creation account of Gen 1 in Job 3 (see, e.g., Schmid, *Hiob*, 36–37).

10. The statement "You [God] have placed [שתה] everything under their [humankind's] feet" in Ps 8:7 seems to be alluded to by the statement "You [God] fix [תשית] your attention on them [humankind]" in Job 7:17.

11. Frevel, "Eine kleine Theologie," 259–60; N. H. Tur-Sinai, *The Book of Job: A New Commentary* (Jerusalem: Kiryath Sepher, 1957), 142.

12. "Damit ist Wort für Wort der positive Sinn der Aussage gekippt und die Aufnahme von Ps 8 zur Parodie unter der Hand mutiert" (Frevel, "Eine kleine Theologie," 260). "Parody" is the word used most frequently to describe the reuse of Ps 8:5–6 in Job 7:17–18 (so, e.g., Illman, "Theodicy in Job," 316; Kynes, "Job and Isaiah 40–55," 98–99; Carol Newsom, *The Book of Job: A Contest of Moral Imaginations*

different ways the root פקד is used in Ps 8:5, where it bears its positive sense "to care for," and in Job 7:18, where, as the context indicates, it has the opposite meaning, "to scrutinize." Although there can be little doubt that Job's complaint parodies the traditional wisdom enshrined in Ps 8, the sufferer does not simply negate or neatly overturn the sense of his source text.[13] While the answer to the rhetorical question in Ps 8:5-6 is that humans are highly exalted creatures whom God has established as nothing less than his vicegerents on earth, the answer to the rhetorical question in Job 7:17-18 is not so much that humans are insignificant creatures, low in status on the cosmic chain of being, but rather that God's scrutiny of Job is much more than he, a mere mortal, can bear. No matter how august God has made humanity—a fact that Job does not seem to deny—Job's experience has made it clear to him that a great gulf exists between himself and his maker, and the cause of this chasm (whether moral or existential) is the focus of his complaint in 7:17-18 and of his debate with his friends. Like Qoheleth, Job is faced with a world that is not as it should be, and he seeks to understand why.[14]

2.1.3. Job 9:2: "How Can Human Beings Be Declared Righteous?"

Job's speech in chapter 7 is followed by a retort from Bildad, according to whom Job's suffering must be the result of sin because God protects the

---

[Oxford: Oxford University Press, 2003], 131; Perdue, *Wisdom in Revolt*, 130; Frevel, "Eine kleine Theologie," 260). Other descriptions include "subversion" ("Subversion": Schmid, *Hiob*, 52) and "reversal" ("Umkehrung": Köhlmoos, *Auge Gottes*, 172). The fact that Job 7:17-18 overturns the sense of Ps 8:5 constitutes one of the strongest arguments for the direction of dependence between these two texts (Kynes, "Job and Isaiah 40-55," 98-100).

13. As Frevel writes, "ohne den positiven Subtext von Ps 8 ist auch die ins Groteske abgerutschte Parodie nicht zu verstehen. Diese ist nicht Ausdruck weisheitlicher Skepsis oder einer angesichts des Leidens entwickelten Verweigerung weisheitlichen Denkens, sondern *argumentatives Mittel*.... Das Menschenbild von Ps 8 bleibt auch für Ijob Paradigma des Menschseins" (Frevel, "Eine kleine Theologie," 262; emphasis original). In this connection, see also Schmid's comment that in Job "die Theologie der Psalmen wird zwar kritisiert, *aber nicht einfach abgewiesen*, sondern dialektisch rezipiert" (Schmid, *Hiob*, 52, emphasis added).

14. Schmid remarks that "Hi 7,17 ... zeigt, dass Hiob bereits in diesem Vers eine verkehrte Welt zeichnet, in der Gott nicht das tut, was er sonst tut, und dem Menschen nicht das zukommen lässt, was ihm sonst zukommt" (Schmid, *Hiob*, 52-53).

righteous (Job 8:5–7, 20a, 21) and punishes the wicked (8:4, 11–19, 20b, 22). Immediately following Bildad's speech is a reply from Job (9:2–10:22), which begins with a sarcastic summary of Bildad's position indicating that Job does not agree at all with the view of his friend:[15]

> אמנם ידעתי כי כן ומה יצדק אנוש עם אל:
> Indeed, I know it is so: How can human beings be declared righteous before God? (Job 9:2)

In addition to being an immediate response to Bildad, this caustic declaration uttered by Job is even more directly a response to Eliphaz's statement in Job 4:17:

> האנוש מאלוה יצדק אם מעשהו יטהר גבר:
> Can human beings be declared righteous before God? Or can people be declared pure before their Maker?

The relevance of these two texts for the present discussion will become apparent below.

2.1.4. Job 15:14: "What Are Human Beings That They Can Be Declared Pure?"

The friends' traditional point of view is reaffirmed by Eliphaz in Job 15:14 in language that, like Job 7:17, alludes to Ps 8:5:

Ps 8:5
> מה אנוש כי תִזְכְּרֶנּוּ ובן אדם כי תפקדנו:

Job 7:17–18
> מה אנוש כי תגדלנו וכי תשית אליו לבך: ותפקדנו לבקרים לרגעים תבחננו:

---

15. On the theology of Job's friends, see recently Urmas Nõmmik, *Die Freundesreden des ursprünglichen Hiobdialogs: Eine form- und traditionsgeschichtliche Studie*, BZAW 410 (Berlin: de Gruyter, 2010), esp. 159–234.

Job 15:14–15

מה אנוש כי יִזְכָּה וכי יצדק ילוד אשה: הן בקדשו [בקדשיו] לא יאמין ושמים לא זַכּוּ בעיניו:

Psalm 8:5 and Job 7:17 and 15:14 are the only texts in the Bible containing the expression מה אנוש כי ("What are human beings that …?"). The use of this rare phrase in all three texts as well as their clear thematic similarity—Job 15:14 deals with the same idea as Job 7:17 and Ps 8:5, the moral and existential place of humankind in God's cosmos—has persuaded most scholars that Job 15:14 alludes to both Job 7:17 and Ps 8:5.[16]

Whereas Job 7:17 challenges, or at least nuances, Ps 8:5 by using similar words (e.g., גדל versus זכר) or the same words but with different meanings (e.g., פקד), Eliphaz's statement in Job 15:14 plays on Ps 8:5 by means of allusive paronomasia. In 15:14, Eliphaz in effect tells Job that the reason he has not found Ps 8:5 to dovetail with his experience (as Job complained in 7:17) is that Job is a sinner. Eliphaz drives home this point by transforming the verb תזכרנו ("you are mindful of them"; from the root זכר, which in the context of Ps 8 denotes a positive, caring regard) to a verb that sounds similar but subverts the meaning of the original context, יזכה ("they can be [made/declared] pure"; from the root זכה, which, given that the implied answer to Eliphaz's rhetorical question is negative, constitutes an accusation of Job).[17] By means of this verbal transformation, Eliphaz casts doubt on one of the main tenets of Israel's wisdom tradition—that God cares for his people, especially the afflicted and the innocent, even in the face of their frailty and transgressions—or at the very least Eliphaz wants Job to know that, though Ps 8:5 may be true *in general*, Job in

---

16. Given that Job 15:14 alludes to Ps 8:5, it seems likely also that Job 15:15 alludes to Ps 8:4.

17. Another play may be present in Job 15:16: does שׁתה ("he drinks") deliberately echo the sound of שַׁתָּה ("he set") in Ps 8:7, which appears also to be alluded to (as noted above) by the word תשית in Job 7:17? (The similarity between שׁתה and שַׁתָּה is enhanced by the *plene* spelling of the latter, so that visually they look alike as well. It must be admitted, however, that the second-person masculine singular suffix conjugation form of שית is rare [occuring elsewhere only in Ps 90:8, where the *ketiv* is שַׁתָּ and the *qere* is שַׁתָּה], and that perhaps it was simply a scribal convention to indicate the suffix -*tâ* by means of the *mater lectionis he* for a hollow root ending in *tav*, such as שית.) Furthermore, Job 34:7 (איוב ישתה לַעַג כמים ["Job who drinks scoffing like water"]) appears to play on Job 15:16 (איש שתה כמים עַוְלָה ["humankind, which drinks wrongdoing like water"]).

particular has foregone God's lovingkindness because of his iniquity. By continuing the allusion to Ps 8:5 found in Job 7:17 and by transforming the source text further by means of paronomasia, Eliphaz's statement in Job 15:14 prompts Job, and thus the reader, to consider whether, or at least to what degree or in what circumstances, the classical doctrine of Ps 8:5 is true. Since Job, as the reader knows, is ultimately innocent, his objection remains, however: if Ps 8:5 is correct in affirming God's care and exaltation of his human creatures, how can this be reconciled with the reality of (innocent) human suffering?[18]

2.1.5. Job 25:4: "How Can a Human Being Be Declared Righteous ... or Pure?"

The textual thread that we have been following up to this point appears one final time in the dialogue between Job and his interlocutors, in the final speech of Job's three friends, Bildad's brief summary of the friends' arguments (Job 25:1–5). The fact that the ideas we have been tracing are recapitulated in this short, final restatement of the friends' arguments reconfirms their centrality to the dialogue between Job and his friends.

As we have seen, Eliphaz's statement in 15:14a (מה אנוש כי יזכה ["What are human beings that they can be made pure?"]) is a direct response to Job's complaint in 7:17a (מה אנוש כי תגדלנו ["What are human beings that you make much of them?"]). In his final summary, Bildad weaves together the verb from Eliphaz's statement in 15:14a (יזכה) with Eliphaz's subsequent statement in 15:14b (וכי יצדק ילוד אשה ["Or those born of woman, that they can be righteous?"]) in order to reaffirm Eliphaz's rejoinder to Job: ומה יזכה ילוד אשה ("How can one born of woman be pure?" [25:4b]). In the preceding line (25:4a), Bildad further reaffirms Eliphaz's position by citing (earnestly) Job's (sarcastic) rejoinder in 9:2 (ומה יצדק אנוש עם אל ["How can human beings be declared righteous before God?"]) to Eliphaz's statement in 4:17 (האנוש מאלוה יצדק ["Can human beings be declared righteous by God?"]).

Bildad's repetition of Eliphaz's arguments continues in 25:5, where he makes an *a fortiori* argument that, if even the heavenly bodies are not pure in God's sight, how much less mortal man: הן עד ירח ולא יאהיל ("Even

---

18. For further discussion of the relationship between Job 7:17–18 and 15:14–16, see Fishbane, "Book of Job," 93–95.

the moon is not bright") in 25:5a echoes Eliphaz's parallel statements הן בעבדיו לא יאמין ("he [God] cannot trust his servants") in 4:18a and הן בקדשו [בקדשיו] לא יאמין ("he [God] cannot trust his holy ones") in 15:15a. Confirmation of this is found in Bildad's next statement (25:5b), וכוכבים לא זכו בעיניו ("and the stars are not pure in his sight"), which clearly parallels Eliphaz's statement ושמים לא זכו בעיניו ("and the heavens are not pure in his sight") in 15:15b.

Bildad's mimicking of Eliphaz's words continues into the beginning of 25:6, which, like 15:16, begins with אף כי ("what, then?" or "how much less?") and then carries on with a derogatory remark about humankind. The words of Bildad's description of humanity in 25:6 and Eliphaz's description of humanity in 15:16 differ, but their spirit is the same. Interestingly, Bildad's excoriation in this verse of "the human being, a worm [תולעה]" (25:6b) may be yet another example of allusive paronomasia, one that plays on Eliphaz's image of "one who who drinks iniquity [עולה] like water" (15:16b). If so, Bildad's rearranging of the letters of Eliphaz's utterance עולה into the word תולעה, which is the last word in the last speech uttered by Job's three friends, is yet another signal that the friends have exhausted their argument and have devolved into pure repetition: all Bildad can do to counter Job at this point is to restate his companions' previous objections to Job, either by repeating their words verbatim, by using synonyms, or by rearranging the letters of their words to reiterate their message.

The central concept uniting the statements by Eliphaz, Bildad, and Job that we have just discussed (4:17; 9:2; 15:14–15; 25:4–5) centers on the roughly synonymous verbs צדק ("to be righteous") and זכה ("to be pure"). What ultimately lies at the heart of their verbal jousting in these texts is the status of mankind, and of Job in particular, before God.[19]

2.1.6. Conclusion

As many scholars have argued, creation is one of the major theological foci of the Hebrew Bible.[20] Further, as Leo Perdue has observed, creation is the basis of the wisdom tradition, and theodicy is one of the wisdom

---

19. The forms יצדק and יזכה may be related by subtle paronomasia: both begin with *yod*, both have a sibilant as their second consonant (*zayin* or *tsade*), and both contain a velar (hard *kaph* or *qoph*).

20. See, e.g., Levenson, *Creation*, passim.

tradition's central concerns.[21] Theodicy and creation therefore go hand in hand, and the allusions to and reverberations of Ps 8:5 in the book of Job—which focuses acutely on the apparent disparity between humanity's exalted status in creation and the pervasiveness of (innocent) suffering—bear this out.[22] The book of Job never seems to deny completely the theology of Ps 8:5. Rather, the book's view, like the world on which it reflects, is complex. Konrad Schmid's words are apropos: "the theology of the Book of Job is not an 'anti-theology' but rather a 'dialectic' theology, i.e., a theology that critically considers any traditional positive statement about God."[23] With the psalmist, the book of Job affirms that human beings occupy a special place in the universe. But how this fact is to be squared with the massive and burdensome reality of human suffering, especially the suffering of those who are apparently innocent, requires sustained struggle and involves great nuance. Profound engagement with the graphic and oral/aural shapes of received traditions and the diverse potentialities or implications of those shapes—changing a letter here or a word there—was one way the authors of the book of Job wrestled with the tradition and with God on these issues. By refracting old words of wisdom through the prism of their poetic skill, these ancient sages demonstrate that the difference between the exaltation of humanity and its depravity, between being a little lower than the angels or one step away from Sheol, is sometimes no greater than the difference between two similar-sounding words.

As is well known, allusion pervades the book of Job—in the form of both the interlocutors' references to each other's speeches and to earlier traditions outside the book—and serves as an important rhetorical device to structure the book and to develop its argument.[24] This book is

---

21. Perdue, *Wisdom in Revolt*, 12.

22. On the question to what degree the issue of innocent suffering is in fact the main problem addressed in the book of Job, however, see Jan Joosten, "La macrostructure du livre de Job et quelques parallèles (Jérémie 45; 1 Rois 19)," in *The Book of Job*, ed. W. A. M. Beuken (Leuven: Peeters, 1994), 400 n. 1; Michael V. Fox, "Job the Pious," *ZAW* 117 (2005): 351–66.

23. Schmid, "Authors of Job," 153. See also Markus Witte, "Does the Torah Keep Its Promise? Job's Critical Intertextual Dialogue with Deuteronomy," in *Reading Job Intertextually*, ed. Katharine Dell and Will Kynes, LHBOTS 574 (New York: Bloomsbury, 2013), 54–65; Witte, "Job in Conversation with the Torah," in *Wisdom and Torah: The Reception of "Torah" in the Wisdom Literature of the Second Temple Period*, ed. Bernd U. Schipper and D. Andrew Teeter, JSJSup 163 (Leiden: Brill, 2013), 81–100.

24. See, e.g., Lyons, "I Also Could Talk"; Newsom, *Book of Job*, esp. 90–168;

THEODICY

equally famous for the virtuosity of its wordplay (both paronomasia and polysemy).[25] We should not therefore be surprised to discover that, in addition to the example that we have just examined, further instances of allusive paronomasia are found in the book of Job. One of these will be the focus of the final section of the present chapter.

2.2. Looking Upon the Punishment—or Prosperity—of the Wicked

2.2.1. Ps 37:34: "You Will Look upon the Destruction of the Wicked"

The forty-verse acrostic poem that is Ps 37 constitutes a sustained meditation on the fate of the righteous and the wicked. The entire psalm consists of interwoven statements concerning the character and destiny of these two groups; the reader is constantly encouraged to think about both groups and to view their fates as corollaries of one another.[26]

The psalm begins with an encouragement not to be angry about evildoers because they will come to ruin (37:1-2). In verses 3-7 the psalmist exhorts his audience to trust in YHWH and to do good, which will lead to YHWH's giving them the desires of their hearts (v. 4) and his vindicating them (v. 6). Although the psalmist recognizes that those who carry out evil schemes (מזמות) do prosper (צלח *hiphil*) (v. 7; cf. vv. 16, 35), he repeatedly advises his audience to avoid wickedness, for in the end, he says, that lifestyle will only lead to ruin (vv. 1-2, 8-9a, 10, 12-13, 15, 17a, 20, 22b, 28d, 34c, 35-36, 38). On the contrary, those who wait on YHWH (קוי יהוה [v. 9]; קוה אל יהוה [v. 34]), the meek (ענוים [v. 11]), those blessed by YHWH (מברכיו [v. 22]), the righteous (צדיקים [v. 29])—they all will "inherit the land" (יירשו ארץ [vv. 9, 11, 22, 29]; לרשת ארץ [v. 34]). Those who trust in YHWH and do his will, though they face affliction (vv. 14, 24, 32), will in the end fare well (vv. 4-6, 17b, 18-19, 23, 25-28, 31, 33, 37, 39-40).[27]

Schmid, *Hiob*, 33–35; Robert Gordis, *The Book of God and Man: A Study of Job* (Chicago: University of Chicago Press, 1965), 169–208.

25. See, e.g., Noegel, *Janus Parallelism*, 18–25.

26. On the structure of Ps 37, see Pierre Auffret, "'Aie confiance en lui, et lui, il agira': Étude structurelle du Psaume 37," *SJOT* 4 (1990): 13–43. On the interweaving of statements about the righteous and the wicked in this psalm, see the chart on 42. Discussion of the psalm's date is found in n. 49 below.

27. On the exegesis of Ps 37 at Qumran and in the New Testament, see, e.g., Beat Weber, *Werkbuch Psalmen I: Die Psalmen 1 bis 72* (Stuttgart: Kohlhammer, 2001), 180.

Like Qoheleth, who is preoccupied with the fate of the righteous and the wicked, the author of Ps 37 emphasizes the role his personal experience has played in shaping his views on the destinies of these two groups (though his conclusions are in some ways opposed to many of those offered by Qoheleth).[28] For example, the psalmist observes that he has seen it go well for the righteous: "I have never seen [לא ראיתי] a righteous man abandoned or his children seeking bread" (v. 25). He has also seen it go ill for the wicked: "I saw [ראיתי] a wicked man, powerful, well-rooted like a robust native tree. Suddenly he vanished and was gone; I sought him [ואבקשהו], but he was not to be found [ולא נמצא]" (vv. 35–36). Just before and just after this statement (in vv. 34 and 37), the psalmist assures his audience that their own observations will confirm what he has seen (ראה). In verse 37, for example, the psalmist exhorts his readers to observe the righteous and to see that they will have a future: "Mark [שמר] the blameless, observe [וראה] the upright, for there is a future for the man of integrity." As a correlative measure, in verse 34 he also encourages his readers to look upon the wicked and to attest that they will have no future: "When the wicked are cut off, you shall see it" (בהכרת רשעים תראה).[29] Although the psalmist has sometimes observed the wicked prosper (vv. 7, 35), his experience indicates that their ultimate fate is destruction, and he seeks to encourage his audience by declaring that their experience will be no different.[30] His last word on the fate of the wicked is, therefore, a summary statement about their demise that sounds similar to verse 34:

---

28. On Ps 37 as a "wisdom psalm," see Avi Hurvitz, "צדיק = חכם בתה' לז ושאלת רקעו החכמתי," in *"Sha'arei Talmon": Studies in the Bible, Qumran, and the Ancient Near East Presented to Shemaryahu Talmon*, ed. Michael Fishbane and Emanuel Tov (Winona Lake, IN: Eisenbrauns, 1992), 131*–35*. (An abridged version of this article was published as "צדיק = 'Wise' in Biblical Hebrew and the Wisdom Connections of Ps 37," in *Goldene Äpfel in silbernen Schalen: Collected Communications to the XIIIth Congress of the International Organization for the Study of the Old Testament, Leuven 1989*, ed. Klaus-Dietrich Schunck and Matthias Augustin, BEATAJ 20 (Frankfurt am Main: Lang, 1992], 109–12.)

29. On the meaning of ראה ב as "look with triumph upon," see Judg 16:27; Pss 22:18; 112:8; 118:7; Ezek 28:17; Obad 12, 13; Mic 7:10.

30. Auffret posits a chiasm in Ps 37:34–36 in which ראיתי at the beginning of v. 35 corresponds to תראה at the end of v. 34 (Auffret, "Aie confiance," 27). This highlights the connection the psalmist makes between his own observations and what he tells his audience their observations will be as well.

ופשעים נשמדו יחדו אחרית רשעים נכרתה ("But transgressors shall be utterly destroyed, the future of the wicked shall be cut off" [v. 38]).[31]

2.2.2. Ps 73:3: "I Look upon the Prosperity of the Wicked"

Psalm 73, a twenty-eight-verse poem that has been called a "little book of Job"[32] and "a mirocosm of Old Testament theology,"[33] shares the focus of Ps 37—the fate of the wicked and the righteous—but Ps 73 presents a more nuanced picture. After an initial declaration that God is good to Israel and to the righteous (v. 1), the author of this psalm questions this doctrine and wrestles with the observation that reality does not always conform to the declaration in Ps 37:34 that "you will look upon the destruction of the wicked."[34] Grappling with the question why the wicked prosper and the

---

31. As Briggs observes, Ps 37 "deals with the same problem as the book of Job; only it takes the earlier position of the friends of Job in their discourses, and does not rise to the higher solution of the discourses of Job himself" (Briggs, *Book of Psalms*, 1:324).

32. "Ps 73, den man auch als 'kleinen Hiob' bezeichnen kann, weist entsprechend auch eine deutliche Nähe zum Hiob-Buch auf" (Beat Weber, *Werkbuch Psalmen II: Die Psalmen 73 bis 150* [Stuttgart: Kohlhammer, 2003], 22). Cf. Walter Brueggemann, "Bounded by Obedience and Praise: The Psalms as Canon," *JSOT* 50 (1991): 85 n. 2.

33. J. Clinton McCann Jr., "Psalm 73: A Microcosm of Old Testament Theology," in *The Listening Heart: Essays in Wisdom and the Psalms in Honor of Roland E. Murphy, O. Carm.*, ed. Kenneth G. Hoglund et al., JSOTSup 58 (Sheffield: JSOT Press, 1987), 247–57. According to McCann, "Psalm 73 is a high point because it contains within itself the tension that is central to the faith of the Old Testament. Since it represents attempts both to legitimate structure and to embrace pain, Psalm 73 is a microcosm of Old Testament theology" (253).

34. According to Brueggemann, Ps 73 "begins a new phase of the Book of Psalms. It does so by reiterating the theological assumption of Psalm 1, but then it moves abruptly against that assumption in its own argument, only to arrive at an affirmative theological conclusion which would evoke and permit praise" (Brueggemann, "Bounded by Obedience," 83; see further 84). So also Beat Weber, who observes that in Ps 73 "die weisheitliche Grundregel von Ps 1, die am Anfang von Ps 73 aufgenommen wird, ist in die Krise geraten. Ihre Wahrheitsfähigkeit muss durch eine Perspektivenerweiterung neu geschenkt und erkämpft werden" (Weber, *Werkbuch Psalmen II*, 22). See also McCann, "Psalm 73," 247. On the continuation of the skeptical point of view expressed in Ps 73 throughout book 3 of the Psalter and the function of Ps 73 in the Psalter as a whole, see Robert L. Cole, *The Shape and Message of Book III (Psalms 73–89)*, JSOTSup 307 (Sheffield: Sheffield Academic, 2000), 15–16, 17 n. 5. On the latter point, see also Walter Brueggemann and Patrick D. Miller, "Psalm 73

righteous suffer, the psalmist laments: "I envied the wanton; I look upon the peace of the wicked" (Ps 73:3).³⁵ The psalmist's locution here is similar to that of Ps 37:34, but his meaning is the opposite:

Ps 37:34
קוה אל יהוה ושמר דרכו וירוממך לרשת ארץ בהכרת רשעים
תראה:

Ps 73:3
כי קנאתי בהוללים שלום רשעים אראה:

These two verses may be related by means of allusion (though, as I will discuss below, if they are genetically related it is difficult to determine the direction of dependence). First, there is a clear thematic correspondence between Pss 37 and 73: both are sustained meditations on the fate of the righteous and the wicked. Second, the two psalms share a distinctive locution: the expression "to look upon the X of the wicked," where a form of the (substantive) adjective רשע is followed directly by the verb ראה, is found in the Bible only in Pss 37:34, 73:3, and 91:8 (this last text will be discussed below).³⁶ In each of these three texts, the word רשע is in the plural form רשעים and the verb ראה is in the prefix conjugation (indeed, the form is the same, תראה, in Pss 37:34 and 91:8—on which see below). These factors suggest that one of these texts may be alluding to the other, though they do not prove this.

If Pss 37:34 and 73:3 are in fact related by means of allusion, it is difficult to determine the direction of dependence.³⁷ The locution שלום רשעים אראה in Ps 73:3 could be modifying the locution בהכרת רשעים תראה in Ps 37:34, adapting the latter to the thought patterns of Ps 73 (i.e., questioning why the wicked prosper). On the other hand, the reverse could be

---

as a Canonical Marker," *JSOT* 72 (1996): 45–56; J. Clinton McCann Jr., *A Theological Introduction to the Book of Psalms: The Psalms as Torah* (Nashville: Abingdon, 1993), 142–43.

35. On the sonic-semantic *inclusio* created by the second half of vv. 3 and 12 of Ps 73, see Cole, *Shape and Message*, 19.

36. Psalm 112:10 is the only other verse in the Bible in which a form of the (substantive) adjective רשע immediately follows the verb ראה; but in this case, רשע is the subject of יראה.

37. On the relative dating of Pss 37 and 73, see n. 49 below.

true: the locution בהכרת רשעים תראה in Ps 37:34 could be modifying the locution שלום רשעים אראה in Ps 73:3, adapting the latter to the thought patterns of Ps 73:3 (i.e., despite what Ps 73 says, the wicked [ultimately] do not prosper and the righteous are ultimately blessed). For the purposes of the present discussion, it is not necessary to determine whether Ps 73:3 alludes to Ps 37:34 or vice versa, or, in fact, even to prove that the texts are genetically related. My main argument, which will be developed below, is that Ps 73:3 (and possibly Ps 37:34 as well) is alluded to by another text, Ps 91:8.

In Ps 73:4–12, the psalmist expands upon his observation in verse 3 in elaborate detail,[38] and in the two verses that follow (vv. 13–14), he states that his own righteousness has brought him nothing but daily suffering.[39] This perspective does not carry through to the end of the psalm, however. Verse 15 marks a major transition, for in this and in the following verses the psalmist recounts how further meditation on the fate of the wicked in the context of God's sanctuary (v. 17)[40] led him to understand that God does bring retribution on evildoers (vv. 18–20, 26) and that God has always been near to the psalmist despite the difficulties of his outward circumstances (vv. 23–24, 26; cf. vv. 25, 28).[41] Therefore, he concludes, his

---

38. Haug observes that Ps 73 contains "one of the most comprehensive descriptions of their [= the wicked's] acts and attitudes in the whole Old Testament" (Kari Storstein Haug, *Interpreting Proverbs 11:18–31, Psalm 73, and Ecclesiastes 9:1–12 in Light of, and as a Response to, Thai Buddhist Interpretations* [Leiden: Brill, 2012], 238). Brueggemann and Miller describe the section in question in words that could have been used to describe Qoheleth, that most famous of skeptics in the Hebrew Bible: "The first extended unit in the psalm (vv. 2–16) portrays the reflection of an Israelite who explored an intentional departure from torah-piety in imitation of 'the wicked' who prospered (v. 3)" (Brueggemann and Miller, "Psalm 73," 46).

39. Lindström characterizes the psalmist's dilemma in Ps 73 thus: "The entire visible world is a single contradiction of the righteous God" (Fredrik Lindström, "Theodicy in the Psalms," in Laato and de Moor, *Theodicy*, 299).

40. On the complexities involved in interpreting Ps 73:17, see McCann, "Psalm 73," 247–48. On the importance of this verse in the psalm as a whole, see Ludger Schwienhorst-Schönberger, "'Bis ich eintrat in die Heiligtümer Gottes' (Ps 73,17): Ps 73 im Horizont biblischer und theologischer Hermeneutik," in *"Gerechtigkeit und Recht zu üben" (Gen 18,19): Studien zur altorientalischen und biblischen Rechtsgeschichte, zur Religionsgeschichte Israels und zur Religionssoziologie; Festschrift für Eckart Otto zum 65. Geburtstag*, ed. Reinhard Achenbach and Martin Arneth, BZABR 13 (Wiesbaden: Harrassowitz, 2009), 387–402.

41. As Brueggemann observes further, the author of Ps 73, like Job, does not

initial envy of the wicked for their prosperity was due to a lack of understanding (vv. 21–22; cf. vv. 2, 15–16).

In the end, the author of Ps 73 reaches a conclusion that is congruous with the declaration of Ps 37:34.[42] In order to reach this conclusion, however, he finds it necessary to grapple intensely with the messiness of reality. What emerges from his struggle is the realization that what is of ultimate importance is not the prosperity of the wicked but rather God's care for the righteous.[43] Furthermore, the psalmist realizes that he can rejoice in his sufferings because it is precisely his affliction that shows that he is beloved by YHWH.[44]

As we have seen, Ps 73 affirms the truth of the correlative realities that the wicked prosper and the righteous suffer and, along with Ps 37:34, affirms another pair of truths, at first glance incongruous with those just mentioned, namely, that God cares for his people and punishes sinners. The author of Ps 73 wrestles with the injustice of the first pair of realities but ultimately finds comfort in the fact that, in the end, God will prove just in judging the righteous and the wicked.[45] The latter perspective—that

---

receive a solution to the issue of theodicy in the form of an explanation concerning human suffering; rather, "it is enough that the God of long-term fidelity is present, caring, powerful and attentive" (Brueggemann, "Bounded by Obedience," 86).

42. The connection on this issue does not only exist between Pss 73 and 37: as various commentators have pointed out, the reflections on the fate of the righteous and the wicked found in Ps 73 carry on those found at the beginning of the Psalter (McCann, *Theological Introduction*, 143; Brueggemann and Miller, "Psalm 73," 52–53; Cole, *Shape and Message*, 26). See also n. 34 above.

43. The psalmist's wrestling with the issue of why the righteous suffer and the wicked prosper has led some to classify Ps 73 as a "wisdom psalm," whereas his ultimate conclusion that God rescues the righteous from suffering has led others to classify the composition as a "song of thanksgiving" (McCann, "Psalm 73," 247). As McCann points out, however: "despite the tension between the two form-critical proposals, both focus on the problem of suffering. Not surprisingly, therefore, scholars who disagree on how to categorize Psalm 73 actually differ little in their assessment of the theological thrust of the psalm" (ibid.).

44. As McCann writes, "the psalmist rejects the traditional understanding of the consequences of maintaining purity of heart"—that is, material blessing—"suggesting that the 'pure in heart' or 'Israel' are those who continue to obey, serve, and praise God even while stricken and troubled" (ibid., 251–52).

45. Beat Weber writes of the psalmist in Ps 73: "Er erkennt, dass die ihm vor Augen stehende Wirklichkeit nicht die ganze Wahrheit umfasst" (Weber, *Werkbuch Psalmen II*, 23).

those who fear God do well and those who spurn God receive their just deserts—which permeates Ps 37 and in the end wins out in Ps 73, appears again in the Psalter in Ps 91, to which we now turn.

2.2.3. Ps 91:8: "You Will Look upon the Punishment of the Wicked"

Like Ps 37, Ps 91 provides a less nuanced perspective on life than Ps 73. But unlike Ps 37—a text that, as mentioned above, devotes equal space to meditation on the destiny of the just and the unjust—Ps 91 focuses almost entirely on the idea that God protects the righteous. Indeed, this theme is elaborated in all but one verse of this sixteen-verse composition. At the very center of the psalm, in verse 8, the psalmist pauses momentarily from his sustained affirmation of God's care for the righteous (vv. 1–7, 9–16) in order to affirm his belief in the correlative reality, that God will bring retribution on the wicked.[46] Here, in Ps 91:8, the psalmist concurs with the thought expressed in Ps 37:34 by employing a turn of phrase similar to the last phrase of that verse and to the last phrase of Ps 73:3, but that states the opposite of what the latter phrase states:

Ps 37:34

קוה אל יהוה ושמר דרכו וירוממך לרשת ארץ בהכרת רשעים תראה:

Ps 73:3

כי קנאתי בהוללים שָׁלוֹם רשעים אראה:

Ps 91:8

רק בעיניך תביט וְשִׁלֻּמַת רשעים תראה:

I have observed that Pss 37:34, 73:3, and 91:8 are connected by the unique phrase "to look upon the X of the wicked."[47] Psalm 91:8 appears to have transformed the word שלום ("peace") from Ps 73:3 into שלמת (the con-

---

46. Some scholars consider v. 8 to be a gloss. See nn. 49 and 50 below.

47. Strengthening the case that שלמת רשעים תראה in Ps 91:8 constitutes an allusion to שלום רשעים אראה in Ps 73:3 are the facts that Ps 73:3 is the only verse in the Bible containing the words ראה ("to see"), רשע ("wicked"), and שלום ("well-being"), and Ps 91:8 is the only verse in the Bible containing the words ראה ("see"), רשע ("wicked"), and שלמה ("recompense").

struct form of שִׁלְמָה), a word that sounds very similar but bears the opposite meaning, "retribution."[48] By doing so the author of Ps 91:8 affirms the idea expressed in Ps 37:34, namely, that God punishes the wicked, using paronomasia to reverse the statement in Ps 73:3, namely, that one might look upon the *peace* of the wicked.[49] Indeed, by phrasing his affirmation of the punishment of the wicked as a direct response to the claim in Ps 73:3 that evil people prosper, the psalmist in Ps 91:8 (much like Job's inter-

---

48. Jacob Weingreen observes the similarity between the exegesis of Ps 73:3 in Ps 91:8 and rabbinic *al tikrei* readings, stating: "It looks as if the Psalmist [in Ps 91:8] was saying: 'Do not read šᵉlôm [the well-being of the wicked] but šillumaṯ [the retribution …]'" (Jacob Weingreen, *From Bible to Mishna: The Continuity of Tradition* [Manchester, UK: Manchester University Press, 1976], 12). I will return briefly in chapter 5 to the similarities between allusive paronomasia in the Bible and rabbinic *al tikrei* readings.

49. Briggs, for example, concluded that Ps 91:8 constitutes a gloss on Ps 73:3 (Briggs, *Book of Psalms*, 1:282). See also Weingreen, *From Bible to Mishna*, 12, who notes the connection and the paronomasia. It is difficult to determine the relative dating of Pss 37, 73, and 91. Hossfeld and Zenger date both Pss 37 and 73 to the fifth century (Frank-Lothar Hossfeld and Erich Zenger, *Die Psalmen: Psalm 1–50*, NEchtB/AT 29 [Würzburg: Echter, 1993], 229; Hossfeld and Zenger, *Psalms 2: A Commentary on Psalms 51–100*, trans. Linda M. Maloney, Hermeneia [Minneapolis: Fortress, 2005], 226). Hossfeld and Zenger do not explicitly suggest a date for Ps 91, but their redactional model of the Psalter implies that they consider it to postdate both Pss 37 and 73 (Hossfeld and Zenger, *Psalms 2*, 5–6). A different relative dating is provided by Briggs, who dates Ps 37 to a time in the postexilic period "before Nehemiah" (Briggs, *Book of Psalms*, 1:325), though he considers Ps 37:34 to be the addition of "an early editor" (1:331) and considers all the psalms of Asaph (including Ps 73) to have been composed "in the early Greek period" (1:lxvi). In Briggs's opinion, Ps 91 "belongs to the late Persian or more probably to the early Greek period" (2:279), though he attributes v. 8 to a "glossator" (2:280–81). Because the conclusions of Hossfeld and Zenger and Briggs regarding the dates of Pss 37, 73, and 91 (and individual verses in these psalms) are necessarily somewhat conjectural—depending as they must on general linguistic, sociological, historical, and theological arguments, or on arguments about the redactional history of the individual psalms in question and of the entire Psalter—the question of the direction of dependence between Pss 37, 73, and 91 can best be addressed by posing the question of function (see Kynes, "Job and Isaiah 40–55"): given the verbal correspondences among these texts, which text seems to be dependent upon and to transform the thought of the others? While in my opinion this question cannot ultimately determine the relative dating of Pss 37 and 73 or of Pss 37 and 91, I believe that it indicates that Ps 91 is more likely later than Ps 73 rather than vice versa.

locutors and adherents of similar "orthodox" theologies)[50] either denies the grievous injustices of life with which the author of Ps 73 grapples or—more likely—considers the ultimate comeuppance of the wicked to be so surpassing a reality compared to the injustice of their prospering that the latter is not even worth mentioning. The view of 91:8 is effectively that of the latter days, the אחרית: whatever injustices God's people experience in this life, in the end God will vindicate his servants by bringing retributive justice on the heads of their oppressors. The paronomasia of the word שלמת in Ps 91:8 on the word שלום in Ps 73:3 transforms the lament of the latter verse so as to bring it into conformity with the overall message of Ps 73, that God will vindicate his people. Thus, Ps 91:8 reads Ps 73 (and possibly also Ps 37) *as a whole* and produces a new statement based on 73:3 that reflects the overall picture that Ps 73 presents.

At this point, it is necessary to say a few words about the textual history of Ps 91:8. The Septuagint (in which this verse is Ps 90:8) reads καὶ ἀνταπόδοσιν ἁμαρτωλῶν ὄψῃ ("and you will look on the retribution of sinners") and therefore appears to reflect the Masoretic Text's ושלמת רשעים תראה. The verse is also attested, however, at Qumran (one time, in Hebrew), in 11QapocrPs, where it reads רק] תביט [בעיניך ותרא]ה שלום [רשע]ים.[51] Although the context of Ps 73:3 indicates that there שלום must mean "peace," if the form שלום is in fact the original reading in Ps 91:8, the context there indicates that these consonants can only be construed as שִׁלּוּם ("recompense"), a word that is attested a couple of times in the MT (in Isa 34:8 and Hos 9:7).[52] (If שלום in Ps 91:8 meant "peace," this verse would completely contradict the rest of the psalm.)

The Septuagint's ἀνταπόδοσιν ("recompense") could therefore reflect either שלום (to be vocalized שִׁלּוּם), the form attested in 11QapocrPs,[53] or שלמת, the form attested in the MT—both of which mean "recompense."

---

50. According to Briggs, "A glossator appends [Ps 91 v.] 8, probably in order to show that God distinguishes between the righteous and the wicked; and that while He delivers those who have made Him their refuge, He does not spare the wicked.... This glossator seems to have held the older opinion, contested in the book of Job, that the wicked and the righteous are carefully discriminated in plagues and other evils" (Briggs, *Book of Psalms*, 2:280–81).

51. 11QapocrPs VI, 9. See Eugene Ulrich, *The Biblical Qumran Scrolls: Transcriptions and Textual Variants* (Leiden: Brill, 2010), 654.

52. The same form also occurs in Mic 7:3, but there it means "bribe."

53. שִׁלּוּם ("recompense, retribution") is also attested elsewhere at Qumran (1QM IV, 12; XVII, 1; 1QH IX, 17).

If שָׁלוֹם is the original reading in Ps 91:8—which would, in fact, make the wordplay with שָׁלוֹם in Ps 73:3 even more remarkable, since the words would differ only on the level of vocalization—a later scribe may have changed the consonantal form שלום (to be read שָׁלוֹם) in Ps 91:8 to שלמת (i.e., שֻׁלֻּמַת) in order to make the meaning of the word absolutely clear.

In addition to constituting an instance of allusive paronomasia with reference to שלום in Ps 73:3, the word שלמת in Ps 91:8 may play on another word in Ps 73. Although I think it would be difficult to prove, it seems possible that in substituting שלמת (the construct form of שלמה) for שלום in his reuse of the phrase שלום רשעים אראה from Ps 73:3, the author of Ps 91:8 may have been reading this phrase in light of Ps 73:19, which says of the wicked: איך היו לשמה כרגע ספו תמו מן בלהות ("How in a moment they are turned *into ruin*, swept away and brought to an end by terrors"). At least one scholar has suggested that לְשַׁמָּה ("[they are turned] into ruin") in this verse plays on שלום in Ps 73:3.[54] If this proposal is correct and if this play was noticed by the author of Ps 91:8, it may be that his use of a form of the word שלמה in Ps 91:8 plays not only on שלום in Ps 73:3 (whose consonants it shares but with which it contrasts starkly in meaning) but also on לשמה in Ps 73:19 (of which שלמה is an anagram and which it resembles in meaning).

2.2.4. Conclusion

The interplay between Pss 37, 73, and 91 on the issue of the fate of the wicked—Do the unjust prosper or receive their just deserts?—reflects an innerbiblical dialogue on this subject that is enriched by the use of allusive paronomasia in Ps 91:8. All three psalms in their present form ultimately voice a similar view on the destiny of the just and the unjust. Psalm 73, however, presents its readers with a more nuanced perspective than the others, one that invites them to trust in the goodness of God, not naively but in full recognition of their experience of the pervasive inequities and heart-wrenching suffering that characterize human experience.

What light can the dialogue among Pss 37, 73, and 91 shed on our understanding of the Psalter as a whole? The fate of the righteous and the wicked was a central concern to those who gave the book of Psalms its final, canonical shape. This can be seen most immediately in the fact that

---

54. Weber, *Werkbuch Psalmen II*, 20.

Ps 1, which was appended to the beginning of the Psalter at a late stage in its redaction in order to form a preface to the entire work, meditates—as do Pss 37, 73, and 91—on the destiny of those who fear God and those who do not.[55] Walter Brueggemann observes that the Psalter begins with the idea that piety leads to prosperity (Ps 1) and ends in unbounded praise of YHWH (Ps 150). He considers the first perspective, as it is expressed in Ps 1 at least, to be "naïve"[56] but discerns as one moves through the Psalter a concerted effort to engage fully with the rawness and complexity of life: "In order to move from Psalm 1 at the beginning to Psalm 150 at the end," he writes, "one must depart from the safe world of Psalm 1 and plunge into the middle of the Psalter where one will find a world of enraged suffering."[57] Whether or not one agrees with Brueggemann's characterization of Ps 1 (I view this psalm as expressing idealism or a future hope or eschatological perspective—as does Ps 91:8—more than reflecting naïveté), his observation on the trajectory of the Psalter as a whole is quite keen.

A number of scholars, including Brueggemann, have suggested that the expressions of human struggle found throughout the Psalter reach a climax in Ps 73, which constitutes a pivotal point in the movement from the monochromatic picture of the righteous versus the wicked painted in Ps 1 to the beautiful polychromatic image of exuberant praise found in Ps 150.[58] This is so because in Ps 73 the psalmist decides to commit himself to serve YHWH not because his piety has led him to *feel* God's care but rather *in spite of the fact that* his righteousness brings him constant suffering and pain. In this way, as Brueggemann observes,

> the dramatic movement of the canon of the Psalms is closely paralleled in the drama of the book of Job. That literature also begins with intense obedience, so that the initial portrayal of Job closely approximates the model of Psalm 1. The poetic middle of the book of Job, like the controversy over *ḥesed* in the Psalter, shows the relation of God and Job in dispute. In the end, in the whirlwind speeches and Job's responses, there is yielding praise, not unlike the concluding doxology of the Psalter.[59]

---

55. See Brueggemann and Miller, "Psalm 73," 53; Brueggemann, "Bounded by Obedience," 64–66.
56. Brueggemann, "Bounded by Obedience," 72.
57. Ibid.
58. See, e.g., ibid., 81; McCann, *Theological Introduction*, 143.
59. Brueggemann, "Bounded by Obedience," 89 n. 1.

Through its wrestling with the relationship between piety and suffering, Ps 73 expresses *in nuce* not only the central theological problem of the book of Job, but indeed, at least according to J. Clinton McCann, of the entire Hebrew Bible as well.[60]

The manner in which Ps 91 harks back to Pss 37 and 73 and plays on the latter text provides a good example of the sophisticated ways in which the scribes of ancient Israel harnessed the power of language in order to demonstrate just how subtle the shades of reality can be and how difficult it can be to reconcile experience and faith. The cognitive dissonance created by the fact that the affirmations "I look upon the peace of the wicked" and "You will look upon the punishment of the wicked" are in fact *both* true in this world is reflected on a linguistic level by the fact that what differentiates the words "peace" (שָׁלוֹם) and "punishment" (שִׁלֻּמָה/שִׁלּוּם) is nothing more than a few breaths. As the author of Ps 73 realized, however, appearances are not always as they seem—they belie a deeper reality. The well-being of the wicked, though genuine, may be fleeting or may in the end lead to ruin. Although the wicked do experience prosperity, according to the author of Ps 73 they do not know the highest kind of peace, that paradoxical beatitude that consists of being close to and cared for by God, even in the midst of suffering.

2.3. Extinguishing the Lamp of the Wicked

2.3.1. Prov 13:9; 24:20: "The Lamp of the Wicked Goes Out"

Three texts in the book of Proverbs portray the downfall of the wicked by employing the image of their lamp being extinguished. Two of these, Prov 13:9 and 24:20, contain the expression נר רשעים ידעך ("The light of the wicked goes out").[61] In both cases, this is the second line of a bicolon. In 13:9, the b-line, ונר רשעים ידעך, is related to the a-line, אור צדיקים ישמח ("The light of the righteous is radiant"),[62] by means of antithetical parallelism. In 24:20, the b-line, נר רשעים ידעך, is related to the a-line, כי לא

---

60. McCann, "Psalm 73," 253. See also Brueggemann, "Bounded by Obedience," 83–84; Weber, *Werkbuch Psalmen II*, 22.

61. On the relationship between Prov 13:9 and 24:20, see Heim, *Poetic Imagination*, 347–53.

62. In Prov 13:9 "the root *ś-m-ḥ* has a double sense, 'rejoice' (its usual meaning) and 'shine' (an archaic but attested usage …). Both senses may be present here in a way

תהיה אחרית לרע ("For there is no future for the evil person"), by means of synonymous parallelism. Both proverbs express the same thought: life goes well for the righteous but, at least in the end, poorly for the wicked. The third proverb that portrays the wicked person's end by utilizing the image of his lamp going out is Prov 20:20: מקלל אביו ואמו ידעך נרו באישון [באשון] חשך ("The one who curses his father and mother—his light goes out in utter darkness").

2.3.2. Job 18:5–6: "Surely the Light of the Wicked Goes Out"

In Job 18, Bildad meditates at length on the theme that the wicked will come to ruin. In the midst of this meditation, which corresponds thematically to the thoughts expressed in Prov 13:9, 20:20, and 24:20, Bildad alludes to these three verses by means of locutions very similar to theirs: גם אור רשעים ידעך ("Surely the light of the wicked goes out" [Job 18:5]) and ונרו עליו ידעך ("His [the wicked person's] lamp goes out" [Job 18:6]). These locutions are either unique to or distinctive of this text and the aforementioned texts from Proverbs. Apart from Job 18:5–6, the nouns נר and רשע and the verb דעך occur together only in Prov 13:9, 24:20, and Job 21:17 (which, as I will argue below, reacts to Job 18:5), and these three words occur together with the word אור only in Job 18:5–6 and Prov 13:9. Furthermore, in addition to the passages just mentioned (Prov 13:9; 24:20; Job 18:5–6; 21:17) the noun נר and the verb דעך are collocated again only in Prov 20:20. By repeating the theology of retribution expressed in Prov 13:9, 20:20, and 24:20, Bildad argues that Job's suffering must be the result of his sin.[63]

2.3.3. Job 21:17: "How Often Does the Lamp of the Wicked Go Out?"

In Job 21:17, Job reacts to Bildad's statements in Job 18:5–6 and questions the theology of retribution that Bildad has learned from the book of

---

that suggests fusion of light and joy" (Michael V. Fox, *Proverbs 10–31*, AB 18B [New York: Doubleday, 2009], 564).

63. According to Michael Fox, the proverb collections in Prov 10–29 "were composed and edited during the monarchy, probably in the eighth to seventh centuries B.C.E." (Fox, *Proverbs 10–31*, 499); so also Clifford: "It is quite probable that all (or a substantial part) of chaps. 10–29 were in circulation before the end of the monarchy" (Richard J. Clifford, *Proverbs*, OTL [Louisville: Westminster John Knox, 1999], 6). According to most scholars, the book of Job is later than this (see n. 6 above).

Proverbs. In Job 21:17–19, Job explicates the thought that, contrary to the view expressed by Bildad and the authors of Prov 13:9, 20:20, and 24:20, the wicked do in fact prosper. In Job 21:17, Job directly rebuts Bildad's statements in Job 18:5–6 by asking, כמה נר רשעים ידעך ("*How often* does the lamp of the wicked go out?" [Job 21:17]).[64] By providing a verbatim citation of the phrase נר רשעים ידעך from Prov 13:9 and 24:20 (which occurs only in these two verses and in Job 21:17),[65] but by prefixing the word כמה ("how often?") to the phrase (which sounds like גם ["surely"] in Job 18:5 but in context expresses the opposite idea), Job argues with the theology of retribution Bildad has drawn from Proverbs.[66]

The Teaching Found in Proverbs concerning "The Lamp of the Wicked"

Prov 13:9

אור צדיקים ישמח ונר רשעים ידעך:

Prov 20:20

מקלל אביו ואמו ידעך נרו באישון [באשון] חשך:

Prov 24:20

כי לא תהיה אחרית לרע נר רשעים ידעך:

---

64. As noted, e.g., by Tur-Sinai, *Book of Job*, 328; Robert Gordis, *The Book of Job: Commentary, New Translation, and Special Studies* (New York: Jewish Theological Seminary of America, 1978), 529.

65. Various scholars recognize the citation in Job 21:17. See, e.g., John Gray, *The Book of Job*, ed. David J. A. Clines, THB 1 (Sheffield: Sheffield Phoenix Press, 2010), 295; Raik Heckl, *Hiob: Vom Gottesfürchtigen zum Repräsentanten Israels; Studien zur Buchwerdung des Hiobbuches und zu seinen Quellen*, FAT 70 (Tübingen: Mohr Siebeck, 2010), 129 n. 402.

66. That Job in 21:17 is replying directly to his friends is further made clear by his description of their position two verses later, "[You say:] 'God is reserving their [wicked people's] punishment for their children'" (Job 21:19a), and by his continued objection to this point of view in the remainder of his speech (Job 21:19b–34). Job 21:19a is sometimes described as a "virtual quotation." For a rejection of this terminology, with helpful bibliography, see Lyons, "I Also Could Talk," 170 n. 6.

Bildad's Reiteration of the Teaching Found in Proverbs concerning "The Lamp of the Wicked"

Job 18:5–6

גַּם אוֹר רְשָׁעִים יִדְעָךְ וְלֹא יִגַּהּ שְׁבִיב אִשּׁוֹ: אוֹר חָשַׁךְ בְּאָהֳלוֹ וְנֵרוֹ עָלָיו יִדְעָךְ:

Job's Objection

Job 21:17

כַּמָּה נֵר רְשָׁעִים יִדְעָךְ וְיָבֹא עָלֵימוֹ אֵידָם חֲבָלִים יְחַלֵּק בְּאַפּוֹ:

Bildad's affirmation of Proverbs's retribution theology can be paraphrased as: "Indeed [גם], what Proverbs teaches concerning the lamp of the wicked proves true! Just look at your suffering, Job—it indicates that you belong to this group." Job's reply, which uses paronomasia to state the opposite, can be paraphrased: "How often [כמה] is what Proverbs teaches concerning the lamp of the wicked actually true? Just look at such people—they frequently are doing just fine!" Since Job's words are vindicated by God at the end of the book (42:7; cf. 21:34; 26:3), from the point of view of the book's final form Job's use of paronomasia to rebut Bildad's theology can be considered a divine revelation that Bildad's affirmation of the retribution theology of Proverbs is mistaken—not in general, necessarily, but at least in the case of Job.

2.3.4. Job 22:17–18: Getting the Last Word

Although Job has the final word on the lamp of the wicked (21:17), his objection to the traditional doctrine as expressed by means of this metaphor is later rebutted in an indirect but brilliant fashion by Eliphaz. Interestingly, just as Job refuted the words of Bildad by means of paronomasia that alluded to Bildad's words, Eliphaz uses paronomasia (that alludes not to Job's words, however, but to the book of Proverbs) in order to construct his counterargument to Job's objection to his friends' position. Immediately following Job's argument in chapter 21 that the wicked prosper is a rejoinder from Eliphaz (22:1–30), who in 22:17–18 cites in detail Job's statements in 21:14–16 concerning the rebellious attitude of the wicked toward God and then, in 22:19, plays on Prov 13:9 in order to contradict Job's allusion in 21:17 to the same verse. Eliphaz's citation of Job's words is as follows:

Job 21:14–16 (Job is speaking)
ויאמרו לאל סור ממנו ודעת דרכיך לא חפצנו: מה שדי כי נעבדנו
ומה נועיל כי נפגע בו: הן לא בידם טובם עצת רשעים רחקה מני:

Job 22:17–18 (Eliphaz is speaking)
האמרים לאל סור ממנו ומה יפעל שדי למו: והוא מלא בתיהם טוב
ועצת רשעים רחקה מני:

Eliphaz agrees here with Job's characterization of the wicked in 21:14–16. For example, in 22:17a, Eliphaz cites with approval the words that Job put in the mouth of the wicked in 21:14a: האמרים לאל סור ממנו ("They say to God, 'Leave us alone!'"). Eliphaz next attributes to the wicked a question, ומה יפעל שדי למו ("What can Shaddai do about it?" [22:17b]), that reflects the language and thought of the question Job puts in the mouth of the wicked in 21:15b, מה שדי כי נעבדנו ("What is Shaddai that we should serve him?"). Eliphaz's subsequent statement, והוא מלא בתיהם טוב ("But it was he who filled their houses with good" [22:18a]), reflects Job's thought in 21:16a, namely, that the wicked prosper only because God allows them to, not because of their own merit (הן לא בידם טובם: "Indeed, their good is not in [i.e., does not come from] their own strength"). Eliphaz's next words, ועצת רשעים רחקה מני ("The thoughts of the wicked are beyond me!" [22:18b]), are a verbatim citation of Job's next words (21:16b).[67]

Several times in 22:17–18, Eliphaz uses paronomasia in order to reformulate Job's words. For example, the verb מלא ("he fills") in Eliphaz's speech contains the consonants of the word לא ("not") from the parallel clause in Job's speech and occupies the syntactic slot corresponding to לא there. Likewise, Eliphaz's use of בתיהם ("their houses") mimics the sounds of Job's בידם ("in their hand"; both words begin with *bet*, end in *mem*, and contain *yod*; and *tav/dalet*—dental voiceless and voiced counterparts—are similar in place of articulation).[68] Furthermore, the verb יפעל in 22:17

---

67. On this clause and for a proposed emendation, see Tur-Sinai, *Book of Job*, 328. On the expression עצת רשעים, see Roland Bergmeier, "Zum Ausdruck עצת רשעים in Ps 1 1 Hi 10 3 21 16 und 22 18," ZAW 79 (1967): 229–32. The phrase עצת רשעים occurs only in the two texts we are considering, Job 21:16 and 22:18, in one other place in Job (10:3), and in Ps 1:1. It seems likely that the verses in Job just cited interact consciously with Ps 1.

68. Because the *yod* in בתיהם is not a consonant but rather a *mater lectionis*, the

appears to play on the sounds of the verbs נועיל and נפגע in Job 21:15.⁶⁹ Thus, in 22:17–18, Eliphaz repeats Job's words from 21:14–16—sometimes augmenting and altering them by means of paronomasia—in order to declare that whatever words one uses, those of Job or words that sound similar, Job's criticism of the wicked is correct.

Eliphaz's agreement with Job ends abruptly in the next verse, 22:19, however, when Eliphaz contradicts Job's statement in 21:17, כמה נר רשעים ידעך ("How often does the lamp of the wicked [actually] go out?"). As I observed above, this statement alludes to Prov 13:9 and 24:20 (as well as, though in a less verbally precise way, to Prov 20:20). In Job 22:19, Eliphaz brilliantly rebuffs Job for casting aspersion on the Proverbs doctrine that the wicked fail by alluding not, as Job did, by using paronomasia to *reverse* the meaning of Prov 13:9*b* but by using paronomasia to *affirm* the meaning of Prov 13:9*a*:

Prov 13:9

אוֹר צַדִּיקִים יִשְׂמָח וְנֵר רְשָׁעִים יִדְעָךְ:

The light of the righteous is radiant, but the lamp of the wicked goes out.

Job 21:17a

כמה נר רשעים ידעך

How often does the lamp of the wicked go out?

Job 22:19a

יִרְאוּ צַדִּיקִים וְיִשְׂמָחוּ

The righteous see [the destruction of the wicked (22:19b–20)] and rejoice.

---

fact that this word and בידם both contain *yod* is only apparent on a graphic level and therefore is not actually an example of paronomasia.

69. As does ילעג in 22:19. Adding to the sonic parallelism between Job 22:18a and 21:16a is the fact that the first word in Job 22:18 (after the conjunction *vav*), הוא, begins with the same letter, *he*, as the first word in Job 21:16, הן. In contrast to my argument that והוא מלא בתיהם טוב in Job 22:18 plays on הן לא בידם טובם in Job 21:16, Tur-Sinai writes of the statement just quoted from Job 22:18: "The outward resemblance to the contention of the friends quoted by Job in XXI, 16, הֵן לֹא בְיָדָם טוּבָם, seems accidental" (Tur-Sinai, *Book of Job*, 344).

In his allusion to Prov 13:9a, Eliphaz changes the word אוֹר ("light" of the righteous) to the paronym יראו ("they [the righteous] will see") and plays on the verb ישׂמח—which in Prov 13:9 is either a *qal* form meaning "[the light of the righteous] is radiant" (or: "rejoices," following the MT) or a *piel* form meaning "[the light of the righteous] causes joy" (if the MT is emended)[70]—by means of the *qal* form וישׂמחו ("they [the righteous] will rejoice"). Eliphaz, having perceived Job's allusion to Prov 13:9, counters it by applying paronomasia to the same verse in order to tell Job that even if one rearranges the letters of the tradition, the truth remains that the wicked fail.

In his rebuttal of Job in 22:19, Eliphaz finds yet another way to reaffirm the wisdom traditions he has inherited (as is so common in his and the other friends' speeches), specifically by reiterating the perspective of Prov 13:9, 20:20, and 24:20 and Bildad's affirmation of those earlier texts in Job 18:5–6. By using antecedent tradition and changing it slightly, Eliphaz's point is that the old doctrine is true, regardless of what words one chooses to express it. Eliphaz's message to Job appears to be, in effect: "No matter how you combine letters to build words, they spell the same message: the righteous succeed and the wicked fail." Eliphaz's reaffirmation of Prov 13:9 by means of allusive paronomasia is made all the more brilliant (even though it proves ultimately to be erroneous) by the fact that in the preceding two verses of his speech, 22:17–18, he uses, as we have seen, allusive paronomasia to rephrase the words of Job himself, not to disagree with Job *but to affirm Job's words as well.*

2.3.5. Conclusion

As in the first example discussed in this chapter, in which the Joban poets problematized a doctrine from the Psalter concerning humanity in general (Ps 8:5), their challenging of statements from the book of Proverbs concerning the fate of the wicked indicates that in their view the inherited tradition on this point required further nuance in the light of Job's innocent suffering. These poets wrestled with the texts from Proverbs by using paronomasia to alter their words when either Job or his friends, or both, allude to them. If, as some have argued, the book of Job constitutes—

---

70. See n. 62 above.

at least on one level—a reflection on Judah's suffering in the exile,⁷¹ the book's wrestling with inherited wisdom may be designed to probe whether the old doctrines could still be considered true given the tragedy of the exile. If so, the allusive paronomasia in the two examples from Job that we have examined in this chapter serves to explore not simply the relationship between God and (innocent) humanity in general but also the relationship between God and his chosen people.

The question of why humans suffer, and especially why God's beloved suffer, is never really answered by the Joban poets, but the rhetorically brilliant ways in which they grapple with this crux are what have made this book of perennial interest to readers and sufferers living in diverse cultures and historical circumstances. If the problem of theodicy cannot be solved, the exploration of this issue that the book of Job provides is— precisely because in its wrestling it does not provide an answer—perhaps the best consolation that can be offered to those living, as Qoheleth puts it, "under the sun."

---

71. Possible evidence for this is found in the fact that Job is afflicted with שחין רע (Job 2:7), an expression that occurs elsewhere only in the covenant curses pronounced against Israel found in Deut 28 (v. 35), and that Job lives 140 years—twice the time of the exile. Alternatively, though not mutually exclusive of the aforementioned interpretive option, Job's 140 years may be intended to indicate that his lifespan is twice the typical lifespan presented in Ps 90:10. In this connection, it is noteworthy that in chapter 42 Job receives double the amount of riches he had in chapter 1; thus his lifespan may have been doubled as well.

3
Judgment

3.1. Setting Babylon on Fire

3.1.1. Jer 17:19–27: Setting Fire to the Gates of Jerusalem

In Jer 17:19–27, YHWH conducts what amounts to a brief covenant ratification ceremony with "the kings of Judah, and all Judah, and all the inhabitants of Jerusalem" (v. 20). First, the deity instructs Jeremiah to command the people to observe the Sabbath (vv. 19–22). Then, after a statement that the people's ancestors failed to heed YHWH's commands (v. 23), the covenant sanctions are laid out before the people: if they obey their divine suzerain, it will go well with them (vv. 24–26), but if they disobey him, they will be destroyed (v. 27). YHWH delivers the covenant curse sanction in the following terms:

והצתי אש בשעריה ואכלה ארמנות ירושלם ולא תכבה׃
I will set fire to its gates; it shall consume the fortresses of Jerusalem and it shall not be extinguished. (Jer 17:27b)

The mention of the burning of Jerusalem's gates here is not accidental; the gates of Jerusalem are a focus in Jer 17:19–27.[1] Jeremiah is told to deliver his message at the "People's Gate" and "in all the gates of Jerusalem" (vv. 19–20). The injunction to obey the Sabbath—the main concern of the pericope—focuses on the command not to bring burdens through the gates of the city, a command that is stated three times (vv. 21, 24, 27).

---

1. Allen notes that the Sabbath and the gates of Jerusalem are both mentioned seven times in these eight verses and observes: "These heptads are surely not coincidental" (Leslie C. Allen, *Jeremiah: A Commentary*, OTL [Louisville: Westminster John Knox, 2008], 208).

If the people obey, Jerusalem will be inhabited for all time, and Davidic kings will enter through the gates of the city in perpetuity (v. 25). In other words, the covenant that YHWH sets before the people in Jer 17:19–27 has as its blessing sanction nothing less than the assurance that YHWH will guarantee the Davidic dynasty forever. As with the covenant treaty in Deuteronomy (31:16–21, 27–29), however, so too here the curse is already sealed on account of the people's recalcitrance (Jer 17:23).

3.1.2. Jer 21:12–14: Setting Fire to the Royal Palace of Jerusalem

Once the Babylonians have started besieging Jerusalem, king Zedekiah wonders if perhaps YHWH will relent from the curses declared earlier by Jeremiah and save the Judeans (Jer 21:2). When Zedekiah consults the prophet on this matter, the latter delivers a tripartite prophecy of doom addressed first to the king (Jer 21:4–7), then to "this people" (21:8–10), and finally to "the house of the king of Judah" (21:11–14). Verses 6–10 of this oracle in particular are reminiscent of the covenant curse sanctions laid out in the book of Deuteronomy, especially the litany of maledictions found in Deut 28:15–68. Jeremiah's language resembles that of Deuteronomy in the specific covenant curses YHWH sets out (Jer 21:6–7, 9) and especially in the offer of a choice between life and death (Jer 21:8), which clearly harks back to Deut 30:15, 19, in which YHWH lays out before Israel, in summary, the choice between life and blessing and curse and death. As in Jer 17, in chapter 21 Jeremiah's prophecy resembles Deuteronomy: no sooner does YHWH offer his people the choice between blessing and curse than he declares that their fate will certainly be the latter (Jer 21:10). Also as in Jer 17, the punishment that closes out the address to "this people" in Jer 21:8–10 is the burning of Jerusalem, and this time the agent of destruction is specified as the king of Babylon:

> כי שמתי פני בעיר הזאת לרעה ולא לטובה נאם יהוה ביד מלך בבל
> תנתן ושרפה באש:
> For I have set my face against this city for evil and not for good—declares the LORD. It shall be delivered into the hands of the king of Babylon, who will destroy it by fire. (Jer 21:10)

In Jer 21:11–14, the address to "the house of the king of Judah," YHWH exhorts the people to obedience (v. 11ab) and then declares that if they fail to obey him he will punish them (vv. 11c–14). This oracle ends, in much the same way as does Jer 17:19–27, with the following statement:

והצתי אש ביערה ואכלה כל סביביה:
I will set fire to its forest; it shall consume all that is around it. (Jer 21:14b)

The gates of Jerusalem, which were the focus of Jer 17:19–27 and the object of burning in 17:27, have given way here to "its [Jerusalem's] forest," a reference either to the royal palace[2] or the area surrounding Jerusalem.[3] The change from the gates of (בשעריה) Jerusalem to the royal forest (ביערה) has been achieved by means of soundplay.[4] This phonic link reinforces the continuity between the judgment declared in Jer 21:14 and that pronounced earlier in 17:27.[5] Furthermore, by reconfiguring the letters of the target of judgment in the earlier text (Jerusalem's *gates*) into a new word that denotes either the city's epicenter or its surroundings (the royal *forest*), the allusive paronomasia in 21:14 either narrows the field of vision of the earlier prophecy (if the palace is in view) or broadens it (if the surrounding area is in view). Either way, the effect is a declaration that the judgment on Jerusalem will surely be total: not only will its gates burn, but the

---

2. See, e.g., William L. Holladay, *Jeremiah 1: A Commentary on the Book of the Prophet Jeremiah, Chapters 1–25*, Hermeneia (Philadelphia: Fortress, 1986), 579.

3. Allen, *Jeremiah*, 243.

4. Although the *ayin*s of יער and שער were probably distinguished orally/aurally (cognate evidence indicates that the *ayin* of יער is *ayin* whereas the *ayin* of שער is *ġayin* [*HALOT*, s.v. יָעַר I, שַׁעַר I]), their pronunciation would still have been sufficiently similar for the two words to create paronomasia. (In fact, however, the /r/ sound following the *ayin* in both cases may have occasioned the two phonemes in question to have been pronounced the same or more closely.) This soundplay is further reinforced by the words ובערה ("and it will burn") and רע ("wickedness") in Jer 21:12. That Jer 21:14 alludes to 17:27 and not vice versa is suggested by the historical situation envisaged in each context: in chapter 17 the Babylonian threat is looming, whereas in chapter 21 the Babylonian onslaught has begun. Both Jer 17:19–27 and 21:1–14 appear to have a redactional history, however, which makes dating individual verses within these pericopes difficult (Allen, *Jeremiah*, 207–8, 237–40). The link between Jer 17:27 and 21:14, including the paronomastic play, obtains regardless of their direction of dependence.

5. Further connecting the two texts is the verb בכה ("to be quenched"), which occurs in 17:27 ("I will set fire to your gates … and it will not be quenched" [ולא תכבה]) and 21:12 ("lest my wrath break forth like fire and burn, with none to quench it" [ואין מכבה]).

city's heart (or the entire area surrounding it) will as well. Moreover, not only has the object of burning shifted as one moves from 17:27 to 21:14; the agent of the destruction has, significantly, shifted as well. Whereas in 17:19–27 the focus was on YHWH as the one who would destroy Jerusalem (no other agent is mentioned), a comparison of verses 10 and 14 of Jer 21 makes it clear that when YHWH says he will destroy Jerusalem, he will do so specifically by means of the historical agent Babylon. This shift, which moves the judgment from the abstract (divine origin) to the concrete (executed by the Babylonians), reinforces its certain arrival and its imminence.

3.1.3. Jer 50:31–32: Setting Fire to the Cities of Babylon

In Jer 50, YHWH issues a fresh threat of burning, but this time the object of punishment is precisely the nation that 21:14 indicated that YHWH would use to punish Judah for her sins, namely, Babylon. That YHWH's judgment on Babylon represents retributive punishment for its treatment of Judah and its spurning of YHWH is stated explicitly in Jer 50:29b:

שלמו לה כפעלה ככל אשר עשתה עשו לה כי אל יהוה זדה אל קדוש ישראל:

Pay her back for her actions, do to her just what she has done; for she has acted insolently against the LORD, the Holy One of Israel.

In the next verse, this talionic perspective is continued through the application to Babylon of an oracle of judgment originally uttered, in Jer 9:20, against Judah and then reapplied, in Jer 49:26, to Damascus—which (along with all the nations mentioned in Jer 46–49) was also destroyed by the Babylonians.[6] By reusing earlier texts, Jer 50:30 reinforces the perspective that Babylon's downfall constitutes its just deserts for its devastating the surrounding nations:[7]

---

6. It is obvious that Jer 50:30 constitutes a citation of 49:26, to which it is almost identical. (The order of these two texts in the book is reversed in LXX, however: Jer 50:30 MT = 27:30 LXX and 49:26 MT = 30:32 LXX.) That both of these verses allude to Jer 9:20 is evident from the fact that all three verses speak about young men (בחורים) dying in the squares (רחובות) and the fact that these three texts are the only verses in the Bible that contain both בחור and רחב.

7. Note also the reuse of the oracle against Edom (which was defeated by Baby-

Jer 9:20 (Babylon destroys Judah)
כי עלה מות בחלונינו בא בארמנותינו להכרית עולל מחוץ **בחורים מרחבות**:

Jer 49:26 (Babylon destroys Damascus)
לכן יפלו **בחוריה ברחבתיה וכל אנשי המלחמה ידמו ביום ההוא** נאם יהוה צבאות:

Jer 50:30 (YHWH destroys Babylon)
לכן יפלו בחוריה ברחבתיה וכל אנשי מלחמתה ידמו ביום ההוא נאם יהוה:

The principle of retribution is expressed yet again in the following two verses, 50:31–32, by means of an allusion to 21:13–14 (which, as was argued above, alludes to 17:27) that serves to bring the judgment declared against Judah in 21:13–14 down on the heads of the Babylonians:

Jer 17:27b
והצתי אש בִּשְׁעָרֶיהָ ואכלה ארמנות ירושלם ולא תכבה:

Jer 21:13–14
הנני אליך ישבת העמק צור המישר נאם יהוה האמרים מי יחת עלינו ומי יבוא במעונותינו: **ופקדתי** עליכם כפרי מעלליכם נאם יהוה **והצתי אש בְּיַעְרָהּ ואכלה כל סביביה**:

Jer 50:31–32
הנני אליך זדון נאם אדני יהוה צבאות כי בא יומך עת **פקדתיך**: וכשל זדון ונפל ואין לו מקים **והצתי אש בְּעָרָיו ואכלה כל סביבתיו**:

The multiple lexical correspondences between Jer 21:14 and 50:32 (as noted immediately above), and especially the fact that these are the only verses in the Bible in which the verb אכל ("to consume") is immediately followed by the words כל ("all") and סביב ("surroundings"), indicate that

---

lon) in Jer 49:19–21 as an oracle against Babylon in Jer 50:44–46 (Alice Ogden Bellis, "Poetic Structure and Intertextual Logic in Jeremiah 50," in *Troubling Jeremiah*, ed. A. R. Pete Diamond, Kathleen M. O'Connor, and Louis Stulman [Sheffield: Sheffield Academic, 1999], 196–99).

Jer 50:32 alludes to Jer 21:14.⁸ In addition, 50:32 builds on the allusive paronomasia in 21:14 by playing on the sounds of ביערה in that verse and thus also on בשעריה in Jer 17:27 (to which ביערה in 21:14 alludes by means of paronomasia).⁹ By rearranging the letters of the object of punishment in Jer 17:27 (Jerusalem's gates: בשעריה) and 21:14 (Jerusalem's "forest": ביערה) into another new word, one denoting Babylon's *cities* (בעריו), the prophet reveals by means of his poetry what YHWH will soon bring about by means of his power: Babylon will be punished for the punishment it meted out to Jerusalem. Jeremiah's reversal of sounds here, which reflects YHWH's reversal of the fates of nations, is a particularly nice example of this prophet fulfilling his commission to stand "over nations and kingdoms, to uproot and to pull down, to destroy and to overthrow, to build and to plant" (Jer 1:10).¹⁰

If there were any doubts that Jer 50:32 pronounces measure-for-measure punishment against Babylon for its treatment of Judah, verses

---

8. Although a variety of dates have been given for the oracle against Babylon in Jer 50–51, and although these chapters have sometimes been seen as the product of extensive redaction, it seems best to follow Holladay and Lundbom in locating most of the material in these chapters late in the career of Jeremiah. Lundbom suggests "a date prior to 594 B.C. for most of the Babylon utterances" in this part of the text (Jack Lundbom, *Jeremiah 37–52*, AB 21C [New York: Doubleday, 2004], 366–67; see also William L. Holladay, *Jeremiah 2: A Commentary on the Book of the Prophet Jeremiah, Chapters 26–52*, Hermeneia [Minneapolis: Fortress, 1989], 401–15, esp. 414). Regarding Jer 50:2–51:58, Allen writes: "The present form of the compositions [i.e., 50:2–46 and 51:1–58] in the common text of LXX and MT reflects a perspective on Babylon later than the time of Jeremiah's prophetic ministry. On the basis of 51:46, they have been dated between 560 and 555. A similar estimate assigns them to the decade before 550, the year Cyrus broke the power of the Medes" (Allen, *Jeremiah*, 509). There can be no doubt that the historical situation envisaged in Jer 50:31–32 (= 27:31–32 LXX), the fall of Babylon, is later than the one envisaged in 17:27 and 21:14—namely, the fall of Jerusalem.

9. The play between בעריו in Jer 50:32 MT (= 27:32 LXX) and ביערה in Jer 21:14 MT (= LXX) was noted by Jean Koenig, *L'herméneutique analogique du judaïsme antique d'après les témoins textuels d'Isaïe*, VTSup 33 (Leiden: Brill, 1982), 16. While the play is present in the MT, it is not represented in the *Vorlage* of LXX. Jer 27:32 LXX (= Jer 50:32 MT) reads καὶ ἀνάψω πῦρ ἐν τῷ δρυμῷ αὐτῆς ["in her forest"] καὶ καταφάγεται πάντα τὰ κύκλῳ αὐτῆς. This reading is identical to that of Jer 21:14 LXX (= MT) except that in 21:14 אכלה is rendered not καταφάγεται ("it will eat up, devour"; as in Jer 27:32 LXX [= 50:32 MT] and 17:27 LXX [= MT]) but ἔδεται ("it will eat"). On the complex relationship between MT and LXX Jeremiah, see Holladay, *Jeremiah 2*, 2–8.

10. See §1.4 above.

41–43 make it absolutely clear that this is what the prophet has in mind. These verses constitute an almost verbatim repetition of the announcement in Jer 6:22–24 that Babylon will sweep down upon Judah but turn this prophecy back on Babylon itself, substituting the name of that nation and its king for Judah and its inhabitants at the decisive point in the oracle:[11]

Jer 6:22–24

כה אמר יהוה הנה עם בא מארץ צפון וגוי גדול יעור מירכתי ארץ׃
קשת וכידון יחזיקו אכזרי הוא ולא ירחמו קולם כים יהמה ועל
סוסים ירכבו ערוך כאיש למלחמה עליך בת צִיּוֹן: שָׁמַעְנוּ אֶת שִׁמְעוֹ
רָפוּ יָדֵינוּ צָרָה הֶחֱזִיקַתְנוּ חִיל כַּיּוֹלֵדָה׃

Jer 50:41–43

הנה עם בא מצפון וגוי גדול ומלכים רבים יערו מירכתי ארץ׃ קשת
וכידן יחזיקו אכזרי המה ולא ירחמו קולם כים יהמה ועל סוסים
ירכבו ערוך כאיש למלחמה עליך בת בָּבֶל: שָׁמַע מֶלֶךְ בָּבֶל אֶת
שִׁמְעָם וְרָפוּ יָדָיו צָרָה הֶחֱזִיקַתְהוּ חִיל כַּיּוֹלֵדָה׃

3.1.4. Conclusion

The theme of YHWH punishing Israel's enemies—specifically, Assyria and Babylon—for their destruction of his people is common in the prophetic literature. Although YHWH himself commands the nations to punish Israel and Judah, he subsequently chastises them for their arrogance in overstepping the bounds of their mandate.[12] The allusive paronomasia in Jer 21:14 and 50:32 invites the reader to contemplate the mystery of the divine plan whereby YHWH disposes of nations, both his chosen people and the foreign nations, according to his sovereign pleasure.

The reversal of Jer 21:14 in 50:32 might imply that at the time the latter text was written, its author—whether the same as or different from the author of Jer 21:14—viewed the judgment on Jerusalem described in the earlier text as unjust. It is also possible, of course, that the perspective of the author of Jer 50:32 is that God was acting righteously in destroying Jerusalem, but now that that judgment has been accomplished, the time

---

11. On the reuse of Jer 6:22–24 in Jer 50:41–43, see Bellis, "Poetic Structure," 179–80, 194–96; John Hill, *Friend or Foe? The Figure of Babylon in the Book of Jeremiah MT* (Leiden: Brill, 1999), 176–77.

12. See, for example, Isa 10, esp. v. 7.

is ripe for the Babylonians to receive their own punishment. The point of Jer 50:32 is not, therefore, to comment directly on the tradition to which it alludes, but rather to show how a threat made by God at an earlier time is being dramatically reactualized in the present, with deadly irony (the former destroyer now becoming the destroyed).

3.2. Denying Oneself on the Day of Atonement

3.2.1. Lev 16:29–31; 23:27–32; Num 29:7–11: The Day of Atonement

The Torah contains three texts describing the Day of Atonement and Israel's obligations for this day (Lev 16:29–31; 23:27–32; Num 29:7–11). Numbers 29:7–11 (possibly the earliest of the three texts)[13] begins with commands to Israel that it observe the Day of Atonement by practicing self-denial (lit., "afflicting themselves"; ועניתם את נפשתיכם)[14] and refraining from work (כל מלאכה לא תעשו) (Num 29:7). The remainder of the passage is devoted to the kinds of offerings that are to be presented on this day (Num 29:8–11).

Like Num 29:7, Lev 16:29–31 commands that Israel practice self-denial and refrain from work on the Day of Atonement (Lev 16:29), but this text puts a much clearer emphasis on these commands than does the former.[15] The importance of these injunctions is highlighted through their being repeated, in reverse order, in Lev 16:31, which provides Lev 16:29–31 with

---

13. Milgrom follows Knohl's conclusion that "Lev 23 seems to have been constructed on Num 28–29, attributed to P (Knohl 1987)" (Jacob Milgrom, *Leviticus 1–16*, AB 3 [New York: Doubleday, 1991], 13; the work cited by Milgrom is Israel Knohl, "The Priestly Torah Versus the Holiness School: Sabbath and the Festivals," *HUCA* 58 [1987]: 65–117). According to Milgrom, Lev 16:29–31 is an "indisputable H passage" (*Leviticus 1–16*, 39) and Lev 23:27–32 is part of a chapter most of which should be attributed to H (ibid., 13). If one follows Milgrom in considering H (exilic) to be the redactor of P (no later than the exilic period), both Lev 16:29–31 and 23:27–32 are later than Num 29:7–11 (ibid., 13, 27).

14. According to Blenkinsopp, the phrase ענה נפש "suggests a deliberate diminution of vital energies in the pursuit of personal catharsis or ascesis" (Joseph Blenkinsopp, *Isaiah 56–66*, AB 19B [New York: Doubleday, 2003], 183). On the meaning of this expression, see further Hrobon, *Ethical Dimension*, 175.

15. The commands to practice self-denial and to observe the Sabbath are given to the whole people; in vv. 32–33, further commands are given to the priests in particular.

a chiastic structure, in the center of which is a statement describing the focus of the Day of Atonement, the cleansing of the people from sin:[16]

  A   And this shall be to you a law for all time. (והיתה לכם לחקת עולם [v. 29a])
      B   You shall practice self-denial. (תענו את נפשתיכם [v. 29b])
          C   You shall do no manner of work. (וכל מלאכה לא תעשו [v. 29c])
              D   For on this day atonement shall be made for you to cleanse you of all your sins; you shall be clean before the LORD. (v. 30)
          C´   It shall be a sabbath of complete rest for you. (שבת שבתון היא לכם [v. 31a])
      B´   You shall practice self-denial. (ועניתם את נפשתיכם [v. 31b])
  A´   It is a law for all time. (חקת עולם [v. 31c])

The third text in the Torah that presents prescriptions for the Day of Atonement is Lev 23:27–32. As in Lev 16:29–31, here too the importance of the commands to practice self-denial (ועניתם את נפשתיכם [vv. 27, 32]) and to refrain from work (וכל מלאכה לא תעשו [vv. 28, 31]) is accentuated by the literary structure of the passage: these commands are repeated at the beginning and the end of the text, and this forms an *inclusio* around a central section, which declares a curse on anyone who fails to obey them (כל הנפש אשר תעשה כל מלאכה [v. 29]; כל הנפש אשר לא תְעֻנֶּה [v. 30]). The final verse in the pericope, verse 32, emphasizes (like Lev 16:31) that the Day of Atonement is a special Sabbath (שבת שבתון). Two rhetorical devices reinforce the importance of this fact: first, an *inclusio* in verse 32 created by שבת שבתון הוא ("it is a special sabbath") at the beginning of the verse and תשבתו שבתכם ("you shall observe your sabbath") at the end of the verse; and, second, paronomasia on these statements achieved by the declaration at the end of the preceding verse (v. 31)—that is, just before the words שבת שבתון at the beginning of verse 32—that the command to refrain from work is a law for all time and is to be observed in every place, in all of Israel's *dwellings* (בכל משבתיכם).

---

16. Milgrom, *Leviticus 1–16*, 39–40, 1057.

To summarize, all three passages about the Day of Atonement found in the Torah contain commands to practice self-denial (ענה נפש) and to refrain from work, and the two Leviticus passages emphasize these commands in a particularly striking way through a variety of literary devices (repetition, chiasm, *inclusio*, and paronomasia).

3.2.2. Isa 58:3, 5, 7, 9–10: The Fast That YHWH Desires

3.2.2.1. Self-Denial

In Isa 58:1–7, YHWH conducts a covenant lawsuit[17] against the postexilic covenant community, which is addressed specifically as "the house of Jacob," a title that in the book of Isaiah connotes the people's sin.[18] YHWH's complaint is that although the community has sought him and obeyed his laws (v. 2), he has not heeded them (v. 3) because in their obedience to the requirements of the law they have neglected the law's essence, practicing

---

17. Isaiah 58 is clearly addressed to a postexilic audience (most likely sixth or fifth century), though it is an open question whether the temple had been rebuilt when this chapter was composed (Hrobon, *Ethical Dimension*, 155–56). Park dates Isa 58 in its entirety to the late postexilic period based on the emphasis on Sabbath observance in vv. 13–14, even though he is aware that many scholars consider these two verses an addition to vv. 1–12 (on which see below); see Kyung-Chul Park, *Die Gerechtigkeit Israels und das Heil der Völker: Kultus, Tempel, Eschatologie und Gerechtigkeit in der Endgestalt des Jesajabuches (Jes 56, 1–8 ; 58, 1–14 ; 65, 17–66, 24)*, BEATAJ 52 (Frankfurt am Main: Lang, 2003), 248. As Leclerc observes, the emphasis on justice in Isa 58 is very much in line with the preaching of Isaiah of Jerusalem (Thomas L. Leclerc, *Yahweh Is Exalted in Justice: Solidarity and Conflict in Isaiah* [Minneapolis: Fortress, 2001], 143). See also Blenkinsopp's comment that "Isaiah 58:1–14 provides one more example of the assimilation of the older prophetic social critique and the forms of speech in which it was expressed to a more discursive and sustained kind of discourse" (Blenkinsopp, *Isaiah 56–66*, 178). Although I am classifying Isa 58:1–7 as a covenant lawsuit, I am aware that many scholars do not think Isa 58 conforms to any particular form-critical *Gattung* (see Hrobon, *Ethical Dimension*, 167). Leclerc's comment is apposite, however: "In effect, in abandoning the justice of their God (58:2), they [the addressees] have abandoned the covenant. This supports the interpretation … that doing justice and righteousness is a précis of covenant responsibility" (Leclerc, *Yahweh Is Exalted*, 142).

18. Childs, following Beuken (Brevard S. Childs, *Isaiah*, OTL [Louisville: Westminster John Knox, 2001], 476).

love of neighbor.[19] This is manifest specifically in their oppressing their laborers (v. 3) and living in a spirit of war with each other (v. 4).[20] The text further specifies that it is particularly because of their failure truly to obey the command to practice self-denial (ענה נפש)—the first of the central commands of the most solemn day of the Israelite year, the Day of Atonement—that YHWH has refused to listen to them (Isa 58:3, 5).[21] The appearance in Isa 58:3, 5 of the rare expression ענה נפש ("to afflict oneself")[22] in conjunction with the terms פשע, שופר, and חטאת argues

---

19. While some interpreters have considered the diatribe in Isa 58 to be antinomian—that is, to contradict the commands in the Torah to practice self-denial (Lev 16:29, 31; 23:27, 29, 32; Num 29:7)—like other prophetic diatribes that appear to criticize the law or sacrifice, the critique here is not of the law per se but rather that the people have been observing the law in the wrong way, that is, without practicing justice and righteousness. Fishbane writes: "The powerful spiritual redefinition of fasting undertaken by the prophet so balances the old cult practices on the edge of rhetorical hyperbole that the hermeneutical tension between the two is taut and unyielding. However, it must be stressed that Isa. 58:1–12 is not antinomian: it neither attempts to weaken nor to reject the Pentateuchal law.... What the prophet ultimately seeks to effect is a social-spiritual extension of an authoritative religious practice" (Fishbane, *Biblical Interpretation*, 305; see further 305–6). See also Childs, *Isaiah*, 476–77; Blenkinsopp, *Isaiah 56–66*, 179; Leclerc, *Yahweh Is Exalted*, 141.

20. Park, noting Neh 5, considers Isa 58 to address a situation in which debt slavery was practiced (Park, *Gerechtigkeit Israels*, 240; see also 248). Hrobon argues, however, that "Isa 58 does not offer any unambiguous evidence of a class-divided society (whether on economic or theological basis [sic]) and of a tension between these classes" (Hrobon, *Ethical Dimension*, 159), a conclusion that is critical of Paul Hanson's position (ibid., 159, 168–69).

21. Of the original audience of Isa 58, Fishbane writes: "One may even wonder whether the attentive ear of the people would have also heard this rebuke as a deliberate allusion to the afflictions of Yom Kippur. Ancient rabbinic tradition surely did hear it this way and assigned chapter 58 as the prophetic lection for the Day of Atonement, when Leviticus 16 is recited as the pentateuchal portion" (Michael Fishbane, "The Hebrew Bible and Exegetical Tradition," in *Intertextuality in Ugarit and Israel*, ed. Johannes C. de Moor, OTS 40 [Leiden: Brill, 1998], 26).

22. Outside of the Day of Atonement passages in the Torah and Isa 58:3, 5, the expression ענה נפש occurs only two other times in the Bible, neither of which appears to allude to the practice of self-denial stipulated for the Day of Atonement. In one of these texts, the phrase occurs in connection with a husband's right to uphold or annul any vow, including a vow to practice self-denial, made by his wife (Num 30:14). The other occurrence is in a psalm of lament in reference to the psalmist's denying himself in fasting on behalf of his enemies, despite their ill treatment of him (Ps 35:13).

strongly for the conclusion that the Day of Atonement and its obligations are in the background of YHWH's speech here.[23]

In order to communicate YHWH's word to the returned exiles who are rebuilding their community in the land, Third Isaiah unpacks, through repeated use of the verb ענה, what he considers to be the true nature of the admonition that the people practice self-denial.[24] True "affliction of oneself" (ענה נפש [vv. 3, 5]), YHWH declares through his prophet, does not simply involve abstention from food and other pleasures, it requires taking the poor (עניים) into one's home (Isa 58:7), giving of oneself to the hungry (ותפק לרעב נפשך [v. 10a]), and satisfying the afflicted soul (נפש נענה תשביע [v. 10b]).[25] The result of this holistic obedience to the command to the postexilic community to afflict (ענה) themselves in this way will

---

23. As argued by Fishbane, *Biblical Interpretation*, 305–6; Hrobon, *Ethical Dimension*, 203. The multiple points of contact between Isa 58 and the Day of Atonement texts are discussed in Hrobon, *Ethical Dimension*, 165, 202–5; Park, *Gerechtigkeit Israels*, 237–39; Fishbane, *Biblical Interpretation*, 305. In fact, as Hrobon and Park observe, Isa 58 combines elements from the Torah's descriptions of the Day of Atonement with its descriptions of the Sabbatical Year and the Year of Jubilee (Park, *Gerechtigkeit Israels*, 237–38; Hrobon, *Ethical Dimension*, 202–5). The relative dating of Isa 58 (postexilic) and the passages in the Torah describing the Day of Atonement presents no difficulties if the latter are dated to the preexilic and exilic periods (preexilic in the case of the P text Num 29:7–11; exilic in the case of the H texts Lev 16:29–31 and Lev 23:27–32). (See n. 13 above.)

24. ענה is but one of several *Leitwörter* in Isa 58, which also include נפש, חפץ, and קרא (Park, *Gerechtigkeit Israels*, 258–65; Fishbane, "Hebrew Bible," 26; Fishbane, *Biblical Interpretation*, 304–5). As Polan points out, in this chapter "the device of repetition not only serves to establish the major themes and motifs of the literary unit, but also develops them in a way which enhances their contextual meaning" (Gregory J. Polan, *In the Ways of Justice toward Salvation: A Rhetorical Analysis of Isaiah 56–59* [New York: Lang, 1986], 241).

25. Park, *Gerechtigkeit Israels*, 267. As Hrobon remarks, ונפש נענה תשביע in v. 10 "reverses the usual idea of 'afflicting one's soul' … by fasting to satisfying 'the soul of an afflicted one'.… Fasting is therefore redirected and reversed—from starving oneself to feeding one's neighbour" (Hrobon, *Ethical Dimension*, 183; see also Leclerc, *Yahweh Is Exalted*, 143; Blenkinsopp, *Isaiah 56–66*, 179). Fishbane puts it well: "True fasting … consists in providing services and sustenance to those who hunger *against their will*" (Fishbane, *Biblical Interpretation*, 304; italics original); see similarly Fishbane, "Hebrew Bible," 26. Hrobon observes further that נפש in the clause just quoted from v. 10 can be understood polysemously not only as "soul" but also as "throat" (the people should give of *themselves* [נפש; v. 10a] to feed the hungry *throat* [נפש; v. 10b]); see Hrobon, *Ethical Dimension*, 183 n. 148, 183–84.

result in YHWH's *answering* (ענה) them when they cry out (v. 9)²⁶ and his satisfying their own souls in parched places (והשביע בצחצחות נפשך [v. 11]).²⁷ Given the repeated use of the root ענה with the meaning "to afflict" in Isa 58:1–12, there can be no doubt that the use of the homophonous root ענה ("to answer") in verse 9 is intended as a polysemous wordplay on the former.²⁸ This play, by which the prophet indicates that the community's proper obedience to its ענה obligation (i.e., to afflict itself) will result in an appropriate ענה response from the deity, constitutes an exegesis of Lev 16:29–31 and 23:27–32 and Num 29:7–11: through repetition of and wordplay on the root ענה, Third Isaiah teases out the full implications of these texts' commands that Israel practice self-denial (ענה) for the community of his own day and also predicts how YHWH will respond (ענה) if they obey.

3.2.2.2. Sabbath

We have just seen that Isa 58 unpacks the nature of the command to practice self-denial (ענה נפש) emphasized in the Torah passages that discuss the Day of Atonement and exploits the *polysemy* of the root ענה (which can mean "to afflict" and "to answer") to promise the restored covenant community that its obedience will result in blessing. Isaiah 58 also alludes to the other major command of the Day of Atonement, Sabbath observance, and appears to use *paronomasia* to apply the same lesson: if the community observes this command, it will be blessed.

---

26. As Polan remarks, "the question in 58:3, why do we humble ourselves (*'nynw*) and God does not know it, is answered in 58:5 with the hint that fasting is not only concerned with humbling (*'nwt*) one's self [*sic*]; in contrast to this, 58:7a points out that in opening one's house to humbled wanderers (*w'nyym mrwdym*) is the way that one's prayer is answered by the Lord (*wYHWH y'nh*, v. 9a). The initial question of a person's humbling of self and not being acknowledged turns upside down to showing [*sic*] that to be answered by God one should care for the individual who is already in a humbled state. Thus the network in which *'nh* recurs moves from question to answer, from dilemma to resolution" (Polan, *Ways of Justice*, 214). Fishbane observes that ענה and other "key terms (particularly חָפֵץ; נֶפֶשׁ; עָנָה, and their variants) echo throughout the piece [Isa 58] in punning allusions" (Fishbane, "Hebrew Bible," 26; see also Fishbane, *Haftarot: The Traditional Hebrew Text with the New JPS Translation* [Philadelphia: Jewish Publication Society, 2002], 393).

27. Park, *Gerechtigkeit Israels*, 267; Hrobon, *Ethical Dimension*, 196.

28. As noted by Polan, *Ways of Justice*, 214.

The mention of the Sabbath in Isa 58 comes in verse 13, where the people are admonished to refrain from trampling the Sabbath day: אִם תָּשִׁיב מִשַּׁבָּת רַגְלֶךָ עֲשׂוֹת חֲפָצֶיךָ בְּיוֹם קָדְשִׁי ("If you refrain from trampling the Sabbath [lit., 'if you turn your foot away from the Sabbath'], from pursuing your affairs on my holy day ..."). Immediately preceding the first part of this statement, in the last line of verse 12, is a promise that the community's obedience will result in its being rebuilt: "You shall be called 'repairer of fallen walls, restorer [משבב] of lanes for habitation [לָשָׁבֶת].'" The presence in close proximity here of the words שֶׁבֶת ("habitation," from the root ישב), שַׁבָּת ("Sabbath"), תָּשִׁיב ("you turn away"), and משבב ("restorer")—the latter two of which are from the root שוב—indicates clearly that these words were used for paronomastic effect,[29] and the soundplay they create forges a strong bond between the command that the community observe the Sabbath and the community's resulting restoration. Furthermore, this paronomasia is likely allusive, in that it appears to echo and build on the statement in Lev 23:31–32 that the Day of Atonement is to be a *special Sabbath* (שבת שבתון) in all of Israel's *dwellings* (בכל משבתיכם).

It should be noted that the paronomasia in Isa 58:12–13 may cross a redactional boundary, since many commentators consider verses 13–14 to be a later addition to verses 1–12.[30] Klaus Koenen has even suggested that

---

29. Klaus Koenen, *Ethik und Eschatologie im Tritojesajabuch: Eine literarkritische und redaktionsgeschichtliche Studie*, WMANT 62 (Neukirchen-Vluyn: Neukirchener Verlag, 1990), 89; Hrobon, *Ethical Dimension*, 199–200; Park, *Gerechtigkeit Israels*, 277 n. 288.

30. Most scholars view vv. 13–14 as a later addition to vv. 1–12 (see especially the discussions in Hrobon, *Ethical Dimension*, 197–205, esp. 197–201, 204; Park, *Gerechtigkeit Israels*, 225–28; Childs, *Isaiah*, 480–81; Koenen, *Ethik und Eschatologie*, 88), a conclusion that appears to be confirmed by the presence of a gap between vv. 12 and 13 in 1QIsa[a] (Koenen, *Ethik und Eschatologie*, 88; Park, *Gerechtigkeit Israels*, 227; Blenkinsopp, *Isaiah 56–66*, 181). However, given the significant thematic and lexical connections between vv. 1–12 and 13–14, the entire chapter can be read as a unity even if vv. 13–14 are a later addition. The literary unity of vv. 1–14 is argued for most extensively by Park, *Gerechtigkeit Israels*, 238–40, 247–49, 275–77 (see also Childs, *Isaiah*, 480–81; Polan, *Ways of Justice*, 225; Leclerc, *Yahweh Is Exalted*, 139–40; Elżbieta M. Obara, *Le strategie di Dio: Dinamiche comunicative nei discorsi divini del Trito-Isaia* [Rome: Gregorian & Biblical Press, 2010], 361). Indeed, v. 13 only strengthens the allusions to the Day of Atonement passages in the Torah present in vv. 1–12 (Hrobon, *Ethical Dimension*, 204–5). Furthermore, as Hrobon writes, "if Isa 58:1–12 is read through the lens of the Sabbath, the Sabbatical year, the Year of Jubilee, and the Day of Atonement regulations in Leviticus, the sabbath concept turns out to be

the word לָשֶׁבֶת ("for habitation") in verse 12 may have acted as a verbal trigger that by means of paronomasia brought the idea of the theme of salvation through Sabbath (שַׁבָּת) observance to the mind of the author of verses 13–14.³¹ Whether verses 13–14 were composed along with verses 1–12 (in which case all four of the paronyms in verses 12 and 13—תָּשִׁיב, מְשַׁבֵּב, משבב, and לָשֶׁבֶת—are original to the text) or verses 13–14 are a secondary addition to verses 1–12 (in which case the words תשיב and מְשַׁבֵּת in verse 13a serve as a redactional link between the later and earlier portions of the text),³² what is important is that in the text's present form the paronomasia links observance of the Sabbath with the postexilic community's restoration (just as earlier in the chapter polysemy links observance of the command for self-denial, the other main command of the Day of Atonement, with YHWH's beneficent response). In this way Third Isaiah or a later redactor unpacks the sound shapes of the words of the tradition in order to interpret them for the present time.

3.2.3. Conclusion

As we have seen, Isa 58 employs allusive polysemy *and* allusive paronomasia in order to emphasize that the postexilic community must exhibit correct behavior with respect to the Torah's commands "to deny oneself" (vv. 6–7, 10ab) and to observe the Sabbath (v. 13) if it wishes to receive blessing from YHWH (vv. 8–9, 10cd–12, 14). This provides a good illustration of what, as Joseph Blenkinsopp observes, is a major difference between Second and Third Isaiah:

> It is noteworthy that, in contrast to the unconditional promises in ch. 40–55, promises are now [in Isa 56–66] conditional on genuine religious observance. We hear no more about an imminent decisive change in Israel's situation as a result of epoch-making international events, and

---

all-encompassing in Isa 58, and vv. 13–14 then come naturally as the chapter's grand finale" (ibid., 205).

31. "Es ist sogar möglich, daß לשבת den Redaktor erst auf die Idee brachte, den ihm wichtigen Gedanken der Sabbatheiligung nachzutragen" (Koenen, *Ethik und Eschatologie*, 89).

32. As suggested by Koenen, *Ethik und Eschatologie*, 89, and followed by Hrobon (*Ethical Dimension*, 199) and Park (*Gerechtigkeit Israels*, 248 n. 193). In Park's view, vv. 13–14 are integral to understanding vv. 1–12 (on which see also n. 30 above).

the assurance of a return from the diaspora seems to have receded into the background.³³

As we will see in the following chapter, Second Isaiah had a penchant for employing allusive paronomasia to refashion the traditions he inherited into proclamations of salvation for the exiles in Babylon. As the present example illustrates, Third Isaiah too used allusive paronomasia (as well as allusive polysemy) in order to fashion his message. Facing a new historical situation, however, he employed the device to transform the tradition in a way that, he believed, constituted the word of YHWH for the covenant community that was now back in the land: unlike the exiles, who could be encouraged by the unconditional promises proclaimed by Second Isaiah, the present community would be blessed only to the extent to which they fulfilled the law.

Nevertheless, as Brevard Childs has correctly observed, Third Isaiah did not consider his message to be opposed to that of Second Isaiah. Rather,

> the promise by Third Isaiah focuses on that part of Second Isaiah's eschatological promise not yet fulfilled.... There is no hint that Third Isaiah understood his role as salvaging the unfulfilled hopes of his predecessor by turning the imagery into pious metaphors of conventional religious speech. His words of promise are still as massive and concrete as before, but he does offer a different application of the promise of salvation in the light of the present dire circumstances of postexilic Jerusalem, which still awaits longingly the full entrance of God's rule in a new age of redemption.³⁴

3.3. Defiling and Defrauding YHWH

Allusive paronomasia appears in several places in the book of Malachi, and here I will discuss three examples. I will treat the first two somewhat briefly, since they have already been described by others; I will devote more space to the third example, which to my knowledge has not hitherto been

---

33. Blenkinsopp, *Isaiah 56–66*, 182. For a nuanced understanding of the relationship between Second and Third Isaiah, as brought out specifically by Isa 58, one that is attentive to both the discontinuities and the continuities between these two corpora, see Childs, *Isaiah*, 478–80.

34. Childs, *Isaiah*, 480.

noticed. Taken together, these examples suggest that allusive paronomasia was an important compositional factor in the book of Malachi.

3.3.1. Mal 3:8–9: An Allusive Etymology for the Children of Jacob

Probably the best-known and clearest example of allusive paronomasia in Malachi is found in the book's third chapter. By this point, the long diatribe that began early in chapter 1 has broadened in scope from an attack on the priests for their improper cultic service (1:6–2:9) to an indictment of the entire postexilic covenant community for their manifold sins against God and one another (2:10–17; 3:5–9, 13–15).[35] In the course of this covenant lawsuit[36] against the people as a whole, the prophet castigates the community—whom he addresses as בני יעקב ("the children of Jacob" [3:6])—for their resemblance to their recalcitrant forebears:

למימי אבתיכם סרתם מחקי ולא שמרתם
From the very days of your fathers you have turned away from my laws and have not observed them. (Mal 3:7)

The specific nature of the apostasy that is in view here is spelled out in the following two verses (3:8–9), where YHWH declares that the people have been defrauding him with respect to tithes and contributions:

היקבע אדם אלהים כי אתם קבעים אתי ואמרתם במה קבענוך
המעשר והתרומה: במארה אתם נארים ואתי אתם קבעים הגוי כלו:

---

35. According to Elie Assis, the book of Malachi is structured in such a way that 1:10–2:9 and 3:7–12 are closely related (Elie Assis, "Structure and Meaning in the Book of Malachi," in *Prophecy and Prophets in Ancient Israel: Proceedings of the Oxford Old Testament Seminar*, ed. John Day, LHBOTS 531 [New York: T&T Clark, 2010], 363–64).

36. Note, however, Redditt's comment regarding the whole of Malachi: "The dominant view is that the book is comprised of a series of question-and-answer speeches, usually called disputation speeches.... Another suggestion is to construe the book as a covenant lawsuit comprised of a series of 'controversies' or legal proceedings. Actually, both constructions are somewhat forced" (Paul Redditt, "Malachi, Book of," in *Eerdmans Dictionary of the Bible*, ed. David Noel Freedman [Grand Rapids: Eerdmans, 2000], 849). Redditt's observation notwithstanding, "lawsuit" does seem to be an appropriate label for at least certain parts of the book.

Ought people to defraud God? Yet you are defrauding me. And you ask, "How have we been defrauding you?" In tithe and contribution. You are suffering under a curse, yet you go on defrauding me—the whole nation of you. (Mal 3:8–9)

As Jon Levenson has observed, the fourfold use of the root קבע ("to defraud") in Mal 3:8–9 appears to constitute a deliberate play on the sounds of the name of the patriarch יעקב ("Jacob"; recall that the community is called בני יעקב a couple of verses earlier), suggesting that the duplicitous actions of the eponymous ancestor are being imitated by his postexilic descendants.[37] Indeed, as Levenson goes on to point out, the juxtaposition of the name יעקב with a paronomastic verb referring to defrauding (קבע) recalls the similar soundplay that characterizes the twin etymologies for Jacob's name provided in Genesis, both of which employ paronomasia to refer to his deception of his older brother.[38] In the first of these etymologies, found in Gen 25:26, Jacob's future supplanting of Esau in the birth order is foreshadowed by his grasping the latter's heel (עקב):

ואחרי כן יצא אחיו וידו אחזת בַּעֲקֵב עשו ויקרא שמו יַעֲקֹב
Then his brother emerged, holding on to the heel of Esau; so they named him Jacob. (Gen 25:26)

In the second etymology, found in Gen 27:36, Jacob's robbing Esau of his status as firstborn is a *fait accompli*; here the swindled elder brother protests to their father Isaac:

ויאמר הכי קרא שמו יַעֲקֹב וַיַּעְקְבֵנִי זה פעמים את בכרתי לקח והנה עתה לקח ברכתי ויאמר הלא אצלת לי ברכה:
Esau said, "Was he, then, named Jacob that he might supplant me these two times? First he took away my birthright and now he has taken away my blessing!" And he added, "Have you not reserved a blessing for me?" (Gen 27:36)

---

37. Jon D. Levenson, *The Death and Resurrection of the Beloved Son: The Transformation of Child Sacrifice in Judaism and Christianity* (New Haven: Yale University Press, 1993), 64.

38. Ibid., 62, 64–65. Levenson demurs regarding the question of whether Mal 3:6–9 alludes to Genesis in particular or rather the traditions about Jacob and Esau that eventually were enshrined in Genesis.

By deliberately alluding to these two texts from Genesis, the soundplay in Malachi's castigation of "the sons of Jacob" (בני יעקב [Mal 3:6]) for defrauding (קבע) the deity (Mal 3:8–9) functions to reinforce the continuity between the transgressions of the postexilic community and those of its ancestors, a sinful kinship referred to explicitly in the previous verse (Mal 3:7).[39]

3.3.2. Mal 1:6–2:9: Inversion of the Priestly Blessing

Thus far we have discussed an example of allusive paronomasia located in the critique of the entire postexilic community found in Mal 2:10–17; 3:5–9, 13–15. This rhetorical device appears in even more baroque fashion earlier in the book, in the judgment on the priests in Mal 1:6–2:9, and it is in this textual unit that both my second and third examples are found.

As Michael Fishbane has pointed out, Malachi's damning tirade against the cultic functionaries for desecrating YHWH and his name through incorrect temple service, which extends from Mal 1:6 to 2:9, constitutes a sustained and relentless overturning of the Priestly Blessing of Num 6:23–27.[40] The goal of this famous benediction, as its conclusion indicates, is the association of God's name with his people:

ושמו את שמי על בני ישראל ואני אברכם:
Thus they shall link my name with the people of Israel, and I will bless them. (Num 6:27)

---

39. Further reinforcement of the connection between the postexilic community and Jacob is found, as Levenson observes, in Mal 2:10: הלוא אב אחד לכלנו הלוא אל אחד בראנו מדוע נבגד איש בְּאָחִיו לחלל ברית אבתינו (ibid., 64). (See also the nearby reference to the community as dwelling in the "tents of Jacob" [Mal 2:12].) In fact, the members of the postexilic community are far worse than their ancestor, for unlike him they have defrauded not only men but God (Mal 3:8–9). The criticism of the postexilic community specifically for their recapitulating Jacob's defrauding of Esau is particularly damning in light of the fact that the book of Malachi opens with YHWH's declaration that he loved Jacob (his people Israel) but hated Esau (the people Edom) (Mal 1:2–5). By defrauding God and each other, the postexilic community has heinously spurned the one who chose them.

40. The Priestly Blessing should be attributed to either P or H (Milgrom, *Leviticus 1–16*, 14). If P, it is preexilic; if H, it is no later than exilic (see n. 13 above). In either case, the Priestly Blessing clearly predates the postexilic book of Malachi (a fact further confirmed by the attestation of the similar formula on the sixth-century Ketef Hinnom amulets).

In uttering the blessing, Aaron and his sons enjoin YHWH to perform six specific actions for his people that will result in the intimate connection just referred to: the priests ask God to bless his people (ברך), to protect them (שמר), to make his face shine on them (האיר פנים), to be gracious to them (חנן), to lift his face toward them (נשא פנים), and to give them peace (שים שלום).[41]

Malachi 1:6–2:9 unravels the sonic threads of Num 6:24–27 and respins them into a devastating judgment against the postexilic priests. The prophet focuses specifically on two of YHWH's actions described in the Priestly Blessing—his being gracious to Israel (חנן) and his shining his face on them (האיר פנים)—and plays with the sounds of these words (especially the verb האיר ["to shine"]) in a number of ways. The result is that the famous blessing given *by* the priests is transformed into a formidable curse *on* them. Despite the example of their ancestor Levi, with whom YHWH made a covenant of life, peace, and reverence (מורא)—which led to Levi's "fearing" YHWH (וייראני [Mal 2:5])—the postexilic priests, with their execrable sacrifices, have "lit the fire" (תאירו) of YHWH's altar "in vain" (חנם) (Mal 1:10). The result of the priests' lack of fealty to the covenant is that those who have spurned the "revered" name (שמי נורא) of YHWH (Mal 1:14) will be "cursed" (ארור) for their cultic infidelities (Mal 1:14) and that YHWH will turn their blessings into "curses" (המארה, וארותי, ארותיה [Mal 2:2]).[42] Through this relentless use of paronomasia to invert the Priestly Blessing's declaration that God will "shine" (האיר) his face on Israel, the prophet reveals that the divine countenance is now darkened in judgment against the postexilic community.[43]

---

41. The close link between God's placing his name (שים שם) on Israel and his bestowing blessing (שים שלום) on them and protecting them (שמר) may be strengthened by the close link in sound between these several phrases.

42. Most of these soundplays are pointed out in Fishbane, *Biblical Interpretation*, 333. To Fishbane's observations I have added the paronomasia on ארור in Mal 1:14 and on מורא and וייראני in 2:5. Fishbane further points out that הפחתם in 1:13 plays on פחתך in 1:8 (ibid., 333). In addition to the paronomasia in Mal 1–2, Fishbane also observes that Malachi plays on the multiple meanings of the expression "to lift up the face," which in the Priestly Blessing refers to YHWH's bestowing of blessing (Num 6:26) but which Malachi uses to refer to the priests' showing of partiality (Mal 2:9).

43. Fishbane sums up the nature of Malachi's exegesis of the Priestly Blessing as follows: "By unfolding the negative semantic range of most of the key terms used positively in the Priestly Blessing, the rotten core and consequences of the language and behaviour of the priests is echoed throughout the diatribe.… Further, in so far as the

3.3.3. Mal 1:11–12: An Interwoven Allusion to Pss 50 and 113

The preceding discussion of two examples of allusive paronomasia in Malachi has made clear that this technique plays a critical role in both of the book's major invectives—the one directed against the entire community that is found in the latter half of the book and the one directed against the priests that is found in the book's first half. I will now consider a further example of allusive paronomasia in the book of Malachi, one that to my knowledge has thus far gone unseen. Like the allusion to the Priestly Blessing, this final example occurs in the diatribe against the priests in Mal 1:6–2:9. Specifically, this pericope contains a combined allusion to two texts from the Psalter, the first of which is a critique of Israel's priests (Ps 50) and the second of which is a declaration of God's greatness (Ps 113). Malachi weaves together the main themes of both of these psalms, employs a distinctive locution found in both of them, and plays on the sounds of—and thereby inverts the meaning of—a key term in the latter psalm. I will first briefly discuss each of these psalms in turn and then show how they are brought together in Mal 1.

3.3.3.1. Ps 50:1–2: Covenant Lawsuit against the Priests

Psalm 50 describes a lawsuit that YHWH brings against his people. The deity appears from Mount Zion in a theophany (vv. 2–3) and summons all the world for judgment (vv. 1, 4, 6–7). The psalm begins as follows:

אל אלהים יהוה דבר ויקרא ארץ ממזרח שמש עד מבאו: מציון מִכְלַל
יפי אלהים הופיע:
God, the LORD God spoke and summoned the world from east to west. From Zion, perfect in beauty, God appeared.[44] (Ps 50:1–2)

---

prophetic speech of Malachi is presented as a divine word, Malachi's speech is revealed to be no less than a divine exegesis of the Priestly Blessing, and a divine mockery of the priests who presume to bless in his name. The sacerdotal language of the Priestly Blessing is thus, by further irony, systematically desecrated and inverted by YHWH himself. The priests, bearers of the cultic blessing, and sensitive to its language, could not have missed the exegetical irony and sarcastic nuance of the prophet's speech" (ibid., 334).

44. That מכלל יפי in Ps 50:2 refers to Zion and not God seems to be indicated by the similar expression כלילת יפי used to describe Jerusalem in Lam 2:15.

Although these verses indicate that the gathering for judgment is universal in scope, the psalm goes on to specify that those assembled are, in particular, God's faithful ones (חֲסִידָי [v. 5a]), "those who made a covenant with me over sacrifice" (כֹּרְתֵי בְרִיתִי עֲלֵי זָבַח [v. 5b]). The mention of sacrifice here reflects its centrality in Israel's covenant with YHWH, as the following verses underscore (vv. 8–14, 23). Furthermore, the fact that the lawsuit that unfolds in this psalm is directed specifically toward those who offer YHWH sacrifices (v. 8) and who recite his law (v. 16) indicates that, though they are not mentioned by name, Israel's priests are evidently the primary target of YHWH's criticism.

Although these cultic personnel recite YHWH's laws (v. 16), they spurn the covenant (v. 17) by breaking the commandments—for example, they steal (v. 18), commit adultery (v. 18), speak deceitfully (v. 19), and speak evil of their neighbor (vv. 19–20). For this reason, YHWH considers even the pleasing sacrifices (v. 8) these priests offer to be gratuitous (vv. 9–13). The kind of sacrifices YHWH truly desires are those accompanied by moral rectitude and dependence on him. Accordingly, he exhorts the priests to sacrifice a thank offering to him (זְבַח לֵאלֹהִים תּוֹדָה [v. 14]; זֹבֵחַ תּוֹדָה יְכַבְּדָנְנִי [v. 23]), to pay their vows (v. 14), and to call upon him in their time of trouble (v. 15). The psalm closes with an affirmation that those who obey the law in this way will see the salvation of God (v. 23).

3.3.3.2. Ps 113:1–4: Praising the Name of YHWH

I turn now to Ps 113, the second text that, as I will seek to demonstrate, is alluded to in Malachi's critique of the priests. This brief poem begins with a volley of hallelujahs:[45]

הללו יה הללו עבדי יהוה הללו את שם יהוה:
Hallelujah! Give praise, O servants of the LORD! Praise the name of the LORD! (Ps 113:1)

As the psalmist proceeds, his focus remains on the name of YHWH and its exaltedness throughout all the world:

---

45. On the so-called "hallelujah redaction" of the latter part of the Psalter, specifically with respect to Ps 113, see Frank-Lothar Hossfeld and Erich Zenger, *Psalms 3: A Commentary on Psalms 101–150*, trans. Linda M. Maloney, Hermeneia (Minneapolis: Fortress, 2011), 3.

יְהִי שֵׁם יהוה מְבֹרָךְ מֵעַתָּה וְעַד עוֹלָם: מִמִּזְרַח שֶׁמֶשׁ עַד מְבוֹאוֹ מְהֻלָּל שֵׁם יהוה:

Let the name of the LORD be blessed now and forever. From east to west the name of the LORD is praised. (Ps 113:2–3)

The chiastic structure of these two verses reinforces the infinite scope, both temporal (v. 2) and geographical (v. 3), of YHWH's renown. Indeed, in the next verse (v. 4) the psalmist declares that YHWH is exalted above all peoples (כל גוים) and then broadens the scope of the deity's glory even further, moving beyond the bounds of the earth to declare that YHWH's splendor is higher even than the heavens. The remainder of the psalm (vv. 5–9) consists of the author extolling YHWH, the great and high God, for his care of the lowly, whom he raises up to greatness. The psalm ends exactly where it began, with an exhortation to praise YHWH (הללו יה [v. 9]), an *inclusio* that again reinforces the universal scope of YHWH's glory.

3.3.3.3. The Use of Pss 50 and 113 in Mal 1

The glory of YHWH's name—which, as we have just seen, is the main subject of Ps 113—is also the central theme of the first half of the book of Malachi. YHWH's exaltedness is first mentioned in Mal 1:5, the conclusion of the book's first pericope (1:2–5), which describes God's electing love of Jacob/Israel and his enmity toward Esau/Edom. This pericope culminates in YHWH's declaration that his destruction of Edom will result in Israel's recognizing the greatness of his name; when the postexilic community looks on Edom's downfall, it will declare: יגדל יהוה מעל לגבול ישראל ("Great is the LORD beyond the borders of Israel!" [1:5]).

The greatness of YHWH's name is also the central theme of the following, much longer pericope, Mal 1:6–2:9—the pericope whose inversion of the Priestly Blessing was discussed above.[46] In contrast to their ancestor Levi, who is extolled for having feared God's name (2:5), the priests of

---

46. Though a discursive unity, Mal 1:6–2:9 can be divided rhetorically into two halves, 1:6–14 and 2:1–9, a distinction signalled especially by the locution ועתה ("and now") at the beginning of 2:1. According to Renker, Mal 1:11–14 should be attributed not to Malachi but to a redactor (Ergänzer); see Alwin Renker, *Die Tora bei Maleachi: Ein Beitrag zur Bedeutungsgeschichte von tôrâ im Alten Testament*, FTS 112 (Freiburg: Herder, 1979), 86. In Renker's opinion, "Der Ergänzer hat seine Thematik nach dem Vorgang von Maleachi herausentwickelt, ist aber im Punkt des Universalismus und

the postexilic community have defiled the deity's name by offering him blemished sacrifices: blind, lame, sick, and stolen animals (1:7, 8, 12–14). The indictment that runs through 1:6–14 climaxes, just as 1:2–5 did, with a declaration of the greatness of God's name:

כי מלך גדול אני אמר יהוה צבאות ושמי נורא בגוים:
For I am a great King—said the LORD of Hosts—and my name is revered among the nations. (Mal 1:14b)

A few verses earlier, in the midst of this indictment (v. 11), YHWH proclaims the greatness of his name in language that, I believe, alludes to both Pss 50 and 113.[47] Malachi 1:11 reads:

כי ממזרח שמש ועד מבואו גדול שמי בגוים ובכל מקום מֻקטר מֻגש לשמי ומנחה טהורה כי גדול שמי בגוים אמר יהוה צבאות:
For from where the sun rises to where it sets, my name is honored among the nations, and everywhere incense and pure oblation are offered to my name; for my name is honored among the nations—said the LORD of Hosts.

The phrase ממזרח שמש (ו)עד מבואו occurs in the Bible only here and in Pss 50 (v. 1) and 113 (v. 3). In my view, Mal 1:11 uses this phrase deliberately in order to call forth to the listener's mind both of these psalms.[48]

---

der Zukunftsschau freier" (86). On the redaction history of Mal 1:6–2:9, see Rainer Kessler, *Maleachi*, HTKAT (Freiburg: Herder, 2011), 133–34.

47. Kessler notes that verses 11 and 14 form an *inclusio*, and "damit wird V 11–14 umklammert und als Sinneinheit innerhalb von Mal 1,6–2,9 kenntlich gemacht, in der es wesentlich um das Fehlverhalten in Jerusalem—zuerst der Priester, dann aber auch der Laien—im Kontrast zur weltweiten Geltung und Anerkennung des JHWH-Namens geht" (Kessler, *Maleachi*, 160; see also 150).

48. The conjunction *vav* prefixed to עד is present in Mal 1:11 but absent in the other two verses. Glazier-McDonald considers the phrase ממזרח שמש (ו)עד מבואו and comparable expressions in the Bible to refer to "a future demonstration of Yahweh's power and greatness to the whole world" (Beth Glazier-McDonald, *Malachi: The Divine Messenger* [Atlanta: Scholars Press, 1987], 60). On the contrary, as Kessler points out, Malachi's use of this phrase harks back to contexts in which the name of YHWH is declared to be praised throughout the world at the present time. Writes Kessler: "Der kultische Hintergrund des Verses setzt voraus, dass der Gottesname jetzt schon 'vom Aufgang der Sonne bis zu ihrem Untergang' gelobt werden soll (Ps 113,

Of course, the occurrence in these three texts of the same phrase (which also occurs outside of the Bible) does not by itself establish any genetic relationship between or among any of them.[49] But my suggestion that the phrase in Mal 1:11 is intended deliberately to recall both Pss 50:1 and 113:3 is confirmed, I believe, by the fact that the larger context of Mal 1:11—that is, Mal 1:6–2:9—weaves together the main themes of both Pss 50 and 113 and plays on a key word from the latter text, inverting its meaning. I will now treat these points in more detail.

As I noted above, in Ps 50 God appears from his sanctuary atop his holy mountain to gather his people, specifically the priests, from every corner of the land (ממזרח שמש עד מבואו) in order to conduct his covenant lawsuit against them. Psalm 113 emphasizes the glory of YHWH's name (שם יהוה), which is mentioned three times in verses 1–3 and which, the psalmist declares, is praised to the ends of the earth: ממזרח שמש עד מבואו מְהֻלָּל שֵׁם יהוה (Ps 113:3). Malachi 1:6–2:9 unites the primary theme of Ps 50 (a covenant lawsuit against priests who break the commandments and whose sacrifices are ineffectual) with the major concern of Ps 113 (the universal renown of YHWH's name). Malachi does this by constructing a covenant lawsuit against priests who spurn torah (Mal 2:6–9) and offer

---

3), weil er eben jetzt schon 'groß ist' und nicht erst künftig groß werden soll" (Kessler, *Maleachi*, 153).

49. Outside the Bible the phrase "from where the sun rises to where it sets" appears most notably in the eighth-century Phoenician Karatepe inscription, where Azatiwadda uses it to refer to the totality of the land in which he settled his people, the Danunians, protected them, and bestowed good things on them: ירחב אנך ארץ עמק אדן למצא שמש ועד מבאי ("I broadened the land of the plain of Adana from the rising of the sun to its setting" [*KAI* 26 I.4–5]); וכן בימתי בכל גבל עמק אדן למצא שמש ועד מבאי ("And [the Danunians] were [there] in my days, on all the borders of the plain of Adana, from the rising of the sun to its setting" [*KAI* 26 II.1–3]). See also ועז אנך ארצת עזת במבא שמש ... ישבם אנך בקצת גבלי במצא שמש ("And I subdued strong lands at the rising of the sun [i.e., the east].... I settled them on the edges of my borders, at the setting of the sun [i.e., the west]" [*KAI* 26 I.18–19]). In the Karatepe inscription, therefore, the phrase "from the rising of the sun to its setting" is associated with peace, goodness, beauty, and the benevolence of the king (cf. *KAI* 26 I.3–6, I.21–II.9). This is similar to the contextual connotations of the phrase in the Bible. O'Brien notes that, "as used in Psalm 50 and in various ancient Near Eastern documents, the phrase 'from the rising of the sun to its setting' stresses the universal power of the sovereign" (Julia O'Brien, *Priest and Levite in Malachi*, SBLDS 121 [Atlanta: Scholars Press, 1990], 65). On the phrase ממזרח שמש (ו)עד מבואו, see also James Swetnam, "Malachi 1,11: An Interpretation," *CBQ* 31 (1969): 201–2.

abominable sacrifices (Mal 1:7–8, 10, 12–14), a lawsuit whose primary concern is the exaltation of God's name (Mal 1:6, 11, 14; 2:1, 5; cf. 1:5). This, along with the use of the phrase ממזרח שמש ועד מבואו in Mal 1:11, strongly suggests that the author of Mal 1:6–2:9 had both Pss 50 and 113 in mind when fashioning his critique of the priests.[50]

The argument for the presence of this double allusion is strengthened by the fact that Mal 1:12, which immediately follows the statement that YHWH's name is exalted ממזרח שמש ועד מבואו (Mal 1:11), drives the prophet's criticism home by using paronomasia to transform the *Leitwort* הלל from Ps 113 into a word that sounds similar but bears the opposite meaning. Whereas the psalmist repeatedly exhorts his audience to praise the name of YHWH (recall particularly the clause מְהֻלָּל שֵׁם יהוה ["the name of YHWH is praised"] in Ps 113:3), the temple community of Malachi's day had, through their cultic infractions, been doing the exact opposite:

גדול שמי בגוים ... כי גדול שמי בגוים אמר יהוה צבאות ואתם מְחַלְּלִים אותו

My name is honored among the nations.... Indeed, my name is honored among the nations—said the LORD of hosts. But you continually *profane* it! (Mal 1:11–12)

The use of the verb חלל ("to profane") here to describe the priests' desecration of God's name plays on, and reverses the meaning of, the key word הלל ("to praise") in Ps 113. More specifically, the word מחללים in the phrase ואתם מחללים אותו in Mal 1:12 appears to play in particular on the word מהלל in the phrase מהלל שם יהוה in Ps 113:3.[51] In addition,

---

50. On the relative dating of these texts, see the next note.

51. The dates of Pss 50 and 113 and Malachi are all a matter of conjecture. Of these three texts, the one whose approximate date is least uncertain is Malachi; although the date of the book is debated, the current scholarly consensus places it in the late sixth or first half of the fifth century (Andrew Hill, *Malachi*, AB 25D [New York: Doubleday, 1998], 83; Redditt, "Malachi," 848). Psalm 50 is very likely postexilic, but beyond this it is difficult to say more (Hossfeld and Zenger, *Die Psalmen*, 309). Based on what he considers ממזרח שמש (ו)עד מבואו to mean in each text, Briggs considers the use of the phrase in Ps 50:1 to be earlier than its use in Ps 113:3 and Mal 1:11 (Briggs, *Book of Psalms*, 1:415). The relative dates proposed for Ps 113 are more problematic for my thesis that Mal 1:11 alludes to Ps 113:3. Hossfeld and Zenger refrain from providing a date for Ps 113 in their commentary on the psalm, though they date the consolidation of Pss 113–118 as a collection to circa 400 BCE (Hossfeld and Zenger, *Psalms 3*,

as Fishbane has noted,⁵² the accusation that the priests are "profaning" (חלל) God's name also plays on, and therefore reinforces the irony of, the prophet's sarcastic call a few verses earlier that the priests "seek" (חלה) God's face (Mal 1:9).

Outside 1:12, the verb חלל appears in the book of Malachi two more times, in 2:10-11, in the lawsuit against the people as a whole. In 2:10, the prophet criticizes the entire community for profaning (חלל) the covenant God made with them,⁵³ as manifested specifically by their mutual mistreatment of one another (נבגד איש באחיו לחלל ברית אבתינו). This faithlessness to one's brother, like the defrauding of God (described, as discussed above, by the root קבע in Mal 3:8-9), likens the members of the postexilic community quite specifically to their wily ancestor Jacob.⁵⁴ In Mal 2:11, Judah is castigated for profaning the sanctuary of YHWH (כי חלל יהודה קדש יהוה). The verb חלל therefore appears at key junctures in the book of Malachi—first in the critique of the priests (1:12) and again in the critique of the entire community (2:10-11)—and thus serves to link the book's two lawsuits. According to the prophet, both the priests and the people as a whole are guilty of profaning God's name, sanctuary, and covenant.

---

3). Briggs dates Ps 113 to the Greek period and concludes that Ps 113:3 in particular "depends upon" Mal 1:11 (Briggs, *Book of Psalms*, 2:388). Whether or not one agrees with Briggs that Ps 113 dates to the Greek period, the lateness of the psalm is evident from the fact that it appears to be a pastiche of various traditions. For example, the first line of Ps 113:2, יהי שם יהוה מברך ("Let the name of the LORD be blessed"), occurs elsewhere in Job 1:12, with a variation in Dan 2:20 (להוא שמה די אלהא מברך מן עלמא ועד עלמא), and thus appears to be a late liturgical formula. While the fact that Ps 113 is a pastiche may weaken the case that Mal 1:11-12 alludes to Ps 113:3 (i.e., Mal 1:11-12 may simply be playing on a liturgical formula that appears in multiple places in the Bible), the conjunction of the phrase ממזרח שמש ועד מבואו in Mal 1:11 with ואתם מחללים אותו in Mal 1:12 constitutes strong evidence that Mal 1:11-12 alludes to ממזרח שמש עד מבואו מהלל שם יהוה in Ps 113:3 and that the combination of the aforementioned phrases in Mal 1:11-12 is not simply a topos.

52. Fishbane, *Biblical Interpretation*, 333.
53. Cf. Mal 2:8.
54. See n. 39 above.

3.3.4. Conclusion

Concerning the priests' spurning of God's name described in Mal 1:12, Andrew Hill has remarked that

> the profanation of Yahweh's Temple has come full circle, in that previously Yahweh gave up his own sanctuary to desecration by the Babylonians as punishment for Israel's apostasy (*měḥallēl ʾet miqdāšî*, Ezek 24:21; cf. Isa 47:6), and now the very guardians of Israel's covenant relationship with Yahweh habitually desecrate his Temple with impure sacrifices (cf. 2:7).[55]

The parallel between the Babylonians' defilement of the first temple and the postexilic priests' defilement of the restored, second temple through their profanation of YHWH's name is all the more damning in the light of YHWH's declaration at the beginning of the book of Malachi that he will glorify his name by making a perpetual ruin of Edom for its complicity with the Babylonians in the destruction of Jerusalem and of the first temple (1:2–4). The haunting implication for the members of the postexilic community is that, if they persist in profaning God's name and sanctuary, he will make a ruin of them as well. Yet, at least according to the latest redaction of the book of Malachi, all hope is not lost: YHWH will rid the community of wickedness (3:1–2, 5), to be sure, specifically through the advent of his messenger, who will purge the temple; but the ultimate purpose of this purge will be to purify the descendants of Levi and to restore the presentation of pleasing offerings (3:3–4). Indeed, though the day of YHWH will come "burning like an oven" (3:19; cf. v. 23), the result will be not only the destruction of the wicked from Israel (3:19, 21), but the flourishing of a remnant who reveres God's name, a restored community on whom the sun of righteousness will rise with healing in its wings (3:20).

---

55. Hill, *Malachi*, 189. In this connection, is it possible that the form מחללים in Mal 1:12 may also play on מכלל in Ps 50:2?

4
Salvation

4.1. Bringing the Destruction of Assyria on Babylon

4.1.1. Nah 2:1: Heralding the Destruction of Nineveh

The book of Nahum consists of an oracle of judgment against Judah's seventh-century foe, the Assyrians, centered on their capital, Nineveh (Nah 1:1). The prophecy opens with a theophanic vision of YHWH (Nah 1:2–6) that develops as a reflection on his character as revealed in Exod 20:5–6 and 34:6–7 (Nah 1:2–3). Meditating on the nature of YHWH expounded on in those traditions, the prophet proclaims that YHWH is a haven for those who trust in him (Nah 1:7) but that the wicked will incur God's overwhelming wrath (Nah 1:6, 8–14).

The prophecy of destruction against the Assyrians in Nah 1 gives way at the beginning of chapter 2 to the image of a messenger heralding the joyous news of peace that has come to Judah on account of Nineveh's downfall:

הנה על ההרים רגלי מבשר משמיע שלום חגי יהודה חגיג שלמי
נדריך כי לא יוסיף עוד לעבור [לעבר] בך בליעל כלה נכרת:

Behold on the mountains the footsteps of one bringing glad tidings, announcing peace! "Celebrate your festivals, O Judah, fulfill your vows. For never again shall worthless men invade you; they will be completely cut off." (Nah 2:1)

The basis for Judah's exaltation is that a shatterer (מפיץ, from the root פוץ) has risen up against Nineveh (Nah 2:2). The prophet exhorts the Assyrians to brace for the onslaught of this foe—whom we know from elsewhere to be the Babylonians—and uses paronomasia to do so, commanding the inhabitants of Nineveh to "man the guard posts [and] watch [צפה, from the root צפה] the road" (Nah 2:2).

4.1.2. Isa 52:1, 7–9: Heralding the Destruction of Babylon

About a century after Nahum's oracle was delivered, the political situation in the region had changed dramatically. Judah had been taken into exile by Nineveh's destroyer, the Babylonians, but now that empire too had come to naught at the hands of a new power, the Persians. Sensing that the principle of transgenerational *talion* upon which Nahum had meditated a few generations earlier (Nah 1:2–3; cf. Exod 20:5; 34:7) was at work again against the oppressing power of his own day, Second Isaiah announced the return of the Judean exiles from their captivity in Babylon by alluding to Nahum's jubilant declaration of the heralding of the fall of Nineveh:

מה נאוו על ההרים רגלי מבשר משמיע שלום מבשר טוב משמיע
ישועה אמר לציון מלך אלהיך:

How lovely on the mountains are the footsteps of one bringing glad tidings, announcing peace, bringing good tidings, announcing salvation, telling Zion: "Your God is king!" (Isa 52:7)

The verbal connections between Nah 2:1a and Isa 52:7 are obvious, and there is universal agreement among scholars that the latter alludes to the former.[1]

Second Isaiah infuses the content of Nah 2:1a with new meaning for his own day not only by applying it to a new situation that resembles the

---

1. For discussion, see, e.g., Patricia Tull Willey, *Remember the Former Things: The Recollection of Previous Texts in Second Isaiah* (Atlanta: Scholars Press, 1997), 116–20; Sommer, *Prophet Reads Scripture*, 82. Nahum 2:1 and Isa 52:7 are the only verses in the Bible that contain the expression על ההרים רגלי מבשר משמיע שלום. Moreover, these are the only two verses in the Bible that contain both the noun רגל and the verb בשר. See further Willey, *Remember the Former Things*, 118. Most scholars date Nahum between 663 (the fall of Thebes) and 612 (the fall of Nineveh); see Klaas Spronk, *Nahum*, HCOT (Kampen: Kok Pharos, 1997), 12–13; Heinz-Josef Fabry, *Nahum*, HTKAT (Freiburg: Herder, 2006), 27–31. As a part of Second Isaiah, Isa 52:1–12 dates, according to critical consensus, to the mid-sixth century (John Goldingay and David Payne, *Isaiah 40–55*, 2 vols., ICC [London: T&T Clark, 2006], 1:28–30; Goldingay and Payne locate Isa 40–55 specifically in the 540s). On the historical context of Isa 40–55, see further Joseph Blenkinsopp, *Isaiah 40–55*, AB 19A (New York: Doubleday, 2002), 92–104.

one envisaged in his source text but also by expanding on the paronomasia present in that text's immediate context (Nah 2:2):

Nah 2:1–2

הנה על ההרים רגלי מבשר משמיע שלום חגי יהודה חגיך שלמי נדריך כי לא יוסיף עוד לעבור [לעבר] בך בליעל כלה נכרת: עלה מֵפִיץ על פניך נצור מצרה צַפֵּה דרך חזק מתנים אמץ כח מאד:

Isa 52:7–9

מה נאוו על ההרים רגלי מבשר משמיע שלום מבשר טוב משמיע ישועה אמר לציון מלך אלהיך: קול צֹפַיִךְ נשאו קול יחדו ירננו כי עין בעין יראו בשוב יהוה ציון: פִּצְחוּ רננו יחדו חרבות ירושלם כי נחם יהוה עמו גאל ירושלם:

As I noted above, Nah 2:2 refers to Assyria's destroyer as a מֵפִיץ ("shatterer," from the root פוץ) and exhorts the Ninevites to "watch [צפה] the road" for the coming onslaught.[2] Isaiah 52:8 applies the root צפה not to Nineveh's but to Jerusalem's צֹפַיִךְ ("watchmen"), who raise their exultant voices and shout for joy at the downfall of Babylon, the very foe against which Nah 2:2 had warned Nineveh's watchmen to be on guard. Isaiah 52:9 then plays on both צפה and its paronym, מפיץ, from Nah 2:2 by declaring that Jerusalem's ruins join its watchmen in "breaking forth" (פצחו, from the root פצח) in exultation over the destruction of the Babylonians.[3] Whereas the Ninevites watched the road for the coming Babylonians (Nah 2:2), Jerusalem's watchmen behold not only the fall of Babylon but also the glorious return of YHWH to Zion (Isa 52:8). Second Isaiah crafts his message by changing the subject of the verb צפה from Judah's enemy, Nineveh, to Judah itself and by using the root פצח, which resembles both צפה and פוץ

---

2. On Babylon as shatterer, see also Jer 51:20, where God addresses Babylon as follows: מפץ אתה לי כלי מלחמה ונפצתי בך גוים והשחתי בך ממלכות. This statement is followed by eight clauses that begin with the words ונפצתי בך ("with you I shattered") followed by the object of shattering (Jer 51:21–23). The result of Babylon's shattering the nations, however—and Judah in particular—is retribution from YHWH: ושלמתי לבבל ולכל יושבי כשדים את כל רעתם אשר עשו בציון לעיניכם ("But I will requite Babylon and all the inhabitants of Chaldea for all the wicked things they did to Zion before your eyes" [Jer 51:24]).

3. Paronomasia is present in the context of Isa 52:9: for example, Shalom Paul notes the "accumulated emphasis on sibilants" in v. 7 (Shalom M. Paul, *Isaiah 40–66: Translation and Commentary* [Grand Rapids: Eerdmans, 2012], 391).

in sound but which replaces the destructive image denoted by the verb פוץ with the positive image of rejoicing.

In addition to the first half of Nah 2:1 being alluded to and transformed by means of allusive paronomasia in Isa 52:8–9, the second half of Nah 2:1 undergoes a similar process in Isa 52:1.[4] In Nah 2:1b, the prophet tells Judah that because of the fall of Nineveh, "never again will worthless men invade you" (לא יוסיף עוד לעבור [לעבר־] בך בליעל), the word בליעל here referring to the Assyrians who had previously invaded Judah (see also Nah 1:11):

Nah 2:1
הנה על ההרים רגלי מבשר משמיע שלום חגי יהודה חגיך שלמי נדריך כי לא יוסיף עוד לַעֲבוֹר־ [לַעֲבָר־] בך בְּלִיַּעַל כלה נכרת:

Isa 52:1
עורי עורי לבשי עזך ציון לבשי בגדי תפארתך ירושלם עיר הקדש כי לא יוסיף יבא בך עוד עָרֵל וטמא:

The allusion to Nah 2:1b in Isa 52:1 involves several minor changes. First, Isa 52:1 moves the adverb עוד to a different place in the clause, and second, it changes the verb עבר ("to invade"; lit., "cross through") to בוא ("to enter"). The syntactic focus of the clause, the enemy, is changed from בליעל ("worthless men") to ערל ("the uncircumcised"), which preserves three out of four of the consonants of the word לעבור from Nah 2:1b (which Isa 52:1 has changed to יבא) and two of the three consonants of בליעל. The change from worthless men (בליעל) invading (לעבור) the land of Judah in Nah 2:1b to the uncircumcised (ערל) and unclean (טמא) entering Jerusalem in Isa 52:1 serves the imagery of the immediate context of the latter passage (where Second Isaiah exhorts Jerusalem to shake off the dust and array herself in fresh, resplendent garments [Isa 52:1–2]) and also prepares the way for the exhortation to the exiles in Isa 52:11 to turn away from Babylon and "touch nothing unclean [טמא] as you *depart* [the opposite of 'enter' in v. 1] from there."[5]

---

4. The quotation of Nah 2:1 in Isa 52:1 is pointed out, e.g., by Willey, *Remember the Former Things*, 119; Paul, *Isaiah 40–66*, 382. For the syntax of Isa 52:1, see Paul, *Isaiah 40–66*, 386.

5. This imagery of uncleanness may also prepare the reader for the uncomely appearance of the servant described in Isa 53:2–3.

Commenting on the relationship between the statements in Nah 2:1 and Isa 52:1, Shalom Paul writes that "there is a very important difference between the two: Nahum couched his prophecies in moral terms … whereas Deutero-Isaiah expresses himself in phrases borrowed from the cultic milieu."[6] According to Paul, the seemingly small change in terminology from בליעל to ערל—which, as I have noted, is achieved by means of allusive paronomasia—signals a democratization of the concept of holiness in the thought of Second Isaiah: "The prophet," writes Paul,

> introduces a revolutionary theological innovation in this chapter: The holy area, which until this time was restricted to the Temple itself, is now expanded to include the entire city. Jerusalem becomes a temple city, and thus strict guidelines to insure its holiness must be introduced.[7]

This vision, as Paul goes on to observe, was carried on at Qumran,[8] and to this it may be added that the New Testament develops this idea as well.[9]

4.1.3. Conclusion

In the seventh century, the prophet Nahum exulted in the fall of Nineveh, an event heralded by a messenger's ringing cry of good news (Nah 2:1). A century later, once Nineveh's destroyer and Judah's next oppressor, Babylon, had fallen, it was a logical step for Second Isaiah to reapply the declaration of the demise of Nineveh to the fall of Babylon. But Second Isaiah went a step further in his reuse of the tradition by playing on the sound and meaning of multiple words in Nahum's prophecy in order to achieve two goals: to demonstrate his agreement with Nahum regarding the validity of the principle of transgenerational *talion* expressed in Israel's earlier traditions and to encourage his community to shift their attention toward the cultic arena as a way of solving the moral problems of their own day. This change of focus, as we have discussed, had far-reaching implications for later communities of both Jews and Christians.

---

6. Paul, *Isaiah 40–66*, 383; see further 386.
7. Ibid., 383.
8. Ibid., 383–84. See also Reinhard G. Kratz, "'The Place Which He Has Chosen': The Identification of the Cult Place of Deut. 12 and Lev. 1 in 4QMMT," *Meghillot* 5–6 (2007): 57–80.
9. This is so particularly in the book of Revelation.

4.2. Creating, De-creating, and Re-creating

4.2.1. Gen 7:11: Water as Weapon

The first physical description of the waters of the Noachian flood appears in Gen 7:11:[10]

> נבקעו כל מעינת תהום רבה וארבת השמים נפתחו
> All the springs of the great deep burst apart, and the floodgates of the sky broke open.

This constitutes a reversal of the creation event, during which the dark deep (תהום) was transformed into an inhabitable cosmos by the wind (or spirit) of God that hovered over the water (Gen 1:2).[11] At this time, too, the upper and lower waters were bounded by a firmament called שמים (Gen 1:6–8), the seas and dry land were separated (Gen 1:9–10), and all the living creatures were assigned to realms that promoted their life, well-being, and ability to reproduce (Gen 1:20–30). All of this—the ordering of the cosmos at creation—YHWH undid when he brought the waters of the flood on the earth.

4.2.2. Ps 74:15: Water as Enemy

In Ps 74, the psalmist laments God's rejection of his people and his failure to stop their foes from persecuting them (vv. 1–11).[12] In Ps 74:13–17, the psalmist recalls God's power in creation, specifically describing God's creative activity in terms of his mythic defeat of the sea monsters and Leviathan (vv. 13–14), in order to appeal to the deity to save his people and

---

10. According to classical documentary models, Gen 7:11 is attributed to P (Claus Westermann, *Genesis 1–11*, trans. John J. Scullion [Minneapolis: Augsburg, 1984], 395), as is Gen 1:1–2:4a, portions of which are discussed below.

11. On the meaning of רוח אלהים in Gen 1:2, see Harry M. Orlinsky, "The Plain Meaning of *ruaḥ* in Gen 1.2," *JQR* 48 (1957): 174–82; Levenson, *Creation*, 84.

12. Although the date of Ps 74 is uncertain, there are good reasons to believe that most of the psalm dates approximately to the sixth century (Hossfeld and Zenger, *Psalms 2*, 243–44). A sixth-century date for Ps 74 would make this text later than Gen 7:11 (P) according to some scholars (most notably Jacob Milgrom, who locates P in the eighth century [Milgrom, *Leviticus 1–16*, 34]), though by no means according to all scholars.

defeat their enemies at the present time (vv. 18-23; cf. v. 12).[13] Although the primeval *Chaoskampf* appears to be in primary view here, this text may also describe YHWH's redemption of Israel at the Red Sea.[14]

Verse 15 continues the description of God's vanquishing his watery foes and in so doing employs language similar to that of Gen 7:11:

אתה בקעת מעין ונחל אתה הובשת נהרות איתן:
You split apart spring and torrent, you dried up mighty rivers. (Ps 74:15)

Genesis 7:11 and Ps 74:15 share vocabulary that occurs together nowhere else, being the only two verses in the Bible that contain both the noun מעין ("spring") and the verb בקע ("burst apart").[15] Furthermore, Gen 7:11 and Ps 74:15 are connected by the use of the similar image of abundant water. What the water refers to in each case, however, differs: whereas in the flood context water was the weapon God used to undo the creational separation between sea and dry land, in Ps 74:15 the water has become YHWH's enemy, the very chaos waters that he tamed at creation.[16] While I am not certain that a genetic relationship exists between

---

13. Psalm 74:12-17 is frequently cited in discussions of *Chaoskampf* in the Bible: e.g., Michaela Bauks, "'Chaos' als Metapher für die Gefährdung der Weltordnung," in *Das biblische Weltbild und seine altorientalischen Kontexte*, ed. Bernd Janowski and Beate Ego, FAT 32 (Tübingen: Mohr Siebeck, 2001), 431-64; Levenson, *Creation*, 11-12; Hans Barstad, *A Way in the Wilderness: The "Second Exodus" in the Message of Second Isaiah* (Manchester: University of Manchester Press, 1989), 28-29. See also J. A. Emerton, "'Spring and Torrent' in Psalm LXXIV 15," in *Volume du Congrès: Genève, 1965*, ed. P. A. H. de Boer, VTSup 15 (Leiden: Brill, 1966), 122-33. On connections between Ps 74:12-15 and the Ugaritic Baal Epic, see William P. Brown, "Joy and the Art of Cosmic Maintenance: An Ecology of Play in Psalm 104," in *"And God Saw that It Was Good": Essays on Creation and God in Honor of Terence E. Fretheim*, ed. Frederick J. Gaiser and Mark A. Throntveit (St. Paul, MN: Luther Seminary, 2006), 23-32.

14. Emerton, "Spring and Torrent," 122-23.

15. On the meaning of the verb בקע in Ps 74:15, see ibid., 125, 129. On the verb בקע, specifically with regard to its use in a *Chaoskampf* context, see Mary K. Wakeman, "The Biblical Earth Monster in the Cosmogonic Combat Myth," *JBL* 88 (1969): 315 n. 10.

16. Jon Levenson notes the verbal and thematic connections between Gen 7:11 and Ps 74:12-17 (Levenson, *Creation*, 10-12). The possibility that Ps 74:15 alludes to Gen 7:11 is strengthened by the fact that Ps 74:17 appears to allude to Gen 8:22. J. A. Emerton has advanced an interpretation of Ps 74:15 that, if correct, would make

these two texts, they do appear to have been read together by a later text, to which I now turn.

4.2.3. Isa 41:18: Water as Source of Life

Both the imagery of abundant water and the distinctive vocabulary that links Gen 7:11 and Ps 74:15 appear in Isa 41:18:

אפתח על שפיים נהרות ובתוך בקעות מעינות אשים מדבר לאגם
מים וארץ ציה למוצאי מים:
I will open up streams on the bare hills and fountains amid the valleys; I will turn the desert into ponds, the arid land into springs of water. (Isa 41:18)

Isaiah 41:18 appears to read Gen 7:11 and Ps 74:15 together and to refashion their vocabulary and imagery into a new message, one of hope for the exiles.[17] Several lexical links bind Isa 41:18 to the two earlier texts. Outside Isa 41:18, the noun מעין ("spring") and the verb פתח ("to open") occur together only in Gen 7:11 and the nouns מעין and נהר ("river") occur together only in Ps 74:15. As mentioned above, Gen 7:11 and Ps 74:15 are the only verses in the Bible that contain both the noun מעין and

---

the link between Ps 74:15 and Gen 7:11 even stronger. Although he argues that the *Chaoskampf* motif is the primary background of Ps 74:15, Emerton proposes that also lying slightly under the surface of this verse is an understanding (shared by other biblical texts) of springs as conduits that drained water from the land, water that would otherwise inundate the earth and undo the natural order (Emerton, "Spring and Torrent," 127–30). If such is a proper understanding of Ps 74:15, this verse, as Emerton observes, describes precisely the opposite of what is envisaged in Gen 7:11, where water wells up from the earth's springs in order to flood the dry ground and de-create the world by re-creating the primeval choas situation: "Ps. lxxxiv 15 tells how God cleft open the springs to let the water descend, just as Gen. vii 11 records that the springs were opened to allow the water to rise.… The whole of Ps. lxxiv 15 describes the removal of the primeval waters from the earth. God cleft open springs, so that the water might descend through them" (129–30).

17. Relative dating of Ps 74:15 and Isa 41:18 is difficult since the texts in which they are found both probably date to the sixth century (on dating Ps 74 and Isa 40–55, see notes 1 and 12 above). According to Patrick, Second Isaiah's new exodus imagery, and the imagery in Isa 41:18 in particular, is derived largely from the Psalter as opposed to other biblical accounts of the exodus (Dale A. Patrick, "Epiphanic Imagery in Second Isaiah's Portrayal of a New Exodus," *HAR* 8 [1984]: 126, 130–31).

the verb בקע ("to split apart"); in the first text the splitting apart of the waters unleashes torrents of destructive deluge death, and in the second text YHWH's splitting apart of the waters constitutes his triumphant victory over his enemies.[18] Isaiah 41:18 cleverly creates a combined allusion to both Gen 7:11 and Ps 74:15 by playing on the sound of the verb בקע: according to Isa 41:18, YHWH will unleash torrents of water so vast that they will fill the valleys, בקעות, which will result in blessing for the exiles:[19]

Gen 7:11bc

ביום הזה נִבְקְעוּ כל מעינת תהום רבה וארבת השמים נפתחו:

Ps 74:15

אתה בָקַעְתָּ מעין ונחל אתה הובשת נהרות איתן:

Isa 41:18ab

אפתח על שפיים נהרות ובתוך בְּקָעוֹת מעינות

By transforming the verb בקע into בקעות, Isa 41:18 takes elements of the imagery of both Gen 7:11 (abundant waters) and Ps 74:15 (YHWH's creational victory) but negates other elements of the imagery of both texts (destruction, splitting apart) in order to forge a new message of re-creation for the exiles of his day.[20] Second Isaiah weaves together the images and

---

18. Or, on Emerton's interpretation, the siphoning off of the chaos waters from the earth in order to establish the boundary between water and dry land (Emerton, "Spring and Torrent," 127–30).

19. Heightening the reader's sensitivity to the presence of allusive paronomasia in Isa 41:18 is the fact that paronomasia permeates the verse: ובתוך and בקעות are paronyms (both contain *bet*, *vav*, and *tav*, and *kaph* and *qoph* are similar in place of articulation), as are בקעות and מעינות (both contain *ayin* and end in ות-). Furthermore, there is paronomasia between ארץ in the last line of Isa 41:18 and ארד in the first line of the next verse (pointed out in Jerome T. Walsh, "Summons to Judgement: A Close Reading of Isaiah xli 1–20," *VT* 43 [1993]: 367).

20. On the connection between creation and redemption, Wakeman writes: "The sea that is *split* that Israel may pass through to independent existence is the monster whom Yahweh defeated that he might create the cosmos. The tendency to assimilate the Reed Sea episode to the ancient battle myth is the result of a feeling that the rescue of Israel is an act of the same creative nature as the separation of the heavens and the earth" (Wakeman, "Biblical Earth Monster," 315, emphasis origi-

words from Gen 7:11 and Ps 74:15, not to describe earth's de-creation by means of a deluge (where water was a weapon) nor God's vanquishing of the primeval chaos monsters in the battle of the original creation (where water was a foe), but rather YHWH's outpouring of water in the wilderness in order to provide a path for the exiles to return to the land of Israel (water is now a means of vivification).[21] Further enriching Second Isaiah's message that YHWH will guide the exiles back to Israel is the probability that Isa 41:18 alludes also to the scene in Num 20:1–13, in which YHWH provides the Israelites with water from the rock to sustain them on their journey through the wilderness to the promised land.[22]

---

nal). Although the purpose of the waters of the flood was to destroy the earth, they also served, as David Gunn observes, to prepare the way for "a new order" (David Gunn, "Deutero-Isaiah and the Flood," *JBL* 94 [1975]: 496). Therefore, the idea of re-creation is latent in the imagery of the destroying flood waters of the Noachian deluge. As Gunn writes, "If Deutero-Isaiah's concern is to proclaim that Yahweh will shortly deliver his people from the chaos of exile into a new order, a new creation, then the pertinence of the flood motif to his proclamation is readily apparent" (ibid., 496–97). Anderson writes that Second Isaiah "in some places links creation and redemption so closely together that one is involved in the other" (Bernhard W. Anderson, "Exodus Typology in Second Isaiah," in *Israel's Prophetic Heritage: Essays in Honor of James Muilenburg*, ed. Bernhard W. Anderson and Walter J. Harrelson [New York: Harper, 1962], 185).

21. See Ulrich Berges, "Der zweite Exodus im Jesajabuch: Auszug oder Verwandlung?" in *Das Manna fällt auch heute noch: Beiträge zur Geschichte und Theologie des Alten, Ersten Testaments; Festschrift für Erich Zenger*, ed. Frank-Lothar Hossfeld and Ludger Schwienhorst-Schönberger, HBS 44 (Freiburg: Herder, 2004), 85. Regarding the trees enumerated in Isa 41:19, Walsh comments that "it is striking that none of the trees is a fruit tree, whereas all are shade trees. This suggests that the images of water and vegetation are not to be understood as an allegory of the restoration of the land of Israel; in that case, the transformation of the desert is to make it not habitable but traversable: in the new creation, water and shade are supplied in the desert for the imminent return of Israel to its homeland" (Walsh, "Summons to Judgement," 367–68). For a contrary view, see Lena-Sofia Tiemeyer, who believes that "Isa 41:17–20 portrays the ecological transformation of Judah" (Lena-Sofia Tiemeyer, *For the Comfort of Zion: The Geographical and Theological Location of Isaiah 40–55* [Leiden: Brill, 2011], 177; see further her discussion and references on 177–78).

22. This allusion was suggested by M. Margaliot ("The Transgression of Moses and Aaron: Num. 20:1–13," *JQR* 74 [1983]: 218 n. 70) and implied by Luis Alonso Schökel, "Isaiah," in *The Literary Guide to the Bible*, ed. Robert Alter and Frank Kermode (Cambridge: Belknap, 1987), 177. Contrast the more skeptical comments in Tiemeyer, *Comfort of Zion*, 177. Strengthening the possibility of an allusion in Isa 41:18 to Num 20:1–13 is the existence of close verbal connections between Isa 41:18

4.2.4. Conclusion

As Dale Patrick has remarked, Second Isaiah "actualized ... latent" meanings in earlier traditions that he reused.[23] This observation can be seen especially clearly in this prophet's use of allusive paronomasia: by subtly changing the sounds of words in his source texts, Second Isaiah unlocked or "actualized" meanings that he perceived to be incipient in the very words, including their sound shapes, used in the earlier texts. Isaiah 41:18 weaves together multiple earlier traditions in order to declare that the same God who created the universe, rescued Israel at the Red Sea, and provided them with water in the wilderness in order to bring them to the promised land and establish them there as his special people will now accomplish a new redemptive re-creation—a second exodus[24]—that will bring the exiles out of their captivity, sustain them on the way back to the land, and reestablish them there as YHWH's chosen people.[25]

---

and Ps 114:8 coupled with the fact that the latter text clearly alludes to Num 20:1–13 (Gottfried Glassner, "Aufbruch als Heimat: Zur Theologie des 114. Psalms," *ZKT* 116 [1994]: 472–79; Barstad, *Way in the Wilderness*, 30–31).

23. Patrick, "Epiphanic Imagery," 138.

24. Although some have denied the presence of exodus imagery in Isa 41:17–20 (Barstad, *Way in the Wilderness*, 26–36, esp. 26–27; Tiemeyer, *Comfort of Zion*, 177, and references there), my argument that Isa 41:18 alludes to Ps 74:15—which, as noted above, may describe not only the original creation but also the exodus—would appear to bolster the view of other scholars that exodus imagery is in fact present in Isa 41:18 and its context (e.g., Anderson, "Exodus Typology," 181, 183). A further, broader consideration in support of the presence of exodus imagery here is that the theme of the new exodus occurs at the beginning and end of Second Isaiah and is prominent throughout this corpus (ibid., 182).

25. On new creation in Isa 41:17–20, see further Carroll Stuhlmueller, *Creative Redemption in Deutero-Isaiah*, AnBib 43 (Rome: Biblical Institute Press, 1970), 70–73; William H. Propp, *Water in the Wilderness: A Biblical Motif and Its Mythological Background* (Atlanta: Scholars Press, 1987), 102–3; Berges, "Zweite Exodus," 83–85; Bradley J. Spencer, "The 'New Deal' for Post-exilic Judah in Isaiah 41,17–20," *ZAW* 112 (2000): 583–97; Joan E. Cook, "Everyone Called by My Name: Second Isaiah's Use of the Creation Theme," in *Earth, Wind, and Fire: Biblical and Theological Perspectives on Creation* (Collegeville, MN: Liturgical Press, 2004), 35–47.

4.3. The Day of Devastation from Shaddai

4.3.1. Isa 13:6, 9: The Day of YHWH against Babylon

Isaiah 13:1–22 presents an oracle of judgment against Babylon.[26] YHWH gathers a mighty host for war (vv. 2–5), and the prophet declares that the terrifying Day of YHWH (vv. 6–9) will come upon the wicked on the earth (v. 9, 11). The judgment is described in cosmic terms: the celestial bodies will go dark (v. 10), heaven and earth will shake (v. 13), the haughty will be brought low (v. 11), and humanity will be destroyed from the earth (v. 12). Although the scope of the judgment appears to be universal in verses 9–16, verses 17–22 focus on Babylon, which, according to the prophet, will be utterly destroyed forever.[27]

The description of devastation in Isa 13:6–9 is bounded by statements that the cosmic convulsions in view constitute the Day of YHWH: הילילו כי קרוב יום יהוה ("Wail, for the day of the LORD is near!" [v. 6]) and הנה יום יהוה בא ("Behold, the day of the LORD is coming!" [v. 9]). The description of this day is given special force by the paronomastic phrase כשד משדי יבוא ("Like devastation from Shaddai it will come!") in verse 6.[28] This soundplay is elaborated in verse 9, which declares that the day is coming "in order to make [לשום] the land a desolation [לשמה], and from it [the land] sinners will be destroyed [ישמיד, an anagram of משדי]."

4.3.2. Ezek 30:2–3: The Day of YHWH against Egypt

Ezekiel 29–32 contains a series of oracles against Egypt. In Ezek 30:2–3, the coming judgment against Egypt at the hands of the Babylonians (Ezek 29:19–20; 30:10–11, 24–25) is described specifically as follows: הילילו הה ליום כי קרוב יום וקרוב יום ליהוה יום ענן עת גוים יהיה ("Wail, alas for the day! For a day is near, indeed, a day of the LORD is near! It will be a day

---

26. For analysis, see the excellent treatment by Joseph Blenkinsopp, *Isaiah 1–39*, AB 19 (New York: Doubleday, 2000), 274–80.

27. On the dynamic between universal and specific judgment in Isa 13, see Anna K. Müller, *Gottes Zukunft: Die Möglichkeit der Rettung am Tag JHWHs nach dem Joelbuch* (Neukirchen-Vluyn: Neukirchener Verlag, 2008), 94; Blenkinsopp, *Isaiah 1–39*, 276–77.

28. Crenshaw, *Joel*, 106; Müller, *Gottes Zukunft*, 38 n. 48; see also Siegfried Bergler, *Joel als Schriftinterpret*, BEATAJ 16 (Frankfurt am Main: Lang, 1988), 37.

of cloud, a time of [invading] peoples" [Ezek 30:2-3]). The language here appears to hark back to Isa 13:6. Most scholars consider a genetic relationship to exist between these two texts, though they debate the direction of dependence (the majority consider Ezek 30:2-3 to allude to Isa 13:6 rather than vice versa).[29] For the purpose of the present discussion, this issue need not be decided; what is important, as I will discuss in more detail presently, is that the book of Joel contains a combined allusion to both of these texts that expands upon the paronomasia in Isa 13:6-9 and that ultimately uses this paronomasia to transform the meaning of this text as well as that of Ezek 30:2-3.

4.3.3. Joel 1:5, 10-11, 13, 15: The Day of YHWH against Judah

Joel 1 paints a stark picture of the devastation that has befallen the land on account of the locust plague. In order to create this scene, the prophet uses a number of rhetorical techniques, including various kinds of wordplay. This wordplay is concentrated in particular in verses 10-12. First, verse 10 contains two instances of assonance: אבלה אדמה ("the earth mourns") and הוביש תירוש ("the new wine is dried up").[30] Second, אכרים ("farm-

---

29. Bergler considers Ezek 30:2-3 to be dependent on Isa 13:6 (Bergler, *Joel als Schriftinterpret*, 138-39). Because Ezek 30:2-3 likely dates to the early sixth century (Moshe Greenberg, *Ezekiel 1-20*, AB 22 [Garden City, NY: Doubleday, 1983], 12) and Isa 13:6, 9 may date to the mid-sixth century, possibly just before the fall of Babylon (Blenkinsopp, *Isaiah 1-39*, 276-78), an argument for direction of dependence based on relative dating is possible but ultimately inconclusive.

30. The soundplays in Joel 1:10 are noted, for example, by Alonso Schökel, *Manual of Hebrew Poetics*, 22, and Crenshaw, *Joel*, 99, 113-14. Of these soundplays Crenshaw writes: "Joel's dirge-like language imitates the heavy blows being reported, falling with hammer-like force" (*Joel*, 99). According to Wolff, "externally the alliterations in vv. 10a and 10bβ show the intensified passion of speech, rooted in the memory of the classic gifts of salvation and of the prophetic threat of their destruction" (Hans Walter Wolff, *Joel and Amos*, trans. Waldemar Janzen, S. Dean McBride Jr., and Charles A. Muenchow, Hermeneia [Philadelphia: Fortress, 1977], 32). The cutting off of the agricultural items listed in Joel 1:10 not only deprives the populace of food but it also destroys the precise agricultural items used in the cult (cf. Joel 1:9, 13); see Crenshaw, *Joel*, 100, 113; Wolff, *Joel and Amos*, 31-32, 34, 36; John Barton, *Joel and Obadiah*, OTL (Louisville: Westminster John Knox, 2001), 53; Müller, *Gottes Zukunft*, 36; Bergler, *Joel als Schriftinterpret*, 59. That is, YHWH's judgment not only creates famine but it also makes it impossible for the people to worship him properly. This is specifically a judgment against the priests. As Barton observes regarding the

ers") and כרמים ("vinedressers") in verse 11 are paronyms. Third, the root יבש ("to dry up") occurs four times in verses 10 and 12 (הוביש [v. 10]; הובישה, יבשו, and הביש [v. 12]), and this is played on by the form הבישו in verse 11, which appears to be derived from the root יבש but which makes more sense if derived from the root בוש ("to be ashamed") since the subject of הבישו is אכרים ("farmers").[31]

A final example of wordplay in Joel 1:10–12 is the paronomastic phrase שֻׁדַּד שָׂדֶה ("the fields are devastated") in verse 10. Each word of this phrase is repeated in the subsequent lines: שֻׁדַּד later in verse 10 in the phrase כי שדד דגן ("for the grain is devastated") and שדה in verse 11 in the phrase כי אבד קציר שדה ("for the crops of the field have perished"). This soundplay is carried on a few verses later in the following declaration: אהה ליום כי קרוב יום יהוה וכשד משדי יבוא ("Alas for the day! For the day of the LORD is near! Indeed, *like devastation from Shaddai* it will come!" [Joel 1:15]). This statement, which, as has plausibly been argued, is the rhetorical and ideological center of the first chapter of the book of Joel and which also points forward in important ways to the following chapters,[32] constitutes a combined allusion to Isa 13:6 and Ezek 30:2–3.[33]

---

destruction of the grain, wine, and oil described in verse 10: "The priests are devastated by this, since for them maintaining the proper cult is a way of life, indeed their whole *raison d'être*" (Barton, *Joel and Obadiah*, 53).

31. Barton, *Joel and Obadiah*, 54; Wolff, *Joel and Amos*, 32; Crenshaw, *Joel*, 100–2, 114; Müller, *Gottes Zukunft*, 27 n. 7, 36; Ronald Simkins, *Yahweh's Activity in History and Nature in the Book of Joel*, ANETS 10 (Lewiston, NY: Mellen, 1991), 138 n. 61. A similar play is found in Hos 2:7 in the phrase הבישה הורתם. According to the Masoretic vocalization, הֹבִישָׁה is a form of יבש ("to dry up"), but given the subject (הורתם ["she who bore them"]) and the verb in the preceding parallel clause (זנתה ["she acted as a harlot"]), deriving הבישה from בוש and translating it as something akin to "she has acted shamefully" makes more sense. In fact, both meanings fit well within the fertility cult language of Hos 1–3.

32. Wolff, *Joel and Amos*, 36; Müller, *Gottes Zukunft*, 29 n. 17, 35 n. 37, 37–38, 90, 195.

33. The book of Joel is famously difficult to date (estimates span the ninth to second centuries; see Barton, *Joel and Obadiah*, 3). I follow Barton and other scholars in dating the book in its final form to the Persian period, with parts of 1:2–2:27 stemming from an earlier time in the postexilic period (ibid., 16–18). Thus, Joel 1:15, as well as the other portions of the book of Joel considered in the present discussion, almost certainly is later than both Ezek 30:2–3 and Isa 13:6–9. Bergler believes that Joel 1:15 alludes to Isa 13:6, 9 (Bergler, *Joel als Schriftinterpret*, 67, 138–39). According to Wolff "the declarations" in Joel 1:15 are "taken over verbatim from Ezek 30:2–3

The allusion is marked in several ways. First, the imperative form הֵילִילוּ ("wail!") is present in both Isa 13:6 and Ezek 30:2 and is used three times in the immediate context of Joel 1:15 (Joel 1:5, 11, 13). Second, the three texts share the rare expression קָרוֹב יוֹם (ל)יהוה ("a/the day of the LORD is near").[34] A further connection between Joel 1:15 and Ezek 30:2-3 is the fact that the words אֲהָהּ and יוֹם occur together only in Joel 1:15 and the words הָהּ (a *hapax legomenon*) and יוֹם occur together only in Ezek 30:2. The clearest indication that Joel 1:15 alludes to Isa 13:6 in particular is the unique appearance in these two texts of the phrase כְּשֹׁד מִשַּׁדַּי יָבוֹא ("like devastation from Shaddai it will come!").[35]

Joel 1, especially in verse 15, transforms the oracles directed against foreign nations in Isa 13 and Ezek 30 into a declaration that the Day of

---

and Is 13:6" (Wolff, *Joel and Amos*, 35; see also 36). Crenshaw notes the similarities between Joel 1:15 and Isa 13:6 and Ezek 30:2-3 but refrains from rendering an explicit judgment on directionality of influence (Crenshaw, *Joel*, 27, 105-6; see his caution on this matter on 28). Barton lists Isa 13:6 and Ezek 30:2 in connection with Joel 1:15 in his chart of "quotations" in the book of Joel, which he simply reproduces from Crenshaw (Crenshaw, *Joel*, 27; Barton, *Joel and Obadiah*, 23), but employs slightly cautious language when describing the relationship between the texts. He writes of Joel 1:15 that "here we seem to have a clear case of dependence on Isa. 13:6" (ibid., 24) and "there seems to be a connection here with Ezek. 30:2" (ibid., 58). Müller recognizes that Joel 1:15 is a citation of Isa 13:6 (Müller, *Gottes Zukunft*, 79, 89-90), but she does not mention Ezek 30:2-3. On allusions to Isa 13 elsewhere in Joel (specifically, in Joel 2:1-11), see ibid., 59-60, 69-91. For broader discussions of quotation and allusion in the book of Joel, see Crenshaw, *Joel*, 26-28; Barton, *Joel and Obadiah*, 22-27; Bergler, *Joel als Schriftinterpret*, 23-32.

34. Aside from Isa 13:6, Ezek 30:2, and Joel 1:15, this and like expressions occur twice elsewhere in Joel (2:1: judgment on Judah; 4:14: judgment on all nations), twice in the first chapter of Zephaniah (Zeph 1:7, 14: judgment on Judah), and in Obad 15 (judgment on all nations).

35. Indeed, the words שֹׁד and שַׁדַּי occur together only in Joel 1:15 and Isa 13:6. Crenshaw translates כְּשֹׁד מִשַּׁדַּי יָבוֹא as "dawning like destruction from the Destroyer" (when translating Joel 1:15; Crenshaw, *Joel*, 84) and as "dawning like devastation from the Devastater [sic]" (when translating Isa 13:6; ibid., 106), in order to bring out the wordplay between שֹׁד and שַׁדַּי, but he admits that "the pun on the divine name El Shaddai ... does not solve the controversial issue of its etymology" (ibid., 106; see likewise Müller, *Gottes Zukunft*, 38 n. 48). See, similarly, Müller, who, following Buber and Rosenzweig, renders the phrase "Wie Gewalt vom Gewaltigen kommt er" (Müller, *Gottes Zukunft*, 28, 38, 89; so also Wolff in his German original, translated into English as: "Like might from the Mighty One it comes" [*Joel and Amos*, 19]).

YHWH is coming against Judah.³⁶ The ravaging locust plague, horrible as it was, portends an even greater judgment against the nation, a message that is developed further in the eschatological sections later in the book of Joel.³⁷ This message is communicated, in part, through Joel's use of soundplay: the paronomasia linking שדד שדה in verse 10 and the phrase שד משדי in verse 15 creates a conceptual link between the locust plague and the Day of YHWH.³⁸

4.3.4. Joel 2:21–23: The Curse Reversed

In Joel 2:18–27 YHWH announces that he will comprehensively reverse the curses wrought and restore the losses incurred by the drought and locust plague described in Joel 1.³⁹ Joel 2:21–24 in particular systematically reverses the drought of Joel 1.⁴⁰ A particularly clear instance of this is the reversal of the lament "Is not food cut off before our very eyes, *joy and gladness* [שמחה וגיל] from the house of our God?" (1:16) in commands to the soil (אדמה) and to the children of Zion (בני ציון), respectively, to rejoice and be glad (גילי ושמחי [2:21]; גילו ושמחו [2:23]) at the restoration of produce and of the rain necessary to make it grow.⁴¹ The statement just quoted from Joel 1:16 follows immediately the declaration in verse 15

---

36. The later parts of the book of Joel universalize the Day of YHWH, bringing the development of this biblical concept to a new stage (Crenshaw, *Joel*, 106; Wolff, *Joel and Amos*, 34; Müller, *Gottes Zukunft*, 60, 196; Bergler, *Joel als Schriftinterpret*, 67, 138–39). Note, though, that according to Müller the scope of the judgment of the Day of YHWH is also universal in Joel 1–2: "Im Joelbuch wird diese universale Bedeutung [of the Day of YHWH] programmatisch, wenn von Anfang an die Ankündigungen von den primären Adressaten, den Bewohnern Jerusalems aus transparent für die ganze Erde ist" (Müller, *Gottes Zukunft*, 95).

37. Crenshaw, *Joel*, 106, 114; Wolff, *Joel and Amos*, 35; but see the comments of Barton, *Joel and Obadiah*, 60–62.

38. Wolff points out that Joel's connecting a current crisis with the coming Day of YHWH constitutes "the early signs of apocalypticism" (Wolff, *Joel and Amos*, 26).

39. See, e.g., Barton, *Joel and Obadiah*, 89; Wolff, *Joel and Amos*, 63. According to Barton, YHWH's declaration in Joel 2:25 that he will repay his people for the locust plague interrupts the flow of the surrounding material and "might be a later insertion" (Barton, *Joel and Obadiah*, 89–90).

40. As Wolff writes, "2:21–24 shows itself to be an assurance oracle answering a plea which corresponds exactly to the laments in 1:16–20" (Wolff, *Joel and Amos*, 63).

41. The nouns שמחה and גיל occur together in the book of Joel only in 1:16 and the verbs שמח and גיל occur together in the book only in 2:21, 23.

that the Day of YHWH is coming "like devastation from Shaddai" (כְּשֹׁד מִשַּׁדַּי), and sandwiched between the twin commands to rejoice and to be glad in 2:21 and 23 is a statement that plays on the sounds of כְּשֹׁד מִשַּׁדַּי but transforms the destruction portended by these words into a jubilant announcement of renewal: "Fear not, beasts of the field [בהמות שָׂדַי], for the pastures of the wilderness have sprouted grass [דשאו]!" (2:22). This exhortation to the beasts of the fields to rejoice is a direct response to the statement מה נאנחה בהמה ("How the beasts groan!") found in 1:18, and it even more clearly reverses the scene presented in 1:20: גם בהמות שדה תערוג אליך כי יבשו אפיקי מים ואש אכלה נאות המדבר ("The very beasts of the field cry out to you; for the watercourses are dried up, and fire has consumed the pastures of the wilderness").[42] The use in the phrase בהמות שדי ("beasts of the field") in 2:22 of the rare poetic term שָׂדַי (which occurs only thirteen times in the Bible), as opposed to the standard term for "field," שָׂדֶה (which occurs 321 times, including in the parallel expression בהמות שדה in Joel 1:20), strengthens the probability that שדי ("field") in 2:22 was intended as a deliberate play on שדי ("Shaddai") in 1:15.[43] The presence of the root דשא ("to sprout") in 2:22, which occurs as a verbal form in only one other place in the Bible, is also a strong indication that the language of this verse was used deliberately for the purpose of creating paronomasia.[44] The effect of this soundplay is to show that embedded in the declaration of devastation in chapter 1 was a latent promise that YHWH would reverse the curse on the land and the people.

---

42. The connection between Joel 2:22 and 1:18, 20 is noted by Wolff, *Joel and Amos*, 63.

43. Interestingly, the phrase בהמות שדי ("beasts of the field") also occurs in Ps 8:8, and it may well be that Joel 2:22 picks up this phrase from the former. A similar play to the one suggested here between Joel 2:22 and 1:15 may be present in Song 2:7 (// 3:5), where, as Zakovitch suggests, the speaker's adjuration of the daughters of Jerusalem בצבאות או באילות השדה ("by gazelles or by hinds of the field") may allude to יהוה) צבאות] ("[YHWH of] Hosts") and אל שדי ("El Shaddai"); see Yair Zakovitch, שיר השירים (Jerusalem: Magnes, 1992), 64.

44. Significantly, the verb דשא in Gen 1:11 describes God's original creation of the earth's vegetation. The fact that the verb דשא is used only there and in Joel 2:22, along with the description of the land in Joel 2:3 as גן עדן ("the garden of Eden"), further enriches the picture of re-creation in Joel 2:22. See further Crenshaw, *Joel*, 153–54; Ulrich Dahmen, *Die Bücher Joel und Amos*, NSKAT 23.2 (Stuttgart: Katholisches Bibelwerk, 2001), 75.

4.3.5. Conclusion

The first chapter of the book of Joel alludes to two earlier prophecies of the Day of YHWH, from Isaiah and Ezekiel, in order to announce that the locust plague that has afflicted Judah is a new manifestation of this dread phenomenon. This message is accentuated through a play on the sounds of the declaration that the day will come "like devastation from Shaddai." The function of the allusive paronomasia here is rather similar to that of the play in Jer 50:32 on Jer 21:14 (see §3.1.3 above), but the progression of the targets of the punishment is the opposite in each case: whereas in Jeremiah the oracle about Jerusalem's destruction (21:14) was transformed into a prophecy about the fall of Babylon (50:32), in Joel 1 oracles about Babylon's and Egypt's destruction (Isa 13:6; Ezek 30:2–3) are transformed into a prophecy about the fall of Judah (Joel 1:15).

Building on the paronomastic reversal of Isa 13:6 in Joel 1:15, Joel 2:22 uses soundplay to weave together a beautiful description of YHWH's undoing of the devastating effects of the plague. As with the example from Jeremiah, here again in Joel 1 and 2 the reader is invited to contemplate the mystery of YHWH's sovereign will, by which he tears down and builds up kingdoms, including that of his own chosen people.

5
Conclusion

My goal in this book has been to demonstrate that a variety of biblical writers used paronomasia allusively—that is, in interaction with antecedent textual traditions from ancient Israel—in order to express and develop their theology, that is, their beliefs about God and his relationship to humanity. Many more examples could have been marshalled in support of this conclusion, but I hope that the admittedly modest number I have discussed have provided sufficient evidence to convince the reader of the soundness of my basic argument.

Taken together, the examples found in the preceding chapters indicate that allusive paronomasia is not limited to a particular biblical book or portion thereof or to a particular subcorpus within the Bible (e.g., the prophetic literature). While all the examples in chapters 2, 3, and 4 come from the Prophets and the Writings, and while several come from Second Isaiah and Job, my selection of case studies is not intended to imply that allusive paronomasia in the Bible is limited to these books or groups of books. Furthermore, although all the examples of allusive paronomasia that I have discussed in this book are found in poetic texts, the device has been documented in prose as well.[1] As I stated in the introduction, I chose to discuss the examples I did because in my view they serve well to illustrate the way multiple biblical authors employed allusive paronomasia to generate their theological discourse.[2]

Given that allusive paronomasia appears to be widespread in the Bible—it is found in multiple books and literary genres, and in both poetry and prose—scholars ought to search for further examples of this rhetorical

---

1. For an example of allusive paronomasia in prose, see n. 30 in chapter 1.
2. As I further noted in the introduction (§1.6), an entirely different set of examples could have been chosen to make the same point.

device in all the biblical books, with the goals of identifying a much larger number of examples than have already come to light and, insofar as it is possible, of classifying them according to how they function to transform their source texts (on this last point, see below). Such analysis would give us a deeper appreciation for the Bible's exquisite literary artistry, increase our understanding of the compositional history of various biblical texts, and help us better grasp how various theological traditions found in the Bible developed.

Despite the apparent pervasiveness of allusive paronomasia in the Bible, it is noteworthy that many of the examples of allusive paronomasia treated in the foregoing chapters are found in late texts (Job, Second and Third Isaiah, Joel, Malachi, and apparently postexilic psalms). Although this could be due to chance (since the examples are in no way comprehensive but are simply illustrative of the device), it suggests that allusive paronomasia, while not limited to late texts, may be preponderant in them. Such a conclusion is in one sense not surprising, since later texts in the Hebrew Bible are, generally speaking, more allusive than earlier ones (not least because they had available to them a larger literary corpus on which to draw than did earlier texts). But this conclusion—which should be treated as tentative until a much larger number of examples of allusive paronomasia have been catalogued and studied—is significant insofar as it suggests that later texts increasingly viewed even the smallest details of the tradition (such as individual phonemes in earlier texts) to be highly significant for interpretation (an attitude that is characteristic of postbiblical interpretation of the Bible, as I will discuss further below).[3]

Indeed, my intention throughout this book has been to show how the allusive use of paronomasia reveals the text-exegetical virtuosity of the biblical writers. By means of even the seemingly minutest of changes (e.g., the alteration of a letter or two in an antecedent text), the biblical writers produced a variety of exegetical effects. As my examples demonstrate, the biblical writers used allusive paronomasia to debate earlier psalmic or wisdom traditions, for instance;[4] to reapply old oracles (of both judgment and salvation) to new situations (whether through reproclamation or

---

3. That scribes of the late biblical period felt free to a certain degree to reproduce earlier texts with alterations is all the more remarkable given that "recent studies in the history of the development of the biblical text have highlighted an increasing trend toward precision of copying" (Carr, *Formation of the Hebrew Bible*, 35).

4. See the examples in chapter 2.

CONCLUSION 121

reversal or a combination of the two);[5] and to proclaim YHWH's covenant lawsuit, with its blessing and curse sanctions, against his people.[6] These are simply a few of the purposes for which the biblical authors employed this literary device, however; they apparently used it to perform many other interpretive functions as well.

This last observation raises the question whether enough examples of allusive paronomasia exist in the Bible for us to be able to create a meaningful system of classification that groups examples according to their exegetical effects or interpretive functions and allows their similarities and differences to be compared on this basis. Benjamin Sommer has helpfully classified examples of allusive soundplay (as well as other allusive devices) found in Isa 40–66 into several broad categories, observing that in this corpus allusive soundplay performs (usually in conjunction with the other devices he discusses) the following functions: reversal, reprediction, repetition of a promise, fulfillment of earlier prophecies, historical recontextualization, and typological linkage.[7] These categories can overlap in any given instance, of course, and Sommer duly notes that in certain texts the allusive soundplay (and other devices) can serve multiple purposes.[8]

When I began working on the present study, my intention was to survey a large number of examples of allusive paronomasia from across the Hebrew Bible and, following Sommer's lead (but also adding new categories to his), to classify and group them according to their function(s). After preparing and sorting a preliminary list of examples in this way, however, it became clear to me that in order to produce a meaningful typology of this kind—one that could accurately reflect the diversity of functions that allusive paronomasia performs in the Bible as a whole, indicate which of these functions are the most and which are the least common, and also demonstrate why some examples are more convincing than others— the number of examples I would have needed to present would have far exceeded what could reasonably fit in one volume.[9] Because producing

---

5. For reproclamation or reapplication of an earlier oracle, see §4.1 and §3.1. For reversal of an earlier oracle, see §4.2. For a combination of reproclamation and reversal, see §4.3.

6. See §3.2.

7. Sommer, *Prophet Reads Scripture*.

8. E.g., ibid., 100–104.

9. Once a relatively large corpus of examples of allusive soundplay in the Hebrew Bible has been established, it would also be interesting to see if any patterns emerged

a study like the one just described does not seem feasible in the present early stage of research on allusive paronomasia, it seemed best to me that the present work should serve the more preliminary—and at this point still necessary—functions, first, of making the basic point that allusive paronomasia is in fact found throughout the Hebrew Bible and, second, of developing a robust method that allows us to identify examples of this device with confidence and to distinguish it from formally similar or identical phenomena. Once scholars have identified a much more substantial number of examples of allusive soundplay from throughout the Bible than has yet been done, we will be in a better position to begin classifying them according to their broad functions and to begin seeing what insights arise from comparing them on this basis.

In addition to the foregoing concerns about the purposes to which allusive paronomasia is put in the Bible, important questions also remain regarding the circumstances under or means by which allusive paronomasia was generated in ancient Israel. In particular, to what degree is the biblical writers' use of allusive paronomasia a purely written phenomenon? That is, were the kinds of sound changes I have discussed in this book sometimes (even perhaps often) not generated through writing but rather the result of oral transmission of the tradition? This question is difficult to answer, and, as David Carr has demonstrated, to posit a fine distinction between written and oral transmission of ancient texts is to create a false dichotomy that does not reflect the complexities of reality.[10] Indeed, from an analysis of "the phenomenon of oral-written cognitive transmission across a broad variety of ancient literatures," Carr concludes that

> this sort of transmission is marked by a set of distinctive variants, "memory variants," which show the transformations typical of texts, transmitted, at least in part, through memory.... The claim made here is simply that the texts of the Hebrew Bible, whatever their often diverse original uses, came down to us through the sorts of transmission processes characteristic of oral-written long-duration literature.[11]

---

when one classified them according to form (as I have done for the similar-sounding words found in parallel texts that I surveyed in the "category 1" section of §1.5.2.2.2).

10. In the Hebrew Bible, as in other ancient literature, Carr remarks, "we see the limits of sharp distinctions between writing and memory" (Carr, *Formation of the Hebrew Bible*, 34).

11. Ibid., 34–35.

Regardless of whether, or to what degree, the alterations to Israel's traditions that I have discussed in this book were the product of writing, orality, or both, their significance can best be appreciated by returning to the question of the intentionality of those who made them, a point I have emphasized throughout this study. In this connection, Carr observes that when studying the transmission of the biblical text

> it is often impossible to separate intentional alteration from unintentional memory shifts in textual transmission, and there are mixed cases, such as places where an exchange of a word or phrase by a scribe might manifest that scribe's unconscious wish to have the text address his or her audience in a particular way.[12]

Although I agree entirely with Carr's judgment here, I have nevertheless argued that in at least some cases one can demonstrate with a high degree of probability that the changes the biblical tradents made to the traditions they inherited (specifically, their playing on the sounds of words in their source texts) were intentional and that the best proof of this in any given instance is the demonstration that the change in question performs a clear, meaningful function.[13]

That the biblical writers could produce significant exegetical payoff by changing or rearranging the sounds of even a single word from the textual tradition they inherited indicates that they considered that tradition—even in its tiniest details—to contain (sometimes multiple) developing meanings and to be significant not only for the past but also, and perhaps especially, for the present and the future. Such an understanding of ancient Israel's textual traditions is, of course, amply attested in postbiblical literature as well. Indeed, paronomasia continued to be a productive exegetical principle for later communities interpreting the biblical text. In this regard, one thinks especially of the use of paronomasia as an exegetical device at Qumran,[14] in

---

12. Ibid., 36.
13. See §1.5.2.1.4.
14. Examples of paronomasia as an exegetical device in Pesher Habakkuk can be found in L. H. Silberman, "Unriddling the Riddle: A Study in the Structure and Language of the Habakkuk Pesher (1 Q p Hab)," *RevQ* 3 (1961): 323–64. According to Silberman, "the commentator [who wrote Pesher Habakkuk] viewed the prophetic text as a vision whose meaning, already known in fact, was to be unriddled. The method used was that of establishing a relationship between the 'events' in the history of the community and the biblical text *by means of literary devices that depended, for the most*

the New Testament,[15] and in the midrashim,[16] especially those involving *al tikrei* readings.[17] Increased recognition of the degree to which allusive paronomasia occurs in the Bible as a productive principle of exegesis raises the question to what extent these later communities' use of soundplay (as well as other kinds of wordplay) to interpret the biblical text constitutes an organic outgrowth of the compositional practices that shaped the Bible itself.[18] A fruitful and illuminating avenue of research in this regard would

---

part, upon auditory word-plays" (334; emphasis added). For paronomasia (as well as other kinds of wordplay) as an exegetical device in Pesher Nahum (and elsewhere at Qumran), see Gregory L. Doudna, *4Q Pesher Nahum: A Critical Edition*, JSPSup 35, CIS 8 (Sheffield: Sheffield Academic, 2001), 253–65, and Shani L. Berrin, *The Pesher Nahum Scroll from Qumran: An Exegetical Study of 4Q169*, STDJ 53 (Leiden: Brill, 2004). As James Harding has observed, "wordplay, *sometimes between words some considerable distance apart*, is a crucial literary device within the 'sectarian' scrolls" (James E. Harding, "The Wordplay between the Roots *ksl* and *skl* in the Literature of the Yaḥad," *RevQ* 19 [1999]: 80; emphasis added). See also Michael Fishbane, "Use, Authority, and Interpretation of Mikra at Qumran," in *Mikra: Text, Translation, Reading, and Interpretation of the Hebrew Bible in Ancient Judaism and Early Christianity*, ed. Martin J. Mulder (Philadelphia: Fortress, 1988), 374–75.

15. For an interesting example, see E. Earle Ellis, "Biblical Interpretation in the New Testament Church," in *Mikra: Text, Translation, Reading, and Interpretation of the Hebrew Bible in Ancient Judaism and Early Christianity*, ed. Martin J. Mulder (Philadelphia: Fortress, 1988), 704.

16. Among the rabbis, "many of the methods and literary forms used in interpreting nonlegal biblical verses have to do with philological play, for indeed the play on words is one of the main features of rabbinic exegesis" (Carol Bakhos, "Midrash, Midrashim," in *The Eerdmans Dictionary of Early Judaism*, ed. John J. Collins and Daniel C. Harlow [Grand Rapids: Eerdmans, 2010], 946). See also Howard Eilberg-Schwartz, "Who's Kidding Whom? A Serious Reading of Rabbinic Word Plays," *JAAR* 55 (1987): 765–88.

17. On *al tikrei* see, e.g., Carmel McCarthy, *The Tiqqune Sopherim and Other Theological Corrections in the Masoretic Text of the Old Testament* (Göttingen: Vandenhoeck & Ruprecht, 1981), esp. 139–66. On the continuity between the interpretive exploitation of variant spellings in Qumran pesharim and rabbinic *al tikrei* midrashim, see Shemaryahu Talmon, "Aspects of the Textual Transmission of the Bible in the Light of Qumran Manuscripts," in *Qumran and the History of the Biblical Text*, ed. Frank Moore Cross and Shemaryahu Talmon (Cambridge: Harvard University Press, 1975), 226–63, esp. 256–59, 263.

18. See, e.g., Isaac Leo Seeligmann, "Voraussetzungen der Midraschexegese," in *Congress Volume: Copenhagen, 1953*, VTSup 1 (Leiden: Brill, 1953), 150–81; Shemaryahu Talmon, "The Ancient Hebrew Alphabet and Biblical Text Criticism," in *Mélanges Dominique Barthélemy: Études bibliques offertes à l'occasion de son 60ᵉ anni-

be to examine the formal and functional similarities and differences that obtain between allusive paronomasia in the Bible and the use of soundplay (and other kinds of wordplay) in the exegesis of biblical texts in the pesharim and midrashim.

Considering the other end of the historical spectrum, the biblical writers were themselves heirs to an ancient scribal tradition that used paronomasia as a hermeneutical device, as is attested especially in Mesopotamian omen collections[19] and dream interpretation.[20] Therefore, the Bible's use of soundplay for interpretive purposes simply represents one (protracted) stage in a long historical arc that had deep roots in Mesopotamia and reached its floruit in the writings of the heirs of the biblical tradition, especially the rabbis,[21] a conclusion that is confirmed by the clear connections

---

versaire, ed. Pierre Casetti, Othmar Keel, and Adrian Schenker, OBO 38 (Göttingen: Vandenhoeck & Ruprecht, 1981), 497–530, esp. 500–501; Talmon, "The Textual Study of the Bible: A New Outlook," in *Qumran and the History of the Biblical Text*, ed. Frank Moore Cross and Shemaryahu Talmon (Cambridge: Harvard University Press, 1975), 378–81; Geza Vermes, "Bible and Midrash: Early Old Testament Exegesis," in *From the Beginnings to Jerome*, vol. 1 of *The Cambridge History of the Bible*, ed. Peter R. Ackroyd and Chistopher F. Evans (Cambridge: Cambridge University Press, 1970), 199; Avigdor Shinan and Yair Zakovitch, "Midrash on Scripture and Midrash within Scripture," *ScrHier* 31 (1986): 277; Silberman, "Unriddling the Riddle," 332–33.

19. Jovan Bilbija, "Interpreting the Interpretation: Protasis-Apodosis-Strings in the Physiognomic Omen Series *Šumma Alamdimmû* 3.76–132," in *Studies in Ancient Near Eastern World View and Society Presented to Marten Stol on the Occasion of His 65th Birthday, 10 November 2005, and His Retirement from Vrije Universiteit Amsterdam*, ed. R. J. van der Spek (Bethesda, MD: CDL, 2008), 19–27; C. J. Gadd, "Omens Expressed in Numbers," *JCS* 21 (1967): 52–63; Abraham Winitzer, "The Generative Paradigm in Old Babylonian Divination" (PhD diss., Harvard University, 2006).

20. Scott B. Noegel, "Dreams and Dream Interpreters in Mesopotamia and in the Hebrew Bible (Old Testament)," in *Dreams: A Reader on Religious, Cultural, and Psychological Dimensions of Dreaming*, ed. Kelly Bulkeley (New York: Palgrave, 2001), 45–71; Noegel, *Nocturnal Ciphers: The Allusive Language of Dreams in the Ancient Near East*, AOS 89 (New Haven: American Oriental Society, 2007).

21. As Bakhos observes, "the rabbis were punsters par excellence, and their aural acuity allowed them to move with great facility from one end of the biblical canon to the other in order to voice theological beliefs, to provide fanciful details to laconic biblical stories, to flesh out a patriarch's or a matriarch's moral character, or bring out the immoral character of the likes of Esau and Pharaoh" (Bakhos, "Midrash, Midrashim," 946).

between Mesopotamian exegetical literature and that of Qumran[22] and rabbinic Judaism.[23]

What ultimately underlies the biblical writers' use of allusive paronomasia to express their conceptions about God and his relationship to humanity is a belief in the power of language that permeated the world in which the Bible arose.[24] On the broadest level, then, by focusing on the way the biblical writers used allusive paronomasia to harness language to great exegetical effect, my intention has been to draw attention to how language was conceived of in ancient Israel. In particular, the examples I have discussed in this book—which reflect the ancient Israelite scribes' view that sounds, the smallest units of linguistic expression, have the power to reveal the significance of the past, present, and future—suggest that at least some of the biblical writers viewed language per se not as a merely human phenomenon but as expressive of the character, and indeed the voice, of God, as well as of the destiny of humanity. They apparently also

---

22. See Alex P. Jassen, "The Pesharim and the Rise of Commentary in Early Jewish Scriptural Interpretation," *DSD* 19 (2012): 363–98, in which the author "argues for renewed attention to ancient Near Eastern dream and omen interpretation as the most plausible historical influence on the commentary form as encountered in the pesharim" (363). See also Daniel A. Machiela, "The Qumran Pesharim as Biblical Commentaries: Historical Context and Lines of Development," *DSD* 19 (2012): 313–62.

23. On the Mesopotamian roots of rabbinic exegesis, see A. Cavigneaux, "Aux sources du Midrash: L'herméneutique babylonienne," *AuOr* 5 (1987): 243–55; Stephen J. Lieberman, "A Mesopotamian Background for the So-Called Aggadic 'Measures' of Biblical Hermeneutics?" *HUCA* 58 (1978): 157–225; Jeffrey Tigay, "An Early Technique of Aggadic Exegesis," in *History, Historiography and Interpretation: Studies in Biblical and Cuneiform Literature*, ed. Hayim Tadmor and Moshe Weinfeld (Leiden: Brill, 1983), 169–89. Compare Chaim Milikowsky, "Rabbinic Interpretation of the Bible in the Light of Ancient Hermeneutical Practice: The Question of the Literal Meaning," in *"The Words of a Wise Man's Mouth Are Gracious" (Qoh 10,12): Festschrift for Günter Stemberger on the Occasion of His 65th Birthday*, ed. Mauro Perani, SJ 32 (Berlin: de Gruyter, 2005), 10.

24. Isaac Rabinowitz, *A Witness Forever: Ancient Israel's Perception of Literature and the Resultant Hebrew Bible* (Bethesda, MD: CDL, 1993), esp. 1–25; Sheldon Greaves, "The Power of the Word in the Ancient Near East" (PhD diss., University of California, Berkeley, 1996); Scott B. Noegel, "'Sign, Sign, Everywhere a Sign': Script, Power, and Interpretation in the Ancient Near East," in *Divination and Interpretation of Signs in the Ancient World: The Fifth Annual University of Chicago Oriental Institute Seminar*, ed. Amar Annus (Chicago: Oriental Institute of the University of Chicago, 2010), 143–62; Noegel, *Nocturnal Ciphers*, 36–45.

considered the voice of God to be able to express itself in terms of an ever-evolving tradition, one that was always rooted in the past but that could develop fresh insights (that might be more or less continuous with earlier ones) in response to new circumstances. The fact that the biblical authors espoused such an organic view of how the deity makes himself known should prompt students of the Bible, especially those who approach it from a position of faith, to reflect on whether their own understanding of what constitutes the word of God is characterized by the same dynamism as was that of the biblical writers.

Bibliography

Abasciano, Brian J. *Paul's Use of the Old Testament in Romans 9:1-9: An Intertextual and Theological Exegesis*. London: T&T Clark, 2005.

Allen, Leslie C. *Jeremiah: A Commentary*. OTL. Louisville: Westminster John Knox, 2008.

Alonso Schökel, Luis. "Isaiah." Pages 165–83 in *The Literary Guide to the Bible*. Edited by Robert Alter and Frank Kermode. Cambridge: Belknap, 1987.

———. *A Manual of Hebrew Poetics*. SubBi 11. Rome: Pontifical Biblical Institute, 1988.

Anderson, Bernhard W. "Exodus Typology in Second Isaiah." Pages 177–95 in *Israel's Prophetic Heritage: Essays in Honor of James Muilenburg*. Edited by Bernhard W. Anderson and Walter J. Harrelson. New York: Harper, 1962.

Androphy, Ronald L. "Paronomasia in the Former Prophets: A Taxonomic Catalogue, Description, and Analysis." DHL diss., Jewish Theological Seminary, 2011.

Assis, Elie. "Structure and Meaning in the Book of Malachi." Pages 354–69 in *Prophecy and Prophets in Ancient Israel: Proceedings of the Oxford Old Testament Seminar*. LHBOTS 531. Edited by John Day. New York: T&T Clark, 2010.

Auffret, Pierre. "'Aie confiance en lui, et lui, il agira': Étude structurelle du Psaume 37." *SJOT* 4 (1990): 13–43.

Bakhos, Carol. "Midrash, Midrashim." Pages 944–49 in *The Eerdmans Dictionary of Early Judaism*. Edited by John J. Collins and Daniel C. Harlow. Grand Rapids: Eerdmans, 2010.

Barstad, Hans. *A Way in the Wilderness: The "Second Exodus" in the Message of Second Isaiah*. Manchester: University of Manchester Press, 1989.

Barton, John. "*Déjà Lu:* Intertextuality, Method or Theory?" Pages 2–16 in *Reading Job Intertextually*. Edited by Katharine J. Dell and Will Kynes. LHBOTS 574. New York: Bloomsbury, 2013.

———. *Joel and Obadiah*. OTL. Louisville: Westminster John Knox, 2001.

Bauks, Michaela. "'Chaos' als Metapher für die Gefährdung der Weltordnung." Pages 431–64 in *Das biblische Weltbild und seine altorientalischen Kontexte*. Edited by Bernd Janowski and Beate Ego. FAT 32. Tübingen: Mohr Siebeck, 2001.

Beentjes, Pancratius C. "Inverted Quotations in the Bible: A Neglected Stylistic Pattern." *Bib* 63 (1982): 506–23.

Beetham, Christopher A. *Echoes of Scripture in the Letter of Paul to the Colossians*. Leiden: Brill, 2010.

Bellis, Alice Ogden. "Poetic Structure and Intertextual Logic in Jeremiah 50." Pages 179–99 in *Troubling Jeremiah*. Edited by A. R. Pete Diamond, Kathleen M. O'Connor, and Louis Stulman. Sheffield: Sheffield Academic, 1999.

Bendavid, Abba. מקבילות במקרא. Jerusalem: Carta, 1972.

Ben-Porat, Ziva. "The Poetics of Literary Allusion." *PTL* 1 (1976): 105–28.

Berges, Ulrich. "Der zweite Exodus im Jesajabuch: Auszug oder Verwandlung?" Pages 77–95 in *Das Manna fällt auch heute noch: Beiträge zur Geschichte und Theologie des Alten, Ersten Testaments; Festschrift für Erich Zenger*. Edited by Frank-Lothar Hossfeld and Ludger Schwienhorst-Schönberger. HBS 44. Freiburg: Herder, 2004.

Bergler, Siegfried. *Joel als Schriftinterpret*. BEATAJ 16. Frankfurt am Main: Lang, 1988.

Bergmeier, Roland. "Zum Ausdruck עצת רשעים in Ps 1 1 Hi 10 3 21 16 und 22 18." *ZAW* 79 (1967): 229–32.

Berrin, Shani L. *The Pesher Nahum Scroll from Qumran: An Exegetical Study of 4Q169*. STDJ 53. Leiden: Brill, 2004.

Bilbija, Jovan. "Interpreting the Interpretation: Protasis-Apodosis-Strings in the Physiognomic Omen Series *Šumma Alamdimmû* 3.76–132." Pages 19–27 in *Studies in Ancient Near Eastern World View and Society Presented to Marten Stol on the Occasion of His 65th Birthday, 10 November 2005, and His Retirement from Vrije Universiteit Amsterdam*. Edited by R. J. van der Spek. Bethesda, MD: CDL, 2008.

Blenkinsopp, Joseph. *Isaiah 1–39*. AB 19. New York: Doubleday, 2000.

———. *Isaiah 40–55*. AB 19A. New York: Doubleday, 2002.

———. *Isaiah 56–66*. AB 19B. New York: Doubleday, 2003.

Briggs, Charles A. *The Book of Psalms*. 2 vols. ICC. Edinburgh: T&T Clark, 1906.
Brinks, C. L. "Job and Deutero Isaiah: The Use and Abuse of Traditions." *BibInt* 20 (2012): 407–20.
Brown, William P. "Joy and the Art of Cosmic Maintenance: An Ecology of Play in Psalm 104." Pages 23–32 in *"And God Saw that It Was Good": Essays on Creation and God in Honor of Terence E. Fretheim*. Edited by Frederick J. Gaiser and Mark A. Throntveit. St. Paul, MN: Luther Seminary, 2006.
Brueggemann, Walter. "Bounded by Obedience and Praise: The Psalms as Canon." *JSOT* 50 (1991): 63–92.
Brueggemann, Walter, and Patrick D. Miller. "Psalm 73 as a Canonical Marker." *JSOT* 72 (1996): 45–56.
Carr, David M. *The Formation of the Hebrew Bible: A New Reconstruction*. Oxford: Oxford University Press, 2011.
Casanowicz, Immanuel M. "Paronomasia in the Old Testament." PhD diss., Johns Hopkins University, 1892/1894.
———. "Paronomasia in the Old Testament." *JBL* 12 (1893): 105–67.
Cavigneaux, A. "Aux sources du Midrash: L'herméneutique babylonienne." *AuOr* 5 (1987): 243–55.
Cherry, Russell T., III. "Paronomasia and Proper Names in the Old Testament: Rhetorical Function and Literary Effect." PhD diss., Southern Baptist Theological Seminary, 1988.
Childs, Brevard S. *Isaiah*. OTL. Louisville: Westminster John Knox, 2001.
Clifford, Richard J. *Proverbs*. OTL. Louisville: Westminster John Knox, 1999.
Clines, David J. A., ed. *Dictionary of Classical Hebrew*. 9 vols. Sheffield: Sheffield Phoenix, 1993–2014.
Cole, Robert L. *The Shape and Message of Book III (Psalms 73–89)*. JSOTSup 307. Sheffield: Sheffield Academic, 2000.
Conte, Gian Biagio. *The Rhetoric of Imitation: Genre and Poetic Memory in Virgil and Other Latin Poets*. Translated by Charles Segal. Ithaca: Cornell University Press, 1986.
Cook, Eleanor. "Paronomasia." *PEPP*, 1003–4.
Cook, Joan E. "Everyone Called by My Name: Second Isaiah's Use of the Creation Theme." Pages 35–47 in *Earth, Wind, and Fire: Biblical and Theological Perspectives on Creation*. Collegeville, MN: Liturgical Press, 2004.
Crenshaw, James L. *Joel*. AB 24C. New York: Doubleday, 1995.

Dahmen, Ulrich. *Die Bücher Joel und Amos*. NSKAT 23.2. Stuttgart: Katholisches Bibelwerk, 2001.
Dahood, Mitchell J. "Ebla, Ugarit, and the Bible." Afterword to *The Archives of Ebla: An Empire Inscribed in Clay*, by Giovanni Pettinato. Garden City, NY: Doubleday, 1981.
Delekat, Lienhard. "Zum hebräischen Wörterbuch." *VT* 14 (1964): 7–66.
Doudna, Gregory L. *4Q Pesher Nahum: A Critical Edition*. JSPSup 35. CIS 8. Sheffield: Sheffield Academic, 2001.
Driver, Samuel R., and George B. Gray. *The Book of Job*. ICC. Edinburgh: T&T Clark, 1921.
Eilberg-Schwartz, Howard. "Who's Kidding Whom? A Serious Reading of Rabbinic Word Plays." *JAAR* 55 (1987): 765–88.
Ellis, E. Earle. "Biblical Interpretation in the New Testament Church." Pages 691–725 in *Mikra: Text, Translation, Reading, and Interpretation of the Hebrew Bible in Ancient Judaism and Early Christianity*. Edited by Martin J. Mulder. Philadelphia: Fortress, 1988.
Emerton, J. A. "'Spring and Torrent' in Psalm LXXIV 15." Pages 122–33 in *Volume du Congrès: Genève, 1965*. Edited by P. A. H. de Boer. VTSup 15. Leiden: Brill, 1966.
Fabry, Heinz-Josef. *Nahum*. HThKAT. Freiburg: Herder, 2006.
Fishbane, Michael. *Biblical Interpretation in Ancient Israel*. Oxford: Clarendon, 1985.
———. "The Book of Job and Inner-Biblical Discourse." Pages 86–98 in *The Voice from the Whirlwind: Interpreting the Book of Job*. Edited by Leo Perdue and W. Clark Gilpin. Nashville: Abingdon, 1992.
———. *Haftarot: The Traditional Hebrew Text with the New JPS Translation*. Philadelphia: Jewish Publication Society, 2002.
———. "The Hebrew Bible and Exegetical Tradition." Pages 15–30 in *Intertextuality in Ugarit and Israel*. Edited by Johannes C. de Moor. OTS 40. Leiden: Brill, 1998.
———. "Use, Authority, and Interpretation of Mikra at Qumran." Pages 339–77 in *Mikra: Text, Translation, Reading, and Interpretation of the Hebrew Bible in Ancient Judaism and Early Christianity*. Edited by Martin J. Mulder. Philadelphia: Fortress, 1988.
Foster, Benjamin R. *Before the Muses: An Anthology of Akkadian Literature*. 3rd ed. Bethesda, MD: CDL, 2005.
Fox, Michael V. "Job the Pious." *ZAW* 117 (2005): 351–66.
———. *Proverbs 10–31*. AB 18B. New York: Doubleday, 2009.

Frevel, Christian. "'Eine kleine Theologie der Menschenwürde': Ps 8 und seine Rezeption im Buch Ijob." Pages 244–74 in *Das Manna fällt auch heute noch: Beiträge zur Geschichte und Theologie des Alten, Ersten Testaments; Festschrift für Erich Zenger*. Edited by Frank-Lothar Hossfeld and Ludger Schwienhorst-Schönberger. HBS 44. Freiburg: Herder, 2004.

Gadd, C. J. "Omens Expressed in Numbers." *JCS* 21 (1967): 52–63.

Garsiel, Moshe. *Biblical Names: A Literary Study of Midrashic Name Derivations and Puns*. Ramat Gan: Bar-Ilan University Press, 1991.

———. "Word Play and Puns as a Rhetorical Device in the Book of Samuel." Pages 181–204 in *Puns and Pundits: Word Play in the Hebrew Bible and Ancient Near Eastern Literature*. Edited by Scott B. Noegel. Bethesda, MD: CDL, 2000.

Glassner, Gottfried. "Aufbruch als Heimat: Zur Theologie des 114. Psalms." *ZKT* 116 (1994): 472–79.

Glazier-McDonald, Beth. *Malachi: The Divine Messenger*. Atlanta: Scholars Press, 1987.

Glück, J. J. "Paronomasia in Biblical Literature." *Sem* 1 (1970): 50–78.

Goldingay, John, and David Payne. *Isaiah 40–55*. 2 vols. ICC. London: T&T Clark, 2006.

Gordis, Robert. *The Book of God and Man: A Study of Job*. Chicago: University of Chicago Press, 1965.

———. *The Book of Job: Commentary, New Translation, and Special Studies*. New York: Jewish Theological Seminary of America, 1978.

Gordon, Cyrus H. "Near East Seals in Princeton and Philadelphia." *Or* 22 (1953): 242–50.

———. *Ugaritic Textbook*. AnOr 38. Rome: Pontifical Biblical Institute, 1965.

Gray, John. *The Book of Job*. Edited by David J. A. Clines. THB 1. Sheffield: Sheffield Phoenix, 2010.

Greaves, Sheldon. "The Power of the Word in the Ancient Near East." PhD diss., University of California, Berkeley, 1996.

Greenberg, Moshe. *Ezekiel 1–20*. AB 22. Garden City, NY: Doubleday, 1983.

———. "Job." Pages 283–304 in *The Literary Guide to the Bible*. Edited by Robert Alter and Frank Kermode. Cambridge: Belknap, 1987.

Greenstein, Edward. "Wordplay, Hebrew." *ABD* 6:968–71.

Guillaume, A. "Paronomasia in the Old Testament." *JSS* 9 (1964): 282–96.

Gunn, David. "Deutero-Isaiah and the Flood." *JBL* 94 (1975): 493–508.

Halton, Charles. "Allusions to the Stream of Tradition in Neo-Assyrian Oracles." *ANES* 46 (2009): 50–61.

Harding, James E. "The Wordplay between the Roots *ksl* and *skl* in the Literature of the Yahad." *RevQ* 19 (1999): 69–82.

Haug, Kari Storstein. *Interpreting Proverbs 11:18–31, Psalm 73, and Ecclesiastes 9:1–12 in Light of, and as a Response to, Thai Buddhist Interpretations*. Leiden: Brill, 2012.

Hays, Christopher B. "Echoes of the Ancient Near East? Intertextuality and the Comparative Study of the Old Testament." Pages 20–43 in *The Word Leaps the Gap: Essays on Scripture and Theology in Honor of Richard B. Hays*. Edited by J. Ross Wagner, C. Kavin Rowe, and A. Katherine Grieb. Grand Rapids: Eerdmans, 2009.

Hebel, Udo J. "Towards a Descriptive Poetics of Allusion." Pages 135–64 in *Intertextuality*. Edited by Heinrich F. Plett. RTT 15. Berlin: de Gruyter, 1991.

Hebel, Udo J., ed. *Intertextuality, Allusion, and Quotation: An International Bibliography of Critical Studies*. BIWL 18. Westport, CT: Greenwood, 1989.

Heckl, Raik. *Hiob: Vom Gottesfürchtigen zum Repräsentanten Israels; Studien zur Buchwerdung des Hiobbuches und zu seinen Quellen*. FAT 70. Tübingen: Mohr Siebeck, 2010.

Heim, Knut M. *Poetic Imagination in Proverbs: Variant Repetitions and the Nature of Poetry*. Winona Lake, IN: Eisenbrauns, 2013.

Hill, Andrew. *Malachi*. AB 25D. New York: Doubleday, 1998.

Hill, John. *Friend or Foe? The Figure of Babylon in the Book of Jeremiah MT*. Leiden: Brill, 1999.

Hinds, Stephen. *Allusion and Intertext: Dynamics of Appropriation in Roman Poetry*. New York: Cambridge University Press, 1998.

Holladay, William L. *Jeremiah 1: A Commentary on the Book of the Prophet Jeremiah, Chapters 1–25*. Hermeneia. Philadelphia: Fortress, 1986.

———. *Jeremiah 2: A Commentary on the Book of the Prophet Jeremiah, Chapters 26–52*. Hermeneia. Minneapolis: Fortress, 1989.

Hossfeld, Frank-Lothar, and Erich Zenger. *Die Psalmen: Psalm 1–50*. NEchtBAT 29. Würzburg: Echter, 1993.

———. *Psalms 2: A Commentary on Psalms 51–100*. Translated by Linda M. Maloney. Hermeneia. Minneapolis: Fortress, 2005.

———. *Psalms 3: A Commentary on Psalms 101–150*. Translated by Linda M. Maloney. Hermeneia. Minneapolis: Fortress, 2011.

Hrobon, Bohdan. *Ethical Dimension of Cult in the Book of Isaiah*. BZAW 418. Berlin: de Gruyter, 2010.
Hurvitz, Avi. "צדיק = חכם בתה׳ לז ושאלת רקעו החכמתי." Pages 131*–35* in *"Sha'arei Talmon": Studies in the Bible, Qumran, and the Ancient Near East Presented to Shemaryahu Talmon*. Edited by Michael Fishbane and Emanuel Tov. Winona Lake, IN: Eisenbrauns, 1992.
———. "צדיק = 'Wise' in Biblical Hebrew and the Wisdom Connections of Ps 37." Pages 109–12 in *Goldene Äpfel in silbernen Schalen: Collected Communications to the XIIIth Congress of the International Organization for the Study of the Old Testament, Leuven 1989*. Edited by Klaus-Dietrich Schunk and Matthias Augustin. BEATAJ 20. Frankfurt am Main: Lang, 1992.
Illman, Karl-Johan. "Theodicy in Job." Pages 304–33 in *Theodicy in the World of the Bible*. Edited by Antti Laato and Johannes C. de Moor. Leiden: Brill, 2003.
Jassen, Alex P. "The Pesharim and the Rise of Commentary in Early Jewish Scriptural Interpretation." *DSD* 19 (2012): 363–98.
Joosten, Jan. "La macrostructure du livre de Job et quelques parallèles (Jérémie 45; 1 Rois 19)." Pages 400–404 in *The Book of Job*. Edited by W. A. M. Beuken. Leuven: Peeters, 1994.
Kalimi, Isaac. *Zur Geschichtsschreibung des Chronisten: Literarisch-historiographische Abweichungen der Chronik von ihren Paralleltexten in den Samuel- und Königsbüchern*. Berlin: de Gruyter, 1995.
Kessler, Rainer. *Maleachi*. HThKAT. Freiburg: Herder, 2011.
Knohl, Israel. "The Priestly Torah versus the Holiness School: Sabbath and the Festivals." *HUCA* 58 (1987): 65–117.
Koenen, Klaus. *Ethik und Eschatologie im Tritojesajabuch: Eine literarkritische und redaktionsgeschichtliche Studie*. WMANT 62. Neukirchen-Vluyn: Neukirchener Verlag, 1990.
Koenig, Jean. *L'herméneutique analogique du judaïsme antique d'après les témoins textuels d'Isaïe*. VTSup 33. Leiden: Brill, 1982.
Köhlmoos, Melanie. *Das Auge Gottes: Textstrategie im Hiobbuch*. FAT 25. Tübingen: Mohr Siebeck, 1999.
Kratz, Reinhard G. "Innerbiblische Exegese und Redaktionsgeschichte im Lichte empirischer Evidenz." Pages 126–56 in *Das Judentum im Zeitalter des Zweiten Tempels*. FAT 42. Tübingen: Mohr Siebeck, 2004.
———. "'The Place Which He Has Chosen': The Identification of the Cult Place of Deut. 12 and Lev. 1 in 4QMMT." *Meghillot* 5–6 (2007): 57–80.

Kugel, James A. *The Bible as It Was*. Cambridge: Harvard University Press, 1997.

———. "Early Interpretation: The Common Background of Late Forms of Biblical Exegesis." Pages 9–106 in James A. Kugel and Rowan A. Greer, *Early Biblical Interpretation*. Philadelphia: Westminster, 1986.

Kynes, Will. "Job and Isaiah 40–55: Intertextualities in Dialogue." Pages 94–105 in *Reading Job Intertextually*. Edited by Katharine Dell and Will Kynes. LHBOTS 574. New York: Bloomsbury, 2013.

———. *My Psalm Has Turned into Weeping: The Dialogical Intertextuality of Allusions to the Psalms in Job*. BZAW 437. Berlin: de Gruyter, 2012.

Leclerc, Thomas L. *Yahweh Is Exalted in Justice: Solidarity and Conflict in Isaiah*. Minneapolis: Fortress, 2001.

Leonard, Jeffery M. "Identifying Inner-Biblical Allusions: Psalm 78 as a Test Case." *JBL* 127 (2008): 241–65.

Lester, G. Brooke. "Inner-Biblical Interpretation." Pages 444–53 in vol. 1 of *The Oxford Encyclopedia of Biblical Interpretation*. Edited by Steven L. McKenzie. 2 vols. Oxford: Oxford University Press, 2013.

Levenson, Jon D. *Creation and the Persistence of Evil: The Jewish Drama of Divine Omnipotence*. Princeton: Princeton University Press, 1994.

———. *The Death and Resurrection of the Beloved Son: The Transformation of Child Sacrifice in Judaism and Christianity*. New Haven: Yale University Press, 1993.

Levinson, Bernard M. *Deuteronomy and the Hermeneutics of Legal Innovation*. New York: Oxford University Press, 1997.

———. *Legal Revision and Religious Renewal in Ancient Israel*. Cambridge: Cambridge University Press, 2008.

Lieberman, Stephen J. "A Mesopotamian Background for the So-Called *Aggadic* 'Measures' of Biblical Hermeneutics?" *HUCA* 58 (1978): 157–225.

Lindström, Fredrik. "Theodicy in the Psalms." Pages 256–303 in *Theodicy in the World of the Bible*. Edited by Antti Laato and Johannes C. de Moor. Leiden: Brill, 2003.

Lundbom, Jack. *Jeremiah 37–52*. AB 21C. New York: Doubleday, 2004.

Lyons, Michael A. "'I Also Could Talk as You Do' (Job 16:4): The Function of Intratextual Quotation and Allusion in Job." Pages 169–77 in *Reading Job Intertextually*. Edited by Katharine Dell and Will Kynes. LHBOTS 574. New York: Bloomsbury, 2013.

———. "Marking Innerbiblical Allusion in the Book of Ezekiel." *Bib* 88 (2007): 245–50.

Machiela, Daniel A. "The Qumran Pesharim as Biblical Commentaries: Historical Context and Lines of Development." *DSD* 19 (2012): 313–62.

Margaliot, M. "The Transgression of Moses and Aaron: Num. 20:1–13." *JQR* 74 (1983): 196–228.

McCann, J. Clinton, Jr. "Psalm 73: A Microcosm of Old Testament Theology." Pages 247–57 in *The Listening Heart: Essays in Wisdom and the Psalms in Honor of Roland E. Murphy, O. Carm.* Edited by Kenneth G. Hoglund, Elizabeth F. Huwiler, Jonathan T. Glass, and Roger W. Lee. JSOTSup 58. Sheffield: JSOT Press, 1987.

———. *A Theological Introduction to the Book of Psalms: The Psalms as Torah.* Nashville: Abingdon, 1993.

McCarthy, Carmel. *The Tiqqune Sopherim and Other Theological Corrections in the Masoretic Text of the Old Testament.* Göttingen: Vandenhoeck & Ruprecht, 1981.

McCreesh, Thomas P. *Biblical Sound and Sense: Poetic Sound Patterns in Proverbs 10–29.* JSOTSup 128. Sheffield: Sheffield Academic, 1991.

Menn, Esther M. "Inner-Biblical Exegesis in the Tanak." Pages 55–79 in *The Ancient Period.* Vol. 1 of *A History of Biblical Interpretation.* Edited by Alan J. Hauser and Duane F. Watson. Grand Rapids: Eerdmans, 2003.

Milgrom, Jacob. *Leviticus 1–16.* AB 3. New York: Doubleday, 1991.

Milikowsky, Chaim. "Rabbinic Interpretation of the Bible in the Light of Ancient Hermeneutical Practice: The Question of the Literal Meaning." Pages 7–28 in *"The Words of a Wise Man's Mouth Are Gracious" (Qoh 10,12): Festschrift for Günter Stemberger on the Occasion of His 65th Birthday.* Edited by Mauro Perani. SJ 32. Berlin: de Gruyter, 2005.

Miller, Geoffrey D. "Intertextuality in Old Testament Research." *CBR* 9 (2011): 283–309.

Morier, Henri. "Paronomase." Pages 868–71 in *Dictionnaire de poétique et de rhétorique.* 5th ed. Paris: Presses Universitaires de France, 1998.

Müller, Anna K. *Gottes Zukunft: Die Möglichkeit der Rettung am Tag JHWHs nach dem Joelbuch.* Neukirchen-Vluyn: Neukirchener Verlag, 2008.

Newsom, Carol. *The Book of Job: A Contest of Moral Imaginations.* Oxford: Oxford University Press, 2003.

Noble, Paul R. "Esau, Tamar, and Joseph: Criteria for Identifying Inner-Biblical Allusions." *VT* 52 (2002): 219–52.

Noegel, Scott B. "Dreams and Dream Interpreters in Mesopotamia and in the Hebrew Bible (Old Testament)." Pages 45–71 in *Dreams: A Reader* on *Religious, Cultural, and Psychological Dimensions of Dreaming*. Edited by Kelly Bulkeley. New York: Palgrave, 2001.

———. "Drinking Feasts and Deceptive Talk: Jacob and Laban's Double Talk." Pages 163–80 in *Puns and Pundits: Word Play in the Hebrew Bible and Ancient Near Eastern Literature*. Edited by Scott B. Noegel. Bethesda, MD: CDL, 2000.

———. *Janus Parallelism in the Book of Job*. JSOTSup 223. Sheffield: Sheffield Academic, 1996.

———. *Nocturnal Ciphers: The Allusive Language of Dreams in the Ancient Near East*. AOS 89. New Haven: American Oriental Society, 2007.

———. "Paronomasia." *EHLL* 3:24–29.

———. Preface to *Puns and Pundits: Word Play in the Hebrew Bible and Ancient Near Eastern Literature*. Edited by Scott B. Noegel. Bethesda, MD: CDL, 2000.

———. "'Sign, Sign, Everywhere a Sign': Script, Power, and Interpretation in the Ancient Near East." Pages 143–62 in *Divination and Interpretation of Signs in the Ancient World: The Fifth Annual University of Chicago Oriental Institute Seminar*. Edited by Amar Annus. Chicago: Oriental Institute of the University of Chicago, 2010.

———. "'Word Play' in Qoheleth." *JHS* 7 (2007): 2–28.

Nõmmik, Urmas. *Die Freundesreden des ursprünglichen Hiobdialogs: Eine form- und traditionsgeschichtliche Studie*. BZAW 410. Berlin: de Gruyter, 2010.

Obara, Elżbieta M. *Le strategie di Dio: Dinamiche comunicative nei discorsi divini del Trito-Isaia*. Rome: Gregorian & Biblical Press, 2010.

O'Brien, Julia. *Priest and Levite in Malachi*. SBLDS 121. Atlanta: Scholars Press, 1990.

Orlinsky, Harry M. "The Plain Meaning of *ruaḥ* in Gen 1.2." *JQR* 48 (1957): 174–82.

Park, Kyung-Chul. *Die Gerechtigkeit Israels und das Heil der Völker: Kultus, Tempel, Eschatologie und Gerechtigkeit in der Endgestalt des Jesajabuches (Jes 56, 1–8 ; 58, 1–14 ; 65, 17–66, 24)*. BEATAJ 52. Frankfurt am Main: Lang, 2003.

Pasco, Allan H. *Allusion: A Literary Graft*. Toronto: University of Toronto Press, 1994.

Patrick, Dale A. "Epiphanic Imagery in Second Isaiah's Portrayal of a New Exodus." *HAR* 8 (1984): 125–41.

Paul, Shalom M. *Isaiah 40–66: Translation and Commentary*. Grand Rapids: Eerdmans, 2012.

Perdue, Leo. *Wisdom in Revolt: Metaphorical Theology in the Book of Job*. JSOTSup 112. Sheffield: Almond Press, 1991.
Perri, Carmela. "On Alluding." *Poetics* 7 (1978): 289–307.
Polan, Gregory J. *In the Ways of Justice toward Salvation: A Rhetorical Analysis of Isaiah 56–59*. New York: Lang, 1986.
Pope, Marvin H. *Job*. AB 15. Garden City, NY: Doubleday, 1973.
Propp, William H. *Water in the Wilderness: A Biblical Motif and Its Mythological Background*. Atlanta: Scholars Press, 1987.
Rabinowitz, Isaac. *A Witness Forever: Ancient Israel's Perception of Literature and the Resultant Hebrew Bible*. Bethesda, MD: CDL, 1993.
Redditt, Paul. "Malachi, Book of." Pages 848–49 in *Eerdmans Dictionary of the Bible*. Edited by David Noel Freedman. Grand Rapids: Eerdmans, 2000.
Regt, L. J. de. "Wordplay in the OT." *NIDB* 5:898–900.
Rendsburg, Gary A. "Alliteration." *EHLL* 1:86–87.
———. "Word Play in Biblical Hebrew." Pages 137–62 in *Puns and Pundits: Word Play in the Hebrew Bible and Ancient Near Eastern Literature*. Edited by Scott B. Noegel. Bethesda, MD: CDL, 2000.
Renker, Alwin. *Die Tora bei Maleachi: Ein Beitrag zur Bedeutungsgeschichte von tôrâ im Alten Testament*. FTS 112. Freiburg: Herder, 1979.
Rollston, Christopher. "*Ad Nomen Argumenta*: Personal Names as Pejorative Puns in Ancient Texts." Pages 367–86 in *In the Shadow of Bezalel: Aramaic, Biblical, and Ancient Near Eastern Studies in Honor of Bezalel Porten*. Edited by Alejandro F. Botta. Leiden: Brill, 2012.
Sasson, Jack M. "Wordplay in the OT." *IDBSup*, 968–70.
Schmid, Konrad. "Auslegte Schrift als Schrift: Innerbiblische Schriftauslegung und die Frage nach der theologischen Qualität biblischer Texte." Pages 115–29 in *Die Kunst des Auslegens: Zur Hermeneutik des Christentums in der Kultur der Gegenwart*. Edited by Reiner Anselm, Stephan Schleissing, and Klaus Tanner. Frankfurt am Main: Lang, 1999.
———. "The Authors of Job and Their Historical and Social Setting." Pages 145–53 in *Scribes, Sages, and Seers: The Sage in the Eastern Mediterranean World*. Edited by Leo G. Perdue. FRLANT 219. Göttingen: Vandenhoeck & Ruprecht, 2008.
———. *Hiob als biblisches und antikes Buch: Historische und intellektuelle Kontexte seiner Theologie*. Stuttgart: Katholisches Bibelwerk, 2010.
———. "Innerbiblische Schriftauslegung: Aspekte der Forschungsgeschichte." Pages 5–34 in *Schriftgelehrte Traditionsliteratur: Fallstu-

dien zur innerbiblischen Schriftauslegung im Alten Testament. FAT 77. Tübingen: Mohr Siebeck, 2011.

———. "Innerbiblische Schriftdiskussion im Hiobbuch." Pages 243–66 in *Schriftgelehrte Traditionsliteratur: Fallstudien zur innerbiblischen Schriftauslegung im Alten Testament.* FAT 77. Tübingen: Mohr Siebeck, 2011.

———. *The Old Testament: A Literary History.* Translated by Linda M. Maloney. Minneapolis: Fortress, 2012.

———. "Schriftgelehrte Arbeit an der Schrift: Historische Überlegungen zum Vorgang innerbiblischer Exegese." Pages 35–60 in *Schriftgelehrte Traditionsliteratur: Fallstudien zur innerbiblischen Schriftauslegung im Alten Testament.* FAT 77. Tübingen: Mohr Siebeck, 2011.

Schorch, Stefan. "Between Science and Magic: The Function and Roots of Paronomasia in the Prophetic Books of the Hebrew Bible." Pages 205–22 in *Puns and Pundits: Word Play in the Hebrew Bible and Ancient Near Eastern Literature.* Edited by Scott B. Noegel. Bethesda, MD: CDL, 2000.

Schwienhorst-Schönberger, Ludger. "'Bis ich eintrat in die Heiligtümer Gottes' (Ps 73,17): Ps 73 im Horizont biblischer und theologischer Hermeneutik." Pages 387–402 in *"Gerechtigkeit und Recht zu üben" (Gen 18,19): Studien zur altorientalischen und biblischen Rechtsgeschichte, zur Religionsgeschichte Israels und zur Religionssoziologie; Festschrift für Eckart Otto zum 65. Geburtstag.* Edited by Reinhard Achenbach and Martin Arneth. BZABR 13. Wiesbaden: Harrassowitz, 2009.

Seeligmann, Isaac Leo. "Voraussetzungen der Midraschexegese." Pages 150–81 in *Congress Volume: Copenhagen, 1953.* VTSup 1. Leiden: Brill, 1953.

Seidel, Moshe. "Parallels between the Book of Isaiah and the Book of Psalms." *Sinai* 38 (1955–1956): 149–72, 229–42, 272–80, 333–55. (Hebrew)

Shaw, David. "Converted Imaginations? The Reception of Richard Hays's Intertextual Method." *CBR* 11 (2013): 234–45.

Shinan, Avigdor, and Yair Zakovitch. *From Gods to God: How the Bible Debunked, Suppressed, or Changed Ancient Myths and Legends.* Lincoln: University of Nebraska Press, 2012.

———. "Midrash on Scripture and Midrash within Scripture." *ScrHier* 31 (1986): 259–77.

Silberman, L. H. "Unriddling the Riddle: A Study in the Structure and Language of the Habakkuk Pesher (1 Q p Hab)." *RevQ* 3 (1961): 323–64.
Simkins, Ronald. *Yahweh's Activity in History and Nature in the Book of Joel*. ANETS 10. Lewiston, NY: Mellen, 1991.
Snell, Daniel C. *Twice-Told Proverbs and the Composition of the Book of Proverbs*. Winona Lake, IN: Eisenbrauns, 1993.
Sommer, Benjamin D. "Exegesis, Allusion and Intertextuality in the Hebrew Bible: A Response to Lyle Eslinger." *VT* 46 (1996): 479–89.
———. *A Prophet Reads Scripture: Allusion in Isaiah 40–66*. Stanford, CA: Stanford University Press, 1998.
Spencer, Bradley J. "The 'New Deal' for Post-Exilic Judah in Isaiah 41,17–20." *ZAW* 112 (2000): 583–97.
Spronk, Klaas. *Nahum*. HCOT. Kampen: Kok Pharos, 1997.
Sternberg, Meir. *The Poetics of Biblical Narrative: Ideological Literature and the Drama of Reading*. Bloomington: Indiana University Press, 1985.
Stromberg, Jacob. *An Introduction to the Study of Isaiah*. London: T&T Clark, 2011.
Strus, Andrzej. *Nomen-omen: La stylistique sonore des noms propres dans le Pentateuque*. AnBib 80. Rome: Biblical Institute Press, 1978.
Stuhlmueller, Carroll. *Creative Redemption in Deutero-Isaiah*. AnBib 43. Rome: Biblical Institute Press, 1970.
Swetnam, James. "Malachi 1,11: An Interpretation." *CBQ* 31 (1969): 200–209.
Talmon, Shemaryahu. "The Ancient Hebrew Alphabet and Biblical Text Criticism." Pages 497–530 in *Mélanges Dominique Barthélemy: Études bibliques offertes à l'occasion de son 60ᵉ anniversaire*. Edited by Pierre Casetti, Othmar Keel, and Adrian Schenker. OBO 38. Göttingen: Vandenhoeck & Ruprecht, 1981.
———. "Aspects of the Textual Transmission of the Bible in the Light of Qumran Manuscripts." Pages 226–63 in *Qumran and the History of the Biblical Text*. Edited by Frank Moore Cross and Shemaryahu Talmon. Cambridge: Harvard University Press, 1975.
———. "The Textual Study of the Bible: A New Outlook." Pages 321–400 in *Qumran and the History of the Biblical Text*. Edited by Frank Moore Cross and Shemaryahu Talmon. Cambridge: Harvard University Press, 1975.
Tiemeyer, Lena-Sofia. *For the Comfort of Zion: The Geographical and Theological Location of Isaiah 40–55*. Leiden: Brill, 2011.

Tigay, Jeffrey. "An Early Technique of Aggadic Exegesis." Pages 169–89 in *History, Historiography and Interpretation: Studies in Biblical and Cuneiform Literature*. Edited by Hayim Tadmor and Moshe Weinfeld. Leiden: Brill, 1983.

Tooman, William A. *Gog of Magog: Reuse of Scripture and Compositional Technique in Ezekiel 38–39*. FAT 2/52. Tübingen: Mohr Siebeck, 2011.

Tull, Patricia K. "Intertextuality and the Hebrew Scriptures." *CurBS* 8 (2000): 59–90.

Tur-Sinai, N. H. *The Book of Job: A New Commentary*. Jerusalem: Kiryath Sepher, 1957.

Ulrich, Eugene. *The Biblical Qumran Scrolls: Transcriptions and Textual Variants*. Leiden: Brill, 2010.

Vermes, Geza. "Bible and Midrash: Early Old Testament Exegesis." Pages 199–231 in *From the Beginnings to Jerome*. Vol. 1 of *The Cambridge History of the Bible*. Edited by Peter R. Ackroyd and Christopher F. Evans. Cambridge: Cambridge University Press, 1970.

Wakeman, Mary K. "The Biblical Earth Monster in the Cosmogonic Combat Myth." *JBL* 88 (1969): 313–20.

Walsh, Jerome T. "Summons to Judgement: A Close Reading of Isaiah xli 1–20." *VT* 43 (1993): 351–71.

Watson, Wilfred G. E. *Classical Hebrew Poetry: A Guide to Its Techniques*. 2nd ed. Edinburgh: T&T Clark, 2004.

Weber, Beat. *Werkbuch Psalmen I: Die Psalmen 1 bis 72*. Stuttgart: Kohlhammer, 2001.

———. *Werkbuch Psalmen II: Die Psalmen 73 bis 150*. Stuttgart: Kohlhammer, 2003.

Weingreen, Jacob. *From Bible to Mishna: The Continuity of Tradition*. Manchester, UK: Manchester University Press, 1976.

Westermann, Claus. *Genesis 1–11*. Translated by John J. Scullion. Minneapolis: Augsburg, 1984.

Wetzsteon, Rachel. "Allusion." *PEPP*, 42–43.

Weyde, Karl W. "Inner-Biblical Interpretation: Methodological Reflections on the Relationship between Texts in the Hebrew Bible." *SEÅ* 70 (2005): 287–300.

Willey, Patricia Tull. *Remember the Former Things: The Recollection of Previous Texts in Second Isaiah*. Atlanta: Scholars Press, 1997.

Willi, Thomas. *Die Chronik als Auslegung: Untersuchungen zur literarischen Gestaltung der historischen Überlieferung Israels*. FRLANT 106. Göttingen: Vandenhoeck & Ruprecht, 1972.

Winitzer, Abraham. "The Generative Paradigm in Old Babylonian Divination." PhD diss., Harvard University, 2006.

Witte, Markus. "Does the Torah Keep Its Promise? Job's Critical Intertextual Dialogue with Deuteronomy." Pages 54–65 in *Reading Job Intertextually*. Edited by Katharine Dell and Will Kynes. LHBOTS 574. New York: Bloomsbury, 2013.

———. "Job in Conversation with the Torah." Pages 81–100 in *Wisdom and Torah: The Reception of "Torah" in the Wisdom Literature of the Second Temple Period*. Edited by Bernd U. Schipper and D. Andrew Teeter. JSJSup 163. Leiden: Brill, 2013.

Wolde, E. J. van. "Trendy Intertextuality?" Pages 43–49 in *Intertextuality in Biblical Writings: Essays in Honour of Bas van Iersel*. Edited by Sipka Draisma. Kampen: Kok, 1989.

Wolff, Hans Walter. *Joel and Amos*. Translated by Waldemar Janzen, S. Dean McBride Jr., and Charles A. Muenchow. Hermeneia. Philadelphia: Fortress, 1977.

Zakovitch, Yair. "Inner-Biblical Interpretation." Pages 27–63 in *A Companion to Biblical Interpretation in Early Judaism*. Edited by Matthias Henze. Grand Rapids: Eerdmans, 2012.

———. שיר השירים. Jerusalem: Magnes, 1992.

Ancient Sources Index

Hebrew Bible/Old Testament

Genesis
1	46
1:1–2:4	40, 106
1:2	40, 106
1:6–8	106
1:9–10	106
1:11	117
1:20–30	106
1:26–31	44
7:11	106–10
8:22	107
10:3	32, 35
10:23	34
25:26	90
27:36	90

Exodus
20:5	102
20:5–6	101
32:25	11
34:6–7	101
34:7	102
40:9	24

Leviticus
16	83
16:29–31	80–85
16:31	80–81
23	80
23:27–32	80–85
23:31–32	86

Numbers
6:23–27	91–92
6:26	92
20:1–13	110–11
25	11
28–29	80
29:7	80, 83
29:7–11	80, 84–85
30:14	83

Deuteronomy
28:15–68	74
28:35	71
30:15	74
30:19	74
31:16–21	73
31:27–29	73

Joshua
24:30	32
24:31	34

Judges
2:7	34
2:9	32
16:27	54

1 Samuel
31:9	33
31:12	33–34

2 Samuel
5:18	34
5:19	35
5:22	34

2 Samuel (cont.)		14:10	35
6:5	34–35	14:13	34
6:7	34	15:27	35
6:14	35	15:28	34
6:16	34	15:29	34
7:7	33	16:27	33, 35
7:11	34	17:6	33
7:19	35	17:10	34
7:24	33	17:17	35
8:1	33	17:22	33
8:3	33	18:1	33
8:8	34	18:3	33
8:12–13	32	18:11–12	32
8:13	35	18:12	35
10:8	33	19:9	33
10:16	34	19:17	34
10:17	34	20:3	33, 35
12:31	33, 35	20:5	33
21:19	33	20:6	34
21:20	33	21:10	33
23:10	34	21:11–12	33
23:13	34	21:17	35
23:21	34		
24:12	33	2 Chronicles	
24:13	33	8:8	34
24:17	35		
		Nehemiah	
1 Kings		5	83
9:21	34		
		Job	
2 Kings		1	71
20:13	33, 36	1:12	99
		2:7	71
1 Chronicles		3	46
1:6	32, 35	4:17	48, 50–51
1:17	34	4:18	51
8:8	34	7	47
10:9	33	7:17	48–50
10:12	33–34	7:17–18	44–48, 50
11:14	34	8:4	48
11:15	34	8:5–7	48
11:23	35	8:11–22	48
13:8	34–35	9:2	47–48, 50–51
13:10	34	9:2–10:22	48
14:9	34	10:3	68

ANCIENT SOURCES INDEX

15:14	27–29, 48–50	37	53–56, 58–64
15:14–15	49, 51	37:7	53–54
15:14–16	50	37:25	53–54
15:15	49–50	37:34	53–60
15:16	49, 51	37:35–36	53–54
18	65	37:37	53–54
18:5–6	65–67, 70	37:38	53, 55
21	67	50	93–98
21:14–16	67–69	50:1	96–98
21:15	69	50:1–2	93
21:16	69	50:2	100
21:17	65–67, 69	50:2–4	93
21:17–19	66, 69	50:5	94
21:19–34	66	50:6–7	93
21:34	67	50:8–14	94
22:1–30	67	50:15–20	94
22:17–18	67–70	50:23	94
22:19	67, 69–70	54:5	32
22:19–20	69	73	55–64
25:1–5	50	73–89	55
25:4	50–51	73:1	55
25:5	50–51	73:2	58
25:6	51	73:2–16	57
26:3	67	73:3	55–57, 59–62
26:13	39–40	73:4–12	57
34:7	49	73:12	56
42	71	73:13–14	57
42:7	67	73:15	57
		73:15–16	58
Psalms		73:17	57
1	55, 63	73:18–20	57
1:1	68	73:19	62
3–14	44	73:21–22	58
8	45–47, 49	73:23–24	57
8:4	49	73:25	57
8:5	27–29, 43–50, 52, 70	73:26	57
8:5–6	46–47	73:28	57
8:5–9	44	74	106, 108
8:6	43	74:1–11	106
8:7	46, 49	74:12	107
8:8	117	74:13–17	106–7
15:5	38–39	74:15	106–11
22:18	54	74:17	107
31:23	24–25, 33	74:18–23	107
35:13	83	77:18	33

Psalms (cont.)

86:14	32	13:6–9	112–14
90:8	49	13:9	112
90:10	71	24–27	40
91	59–60, 62–64	27:1	39–40
91:1–7	59	34:8	61
91:8	56–57, 59–63	39:2	33, 36
91:9–16	59	40–55	22, 87–88, 102, 105, 108, 110–11
96:6	33, 35	40–66	11, 24, 26, 103–5, 121
112:8	54	41:17–20	110–11
112:10	56	41:18	108–11
113	93–99	41:19	110
113–118	98	47:6	100
113:1	94	47:8	33
113:1–3	97	50:8	26
113:1–4	94–95	52:1	102, 104–5
113:2	99	52:1–2	104
113:2–3	95	52:1–12	102
113:3	96–99	52:7	102
113:5–9	95	52:7–9	102–3
114:8	111	52:8–9	103–4
115:4–6	37–39	52:11	104
115:8	37–39	53:2–3	104
118:7	54	56–66	84–88
135:15–18	37–39	58	82–88
150	63	58:1–7	82
		58:1–12	82–83, 85–87
Proverbs		58:2	82
10–29	65	58:3	82–85
13:9	64–67, 69–70	58:4	83
15:17–19	27–29, 36	58:5	82–85
20:20	65–66, 69–70	58:7	82, 84–85
24:20	64–66, 69–70	58:9	85, 87
29:21–22	27–29, 36	58:9–10	82
		58:10	84, 87
Song of Songs		58:11	85, 87
2:7	117	58:12	86–87
3:5	117	58:13	86–87
		58:13–14	82, 86–87
Isaiah			
10	79	Jeremiah	
10:7	79	1:10	14–15, 78
13	112, 115	1:11–12	14–15
13:1–22	112	1:13–14	15
13:6	112–15, 118	2:22	40

4:13	37	18:17	38–39
6:22–24	79	24:21	100
9:20	76–77	28:17	54
17:19–27	73–76	29–32	112
17:27	73, 75–78	29:19–20	112
19:1	15	30:2–3	112–15, 118
19:7	15	30:10–11	112
20:12	26	30:24–25	112
21:1–14	75	38–39	22
21:2	74		
21:4–7	74	Daniel	
21:8–10	74	2:20	99
21:10	74–76	9:14	15
21:11–14	74–75		
21:12	75	Hosea	
21:13–14	77	1–3	114
21:14	75–79, 118	2:7	114
31:28	15	9:7	61
44:27	15		
46–49	76	Joel	
49:19–21	77	1	113, 115–18
49:26	76–77	1–2	116, 118
50–51	78	1:2–2:27	114
50:2–51:58	78	1:5	113
50:29	76	1:9	113
50:30	76–77	1:10	113–16
50:31–32	76–78	1:10–12	113–15
50:32	77–80, 118	1:13	113, 115
50:41–43	79	1:15	113–18
50:44–46	77	1:16	116
51:20	103	1:16–20	116
51:21–23	103	1:18	117
51:24	103	1:20	117
51:46	78	2:1	115
		2:1–11	115
Lamentations		2:3	117
1:20	10–11	2:18–27	116
1:21	24	2:21–24	116–17
2:11	10–11	2:22	117–18
2:15	93	2:25	116
3:54	24–25, 33	4:14	115
3:56	25		
		Amos	
Ezekiel		8:1–2	14–15
18:13	38–39		

Obadiah		1:10	92, 98
12	54	1:10–2:9	89
13	54	1:11	96–99
15	115	1:11–12	93, 98–99
		1:11–14	95–96
Jonah		1:12	98–100
2:3	25	1:12–14	98
2:5	24–25, 33	1:13	92
2:6	25	1:14	92, 96, 98
		2:1	95, 98
Micah		2:1–9	95
7:3	61	2:2	92
7:10	54	2:5	92, 95, 98
		2:6–9	97
Nahum		2:7	100
1:1	101	2:8	99
1:2–3	102	2:9	92
1:2–6	101	2:10	91, 99
1:7	101	2:10–11	99
1:8–14	101	2:10–17	89, 91
1:11	104	2:12	91
2:1	101–5	3:1	40
2:2	101–3	3:1–2	100
		3:2	40
Habakkuk		3:3	40
1:8	37	3:3–4	100
3:10	33	3:5	100
		3:5–9	89, 91
Zephaniah		3:6	89, 91
1:7	115	3:6–9	90
1:14	115	3:7	89, 91
2:15	33	3:7–12	89
		3:8–9	89–91, 99
Malachi		3:13–15	89, 91
1	89, 93	3:19–21	100
1–2	92		
1:2–5	91, 95–96, 100	Ugaritic Literature	
1:5	95, 98		
1:6	98	*KTU*	
1:6–14	95–96	1.5 I 1–2	40
1:6–2:9	89, 91–93, 95–98		
1:7	96	Phoenician Karatepe Inscription	
1:7–8	98		
1:8	92, 96	*KAI*	
1:9	99	26 I.3–6	97

26 I.4–5	97
26 I.18–19	97
26 I.21–II.9	97
26 II.1–3	97

Septuagint

Psalms
90:8 [91:8]	61

Jeremiah
27:30 [50:30 MT]	76
27:31–32 [50:31–32 MT]	78
30:32 [49:26 MT]	76

Qumran

11QapocrPs
IV, 9	61

1QH
IX, 17	61

1QM
IV, 12	61
XVII, 1	61

1QIsa^a
Isa 58:12–13	86

Modern Authors Index

Abasciano, Brian J. 4
Allen, Leslie C. 73, 75, 78
Alonso Schökel, Luis 8, 110, 113
Anderson, Bernhard W. 110–11
Androphy, Ronald L. 6–8, 11
Assis, Elie 89
Auffret, Pierre 53–54
Bakhos, Carol 124–25
Barstad, Hans 107, 111
Barton, John 4, 113–16
Bate, W. J. 6
Bauks, Michaela 107
Beentjes, Pancratius C. 39
Beetham, Christopher A. 20–21, 42
Bellis, Alice Ogden 77, 79
Bendavid, Abba 31
Ben-Porat, Ziva 19
Berges, Ulrich 110–11
Bergler, Siegfried 112–13, 115–16
Bergmeier, Roland 68
Berrin, Shani L. 124
Beuken, Willem H. 82
Bilbija, Jovan 125
Blenkinsopp, Joseph 80, 82–84, 86–88, 102, 112–13
Bloom, Harold 6
Briggs, Charles A. 44, 55, 60–61, 98–99
Brinks, C. L. 45
Brown, William P. 107
Brueggemann, Walter 55–58, 63–64
Carr, David M. 27, 120, 122–23
Casanowicz, Immanuel M. 8
Cavigneaux, A. 126
Cherry, Russell T., III 16
Childs, Brevard S. 82–83, 86, 88

Clifford, Richard J. 65
Cole, Robert L. 55–56, 58
Conte, Gian Biagio 4–5
Cook, Eleanor 7, 16, 28, 39
Cook, Joan E. 111
Crenshaw, James L. 21, 112–17
Dahmen, Ulrich 117
Dahood, Mitchell J. 39
Delekat, Lienhard 25
Doudna, Gregory L. 124
Driver, Samuel R. 44–45
Eilberg-Schwartz, Howard 124
Ellis, E. Earle 124
Emerton, J. A. 107–9
Eslinger, Lyle 5
Fabry, Heinz-Josef 102
Fishbane, Michael 2, 6, 44–45, 50, 83–85, 91–93, 99, 124
Foster, Benjamin R. 8
Fox, Michael V. 52, 64–65
Frevel, Christian 43–47
Gadd, C. J. 125
Garsiel, Moshe 6, 16, 34
Glassner, Gottfried 111
Glazier-McDonald, Beth 96
Glück, J. J. 8
Goldingay, John 102
Gordis, Robert 53, 66
Gordon, Cyrus H. 39
Gray, George B. 44–45
Gray, John 66
Greaves, Sheldon 126
Greenberg, Moshe 46, 113
Greenstein, Edward 8, 10–11, 14, 16, 23
Guillaume, A. 8

Gunn, David	110	Menn, Esther M.	2
Halton, Charles	19	Milgrom, Jacob	80–81, 91, 106
Hanson, Paul	83	Milikowsky, Chaim	126
Harding, James E.	124	Miller, Geoffrey D.	2, 4, 19
Haug, Kari Storstein	57	Miller, Patrick D.	55–58, 63
Hays, Christopher B.	4, 19	Morier, Henri	11–12
Hays, Richard B.	4	Müller, Anna K.	112–16
Hebel, Udo J.	19	Newsom, Carol	46, 52
Heckl, Raik	66	Noble, Paul R.	20
Heim, Knut M.	27, 64	Noegel, Scott B.	6–12, 14, 24, 53, 125–26
Hill, Andrew	98, 100	Nõmmik, Urmas	48
Hill, John	79	Obara, Elżbieta M.	86
Hinds, Stephen	4, 20	O'Brien, Julia	97
Holladay, William L.	75, 78	Orlinsky, Harry M.	106
Hossfeld, Frank-Lothar	60, 94, 98–99, 106	Park, Kyung-Chul	82–87
Hrobon, Bohdan	20, 80, 82–87	Pasco, Allan H.	2, 5, 19–20
Hurvitz, Avi	54	Patrick, Dale A.	108, 111
Illman, Karl-Johan	45–46	Paul, Shalom M.	103–5
Jassen, Alex P.	126	Payne, David	102
Joosten, Jan	52	Perdue, Leo	46–47, 51–52
Kalimi, Isaac	31, 34–35	Perri, Carmela	19
Kessler, Rainer	96–97	Pettinato, Giovanni	39
Knohl, Israel	80	Polan, Gregory J.	84–86
Koenen, Klaus	86–87	Pope, Marvin H.	44–45
Koenig, Jean	78	Porten, Bezalel	16
Köhlmoos, Melanie	44–47	Propp, William H.	111
Kratz, Reinhard G.	2, 105	Rabinowitz, Isaac	126
Kristeva, Julia	4	Redditt, Paul	89, 98
Kugel, James A.	1–2	Regt, L. J. de	8, 10, 12, 14, 28–29
Kynes, Will	4, 22, 45–47, 60	Rendsburg, Gary A.	9–10
Leclerc, Thomas L.	82–84, 86	Renker, Alwin	95–96
Leonard, Jeffery M.	19	Rollston, Christopher	16
Lester, G. Brooke	2, 4	Sasson, Jack M.	8, 10–11, 14–15
Levenson, Jon D.	44, 51, 90–91, 106–7	Schmid, Konrad	2, 44–47, 52–53
Levinson, Bernard M.	5–6	Schorch, Stefan	14–15, 31
Lieberman, Stephen J.	126	Schwienhorst-Schönberger, Ludger	57
Lindström, Fredrik	57	Seeligmann, Isaac Leo	124
Lundbom, Jack	78	Seidel, Moshe	39
Lyons, Michael A.	2–3, 5, 39, 52, 66	Shaw, David	4, 18, 21, 42
Machiela, Daniel A.	126	Shinan, Avigdor	32, 125
Margaliot, M.	110	Silberman, L. H.	123–25
McCann, J. Clinton, Jr.	55–58, 63–64	Simkins, Ronald	114
McCarthy, Carmel	124	Snell, Daniel C.	27
McCreesh, Thomas P.	13	Sommer, Benjamin D.	3–5, 11, 20, 22, 24, 26, 102, 121

Spencer, Bradley J.	111
Spronk, Klaas	102
Sternberg, Meir	5
Stromberg, Jacob	40
Strus, Andrzej	16
Stuhlmueller, Carroll	111
Swetnam, James	97
Talmon, Shemaryahu	124–25
Tiemeyer, Lena-Sofia	110–11
Tigay, Jeffrey	126
Tooman, William A.	3, 18–20, 22
Tull, Patricia K.	4
Tur-Sinai, N. H.	11, 46, 66, 68–69
Ulrich, Eugene	61
Vermes, Geza	125
Wakeman, Mary K.	107, 109–10
Walsh, Jerome T.	109–10
Watson, Wilfred G. E.	8
Weber, Beat	53, 55, 58, 62, 64
Weingreen, Jacob	60
Westermann, Claus	106
Wetzsteon, Rachel	3–4, 7, 18–20
Weyde, Karl W.	2
Willey, Patricia Tull	102, 104
Willi, Thomas	36
Winitzer, Abraham	125
Witte, Markus	52
Wolde, E. J. van	4
Wolff, Hans Walter	113–17
Zakovitch, Yair	2, 32, 117, 125
Zenger, Erich	60, 94, 98–99, 106

www.ingramcontent.com/pod-product-compliance
Lightning Source LLC
Chambersburg PA
CBHW021844220426
43663CB00005B/397